The AI Commander

The AI Commander

Centaur Teaming, Command, and Ethical Dilemmas

James Johnson

OXFORD
UNIVERSITY PRESS

Great Clarendon Street, Oxford, OX2 6DP,
United Kingdom

Oxford University Press is a department of the University of Oxford.
It furthers the University's objective of excellence in research, scholarship,
and education by publishing worldwide. Oxford is a registered trade mark of
Oxford University Press in the UK and in certain other countries

Published in the United States of America by Oxford University Press
198 Madison Avenue, New York, NY 10016, United States of America

British Library Cataloguing in Publication Data

Data available

Library of Congress Control Number: 2023943114

ISBN 9780198892182

DOI: 10.1093/oso/9780198892182.001.0001

Pod

Acknowledgments

This publication is the third in a series of books on artificial intelligence and future warfare. In *AI and the Bomb* (Oxford University Press, 2023), I argued that AI is transforming the management and control of nuclear strategy and risk and creating new ways and means to increase the risk of nuclear detonation. *Artificial Intelligence and the Future of Warfare* (Manchester University Press, 2021) demystified the hype surrounding AI in the military context and sketched a picture of how AI-enabled warfare might evolve. This final volume in the trilogy (my "Return of the Jedi") presents a human-centric exploration—particularly the ethical and moral dilemmas—of synthesizing man and machine in future warfare. The volume offers a nuanced critique of human–machine interactions in war, moving the discussion forward from a bifurcated focus on banning "killer robots" and the loss of human agency versus viewing AI as a panacea for human frailties in war. Moreover, it not only accepts the false choice between automation versus humans, but further posits that combining the two is not necessarily the best way forward.

There are many colleagues whose contributions I am grateful for. Among them are James Acton, John Amble, Greg Austin, David Blagden, John Borrie, Ingvild Bode, Lyndon Burford, Jeffrey Ding, Mona Dreicer, Sam Dunin, Ryan Evans, Andrew Futter, Erik Gartzke, Andrea Gilli, Rose Gottemoeller, Rebecca Hersman, Michael Horowitz, Patrick Howell, Keir Lieber, Jon Lindsay, Kenneth Payne, Benoit Pelopidas, Giacomo Persi Paoli, Bill Potter, Daryl Press, Adam Quinn, Andrew Reddy, Philip Reiner, Eric Richardson, Brad Roberts, Mick Ryan, Dan Salisbury, Paul Scharre, John Shanahan, Reuben Steff, Oliver Turner, Chris Twomey, Tom Young, Heather Williams, and Benjamin Zala. My appreciation also goes to the many experts who challenged my ideas, sharpened my arguments, and influenced my thinking as the book evolved.

My new home at the University of Aberdeen is proving a highly supportive research environment. I am blessed to have such generous, thoughtful, and talented colleagues from whom I have learned so much and whose commitment to interdisciplinary collaboration and research-led pedagogy is an inspiration. I thank Michael Smith, Joanne McEvoy, Mervyn Bain, and Lynn Bennie for creating a collegial environment in which such research is possible. As a teacher, I am keenly aware of the debt I owe to my students, some of whom are now colleagues. I learned so much from each of them in the class-room. The book benefits enormously from their comments and critiques. I thank them for their dialogue and insight that improved the book.

I have also enjoyed the generous support of several institutions that I would like to acknowledge, including the James Martin Center for Non-Proliferation Studies, the Project on Nuclear Issues and the International Security Program at the Center for Strategic and International Studies, the Vienna Center for Disarmament and Non-Proliferation, the Center for Global Security Research at Lawrence Livermore Laboratory, the U.S. Naval War College, the UK Deterrence & Assurance Academic Alliance, the International Institute for Strategic Studies, the AutoNorms Project, the Towards a Third Nuclear Age Project, UN Institute for Disarmament Research, The Alan Turing Institute, and the UK Government's Foreign, Commonwealth & Development Office for Artificial Intelligence. If, despite this excellent support, any errors remain undetected, I take full responsibility for them.

I also greatly appreciate the excellent team at Oxford University Press (especially Dominic Byatt and Vicki Sunter) for their professionality, guidance, and support. Not to mention the anonymous reviewers, whose comments and suggestions kept me honest and improved the book. Finally, and most importantly, thanks to my beautiful wife Cindy for her unstinting support, love, and encouragement, without which this book—or indeed any of my work or life as I know it—would be possible. Nothing I could do or say would adequately repay her support and kindness. This book is dedicated to her.

Contents

List of figures and tables

Figures

Tables

Introduction

AI-enabled "centaur warfighting"

What do emerging technologies like artificial intelligence (AI) mean for the role of humans in war?[1] This book addresses the largely neglected question of how the fusion of machines into the war machine will affect the human condition of warfare. Specifically, it investigates the vexing, misunderstood, and at times contradictory, ethical, moral,[2] and normative implications—whether incremental, transformative, or revolutionary—of synthesizing man and machine in future algorithmic warfare, or AI-enabled "centaur warfighting." At the heart of these vexing questions are whether we are inevitably moving toward a situation where AI-enabled autonomous weapons will make strategic decisions in place of humans and thus become the owners of those decisions. Can AI-powered systems replace human commanders? And, more importantly, should they?

Much of the recent literature has revolved around two competing schools of thought. First, those who argue (Human Rights Watch, Future Life Institutes, and Chairperson of the Informal Meeting of Experts, etc.) that powerful computers have ushered in an era of automation that portends dramatic improvements in precision, speed, and reliability which will not only make warfare more humane and safer, but also offer a solution to human cognitive and biological fallibilities in combat. Second, those who argue that a new breed of autonomous weapons (or "killer robots") and AI-enabled machine overlords lack common sense in novel situations and moral responsibility in using lethal force, and thus the potentially catastrophic project should be abandoned.[3] While these juxtaposed views both have their merit, this binary choice misses the nuances of AI-enabled centaur (or "hybrid") teaming, and, in turn, the new challenges for command. Considerations of the potential benefits and risks of autonomous weapons must consider and calibrate according to the likely circumstances for use. Although this book is not devoted to making this case, it considers these "circumstances" as a step toward elucidating, reframing, and, hopefully, remediating the problem.

The AI Commander. James Johnson, Oxford University Press. © James Johnson (2024).
DOI: 10.1093/oso/9780198892182.003.0001

The book considers the rationale of combining these approaches in an attempt to leverage the benefits of both. In doing so, it challenges the assumption that the hybrid teaming model offers an elixir for retaining the presumed reliability, speed, and efficiency of AI-enabled autonomous warfare while simultaneously not sacrificing human cognitive flexibility, control, and moral agency.[4] Instead, the book's premise is that while the autonomy vs. humans discourse is a false dichotomy, a synthesis of the two (i.e., human–machine hybrid teaming) is *not necessarily* a panacea. How useful are human "on the loop" or "in the loop" distinctions to view human-machine interactions? The book argues that the popular "on-the-loop" (i.e., humans in control) and "off-the-loop" (i.e., humans replaced by machines) tropes fail to appreciate the complex and psychological continuum of synthesizing man and machine. Moreover, recent efforts to facilitate "cognitive teaming" through augmentation—that is, computers and humans helping each other to *think*— is not a panacea for *humans* making better decisions during war.[5]

This book is not an exploration of how, why, and to what effect AI and autonomy might affect the character and nature of future warfare—which I and others have discussed elsewhere.[6] Rather, it investigates the human-centric features (human–machine teaming, humanizing/dehumanizing war, techno-military ethics, command decisions, and crisis brinkmanship, etc.) of the burgeoning drive to fuse machines with the quintessential human endeavor of war. Chapter 2, for example, considers the impact of anthropomorphizing AI on human–machine tactical teaming. The book engages with the various counterarguments that challenge the view that replacing humans with machines is necessarily a bad idea. Humans, for instance, make mistakes, often act irrationally, and are predisposed to violence[7]—whereas rational AI agents, free from human emotion, misperceptions, and biases may help make warfare more humane, ethical, and even less likely to occur. AI cannot be just passive and neutral force multipliers of human cognition. Instead, the book argues that they will likely become (either by conscious choice or more likely inadvertently) de facto strategic actors in war—or the "AI commander" problem. In short, AI could transform the role and nature of human warfare, but in very different ways from what most observers currently expect.

How might AI-augmented human–machine interaction affect the role of human command in war? How is AI-enabled warfare changing the way we think about the ethical-political dilemmas—moral judgments about military action and agents—in war? The book uses a "cognitivist" approach—focusing on people's perception of the world as understood through ideas, beliefs (or "cognitive schemas"),[8] attitudes, emotions—to explore these questions as an alternative to existing traditional international relations approaches such as constructivist, strategic theory, and legal-ethical and normative models. The book emphasizes the "mind" (both human and machine) and the mechanisms of thought (intelligence, consciousness, emotion, memory, experience, etc.) to consider the effects of AI and autonomy on the human condition of war. The book's underlying assumptions are three-fold. First, that the drive to synthesize AI technology with military capabilities is irreversible and exponential. Second, that the effects of this phenomenon on human agents in war are neither incontrovertible nor predetermined. Third, that for the foreseeable future, machines cannot reliably complement or augment, let alone replace, the role of humans in command.

2027: Centaur warfighting in the Taiwan Straits

How might AI-augmented human–machine teaming effect a crisis between two nuclear-armed adversaries?[9] Consider the following fictional vignette.[10] In 2027, the ailing helmsman President Xi Jinping, keen to fulfill his "China Dream" and secure his legacy in the Chinese Communist history books, invades Taiwan.

Day 1 of "Operation Island Freedom"

People's Liberation Army Air Force stealth J-20 ("Mighty Dragon") fighters, flanked by a swarm of semi-autonomous AI-powered "loyal wingmen" drones ("Little Dragons") in a well-rehearsed synchronized attack, deploys electronic jamming, cyberattacks, and missile strikes to degrade and destroy Taiwanese medium-to-long-range air defenses, severally degrading its command-and-control downlink stations and radar space-based ISR (intelligence, surveillance, reconnaissance) satellites.[11] Multiple semi-autonomous loitering "barrage swarms"—preprogrammed to avoid being intercepted by an enemy jammer system targeting its satellite link—soak up and destroy the bulk of Taiwan's remaining missile defenses, leaving Taipei virtually defenseless against a Beijing-imposed military quarantine.[12]

Amid this blitzkrieg attack, the "Little Dragons" receive a sensor-cue distress signal from a swarm of autonomous loitering underwater unmanned vehicles (UUVs)—on a surveillance and reconnaissance mission off the coast of Taiwan—who warn them of an imminent threat posed by a US carrier group.[13] With the surviving swarm running low on battery power, optical communications with China's People's Liberation Army Navy (PLAN) command-and-control out of range, and the J-20 pilots occupied with higher-level cognitive functions (devising engagement strategies and selecting and prioritizing targets, etc.), the decision to give the engagement order is left to the "Little Dragons."[14] This decision is made without human input or oversight from PLAN's ground controllers back in mainland China.

Using their AI sensors, the "Little Dragons" give the order—via a buoy on a sea-surface drone to a nuclear-powered attack submarine operating in the Philippine Sea—to activate a swarm of semi-autonomous torpedo UUVs fitted with AI-enhanced sensors in a hibernating state mid-ocean in shallower waters near the Philippines.[15] A successful long-term Chinese military espionage campaign against a major US private defense contractor allowed China to deploy seabed sensors and pre-positioned communication buoys and implement its "smart minefield" operating concept.[16]

On a routine patrol of the South China Seas, somewhere off the coast of the Philippines, the USS Ronald Reagan Nimitz-class carrier's anti-UUV defenses detect aggressive behavior from a swarm of a dozen Chinese bulky torpedo drones. As a preemptive measure, the carrier uses its torpedo decoys to draw the Chinese drones away from the carrier group and then attempts to destroy the swarm with a "hard-kill interceptor."[17] Despite these countermeasures, the carrier group cannot destroy the entire swarm, leaving it vulnerable to the remainder, which heads full speed for the mother ship. The swarm delivers a punishing blizzard of kamikaze attacks, neutralizing the carriers' defenses and rendering it *hors de combat*.

In response to the bolt-from-the-blue attack, the Pentagon authorizes a B-21 Raider long-range strategic bomber[18] on a deterrence mission out of Guam to launch a limited conventional counterstrike on China's Yulin Naval Base, Hainan Island—housing China's submarine nuclear deterrent—designed to degrade but not decapitate PLAN's command-and-control. The bomber is supported by a swarm of "Little Buddy" unmanned combat aerial vehicles,[19] fitted with the latest "Skyborg" AI-powered "virtual copilot" computer brain human–machine interface (a robotic navigator, air-to-air combat tactician, and flight engineer) affectionately known as "R2-D2."[20]

Having developed a high degree of trust in R2-D2 and his swarm "Buddies" during a battery of simulation exercises (e.g., testing augmented reality headsets designed for gaming in visual range dogfighting scenarios), the pilots delegate "lower-level" cognitive functions (details of aircraft maneuver, weapon selection, and engagement tactics, etc.) to their AI teammates.[21] Simulated scenarios demonstrate the ability of "intelligent" autonomous machines to perform tactical decisions faster than humans, taking into consideration more data points and not being distracted or confused by the general fog and chaos of combat.[22] The pilots are particularly enamored with R2-D2's ability to produce a comprehensive real-time air picture and predict enemy air courses of intentions and tactics—reducing the cognitive burden in complex, cross-domain, and beyond-visual range engagements.

From a prioritized list of pre-approved targets, R2-D2 applies the latest AI-driven "Bugsplat" software to optimize the type of attack and weapons to employ, the timings involved, and any deconfliction considerations such as avoiding friendly fire.[23] R2-D2 passes this targeting information on to the Little Buddies, waiting for the green light to attack. With their targets in sight and weapons selections made, R2-D2 orders a pair of Little Buddies to identify and confuse Chinese air defenses using its electronic decoys and AI-driven infrared jammers and dazzlers—transmitting a range of signals of varying fidelity.

Simultaneously, a pair of Little Buddies fitted with a hypersonic cruise missile flying at low-supersonic speed is deployed beyond the pilots' visual range to soak up any undetected Chinese defenses, clearing the way for the B-21's air-to-ground long-range missile strike. To distract and confuse Chinese defenses, R2-D2 generates false anthropomorphic cues (non-aggressive flight maneuvers, concealing bulky mechanical devices, etc.) to suppress the swarms' offensive intentions and magnify their benign ones—causing the Chinese to misinterpret the size, type, timing, and intent of the attack and delaying their response.

Escalation increases with each passing turn. Beijing views the US B-21's operations as designed to undermine its sea-based nuclear deterrent in response to "Operation Island Freedom." Believing it could not risk allowing US forces to frustrate the initial successes of its Taiwanese invasion, China launches a conventional preemptive strike against US forces and bases in Japan and Guam. To signal deterrence, China concurrently detonates a high-altitude nuclear explosion off Hawaii's coast, resulting in an electromagnetic pulse. Time is now of the essence.

The attack is designed to disrupt and disable any unshielded or unprotected electronics on nearby ships or aircraft but not directly damage Hawaii. It is the first use of nuclear weapons in warfare since 1945. Because neither side understood the other's deterrence signaling, redlines, command decision-making processes, or escalation ladders, they could not effectively communicate that their actions were calibrated, proportional, and intended to force de-escalation.

Algorithmic warfare: old champagne in a new bottle?

How, if at all, does AI differ from other disruptive emerging technologies? What follows is a brief overview of the current state of "AI technology"[24] and the potential impact of these advances (e.g., machine learning, computer vision, speech recognition, natural language processing, and autonomous technology, see Figures 0.1–0.4) on military capabilities—in particular, those that interact with and augment human warfighters.[25] Because of the rapidly developing nature of this field, this primer can only provide a snapshot in time. That said, the underlying AI-related technical concepts and analysis described in this section will likely remain applicable for the foreseeable future.

AI research began as early as the 1950s as a broad concept concerned with the science and engineering of making intelligent machines.[26] In the decades that followed, AI research went through several development phases—from early exploitations in the 1950s and 1960s, the "AI summer" during the 1970s, through to the early 1980s, and the "AI winter" after the 1980s. Each of these failed to live up to its initial, and often over-hyped, expectations—particularly when *intelligence* was confused with *utility*.[27] Since the early 2010s, an explosion of interest in the field (or the "AI renaissance") has occurred due to the convergence of four critical enabling developments[28]: the exponential growth in computing processing power and cloud computing; expanded datasets (especially "big-data" sources)[29]; advances in the implementation of machine learning (ML) techniques and algorithms (especially deep "neural networks")[30]; and the rapid expansion of commercial interest and investment in AI technology.[31] Notwithstanding the advances in the algorithms used to construct ML systems, AI experts generally agree that the last decade's progress has had far more to do with increased data availability and computing power than improvements in algorithms per se.[32]

AI is concerned with machines that emulate capabilities usually associated with human intelligence, such as language, reasoning, learning, heuristics, and observation. Today, all practical (i.e., technically feasible) AI applications fall into either the "narrow" category (or "weak AI") or, less so, artificial general intelligence (AGI)—also referred to as "strong AI" or "superintelligence."[33] Narrow AI has been broadly used in a wide range of civilian and military tasks since the 1960s,[34] and involves statistical algorithms (mostly based on ML techniques) that learn procedures by analyzing large training datasets designed to approximate and replicate human cognitive tasks.[35] Narrow AI is the category of AI that this book refers to when it assesses the impact of AI technology in a military context.

Most experts agree that the development of AGI is at least several decades away, if feasible at all.[36] While the potential of AGI research is high, the anticipated exponential gains in the ability of AI systems to provide solutions to problems today are limited in scope. Moreover, these narrow-purpose applications do not necessarily translate well to more complex, holistic, and open-ended environments (i.e., modern battlefields), which exist simultaneously in the virtual (cyber/non-kinetic) and physical (or kinetic) plains.[37] However, that is not to say that the conversation on AGI and its potential impact should be entirely eschewed.[38] If AGI does emerge, then ethical, legal, and normative frameworks will need to be devised to anticipate the implications for what would be a potentially pivotal moment in the course of human history.[39] To complicate matters further, the distinction between narrow and general AI might prove less of an absolute (or binary) measure. Thus, research on narrow AI applications, such as game playing, medical diagnosis, and travel logistics, often results in incremental progress on general-purpose AI—moving researchers closer to AGI.[40]

AI has generally been viewed as a sub-field of computer science, focused on solving computationally complex problems through search, heuristics, and probability. More broadly, AI also draws heavily from mathematics, human psychology, biology, philosophy, linguistics, psychology, and neuroscience (see Figure 0.1).[41]

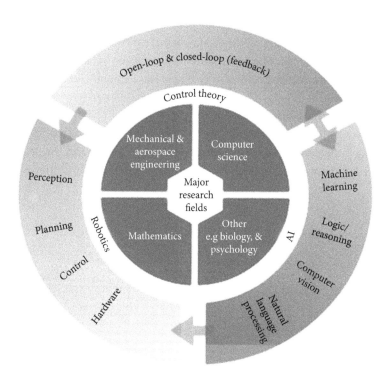

Figure 0.1 Major research fields and disciplines associated with AI

Source: James Johnson, *Artificial Intelligence & the Future of Warfare: USA, China, and Strategic Stability* (Manchester: Manchester University Press, 2021), p. 19

Because of the divergent risks involved and development timeframes in the two distinct types of AI, the discussion in this book is careful not to conflate them.[42] Given the diverse approaches to research in AI, there is no universally accepted definition,[43] which is confusing when the generic term "artificial intelligence" is used to make grandiose claims about its revolutionary impact on military affairs—or revolution in military affairs (RMA).[44] Moreover, if AI is defined too narrowly or too broadly, we risk understating the potential scope of AI capabilities; or, juxtaposed, fail to specify the unique capacity that AI-powered applications might have. A recent US congressional report defines AI as follows:

> Any artificial system that performs tasks under varying and unpredictable circumstances, *without significant human oversight*, or can learn from their experience and improve their performance, may solve tasks requiring human-like perception, cognition, planning, learning, communication, or physical action. (Emphasis added)[45]

Similarly, the UK Ministry of Defence understands AI as:

> A family of general-purpose technologies, any of which may enable machines to perform tasks *normally requiring human or biological intelligence*, especially when the machines learn from data how to do those tasks. (Emphasis added)[46]

AI can be best understood as a universal term for improving the performance of automated systems to solve a wide variety of complex tasks, including[47]: *perception* (sensors, computer vision, audio, and image processing); *reasoning and decision-making* (problem-solving, searching, planning,

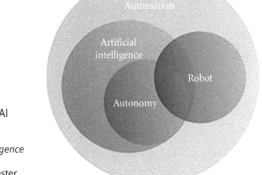

Figure 0.2 The linkages between AI and autonomy

Source: James Johnson, *Artificial Intelligence & the Future of Warfare: USA, China, and Strategic Stability* (Manchester: Manchester University Press, 2021), p. 20

and reasoning); *learning and knowledge representation* (ML, deep networks, and modeling); *communication* (language processing); *automatic* (or autonomous) *systems and robotics* (see Figures 0.1 and 0.2)[48]; and *human–AI collaboration* (humans define the systems' purpose, goals, and context).[49] As a potential enabler and force multiplier of a portfolio of capabilities, therefore, military AI is more akin to electricity, radios, radar, and ISR support systems than a "weapon" per se.[50]

Machine learning is not magic

ML is an approach to software engineering developed during the 1980s and 1990s,[51] based on computational systems that can "learn" and "teach"[52] themselves through a variety of techniques, such as neural networks, memory-based learning, case-based reasoning, decision trees, supervised learning, reinforcement learning, unsupervised learning, and, more recently, generative adversarial networks—which examine how systems that leverage ML algorithms might be tricked or defeated. Consequently, the need for cumbersome human hand-coded programming has been dramatically reduced.[53] From the fringes of AI until the 1990s, advances in ML algorithms with more sophisticated connections (i.e., statistics and control engineering) emerged as one of the most prominent AI methods (see Figure 0.3). In recent years, a subset of ML, deep learning (DL), has become the avant-garde AI software engineering approach, transforming raw data into abstract representations for a range of complex tasks, such as image recognition, sensor data, and simulated interactions (e.g., game playing).[54] The strength of DL is its ability to build complex concepts from simpler representations.[55]

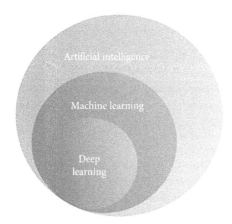

Figure 0.3 Hierarchical relationship: machine learning is a subset of AI, and deep learning is a subset of machine learning

Source: James Johnson, *Artificial Intelligence & the Future of Warfare: USA, China, and Strategic Stability* (Manchester: Manchester University Press, 2021), p. 22

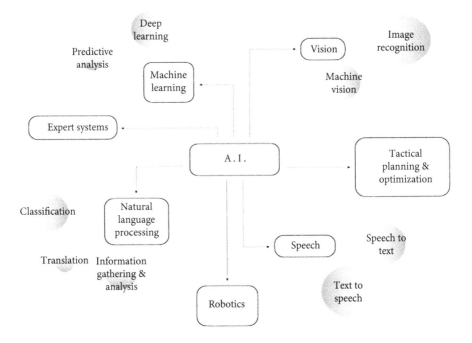

Figure 0.4 The "AI ecosystem"

Source: James Johnson, *Artificial Intelligence & the Future of Warfare: USA, China, and Strategic Stability* (Manchester: Manchester University Press, 2021), p. 23

Alongside the development of AI and ML, a new ecosystem of AI sub-fields and enablers has evolved, including: image recognition; machine vision; predictive analysis and planning; reasoning and representation; natural language representation and processing; robotics; and data classification (see Figure 0.4).[56] In combination, these techniques have the potential to enable a broad spectrum of increasingly autonomous applications, inter alia: big-data mining and analytics; AI voice assistants; language and voice recognition aids; structured query language data-basing; autonomous weapons and autonomous vehicles; and information gathering and analysis, to name a few. One of the critical advantages of ML is that human engineers no longer need to explicitly define the problem to be resolved in a particular operating environment.[57] For example, ML image recognition systems can be used to express mathematically the differences between images, which human hard-coders struggle to do.

ML's recent success can be mainly attributed to the rapid increase in computing power and the availability of vast datasets to train ML algorithms. Today, AI-ML techniques are routinely used in many everyday applications, including: empowering navigation maps for ridesharing software;

by banks to detect fraudulent and suspicious transactions; making recommendations to customers on shopping and entertainment websites; to support virtual personal assistants that use voice recognition software to offer their users content; and to enable improvements in medical diagnosis and scans.[58] While advances in ML-enabled AI applications for ISR performance—used in conjunction with human intelligence analysis—could augur qualitative improvements to weapons systems,[59] four major technical bottlenecks remain unresolved: brittleness; poor quality data (or "garbage in, garbage out"); automated image-detection limitations; and the so-called "black box" (or "explainability") problem-set.[60]

Brittleness problem

Today, AI suffers from several technical shortcomings that should prompt prudence and restraint in the early implementation of AI in a military context—and other safety-critical settings such as transportations and medicine. These shortcomings mean that AI faces asymmetric evaluation against a human operator—that is, the efficacy of autonomous systems deployed will need to be several times higher than humans in safety-critical contexts because any errors will not only impact one unit but may be instantiated exponentially in future iterations.[61]

AI systems are brittle in situations when an algorithm is unable to adapt or generalize to conditions beyond a narrow set of assumptions. That is, AIs do not have the capacity for high-order thinking (or "metacognition") that humans use for understanding the world and their place in it, which includes our beliefs, intuitions, intellect, knowledge of it, and how these arise.[62] Consequently, an AI's computer vision algorithms are unable to recognize an object due to minor perturbations or changes to an environment.[63] Human faces, for example, are notoriously hard for AI-trained facial recognition systems to parse, which has important implications for guidance and targeting systems in autonomous weapons. Thus, researchers are incentivized to develop algorithms (especially neural nets) that have the capacity to make novel inferences and form strong generalizations.[64]

Because "deep-reinforcement-learning" computer vision technology is still a relatively nascent technology, problems have been uncovered which demonstrate the vulnerability of these systems to uncertainty and manipulation.[65] In the case of autonomous cars, AI-ML computer vision does not cope with volatile weather conditions. For example, road lane markings partially covered with snow, or a tree branch partially obscuring a traffic

Figure 0.5 Edge decomposition illustration, courtesy of Wessam Bahnassi,
https://ar.wikipedia.org/wiki/ملف:Find_edges.jpg
[Public domain]

sign—which would be self-evident to a human—cannot be fathomed by a computer vision algorithm because the edges no longer match the system's internal model.[66] Figure 0.5 illustrates how an image can be deconstructed into its edges (i.e., through mathematical computations to identify transitions between dark and light colors): while humans see a tiger, an AI algorithm "sees" sets of lines in various clusters.[67]

ML algorithms are unable to effectively leverage "top-down" reasoning (or "System 2" thinking) to make inferences from experience, episodic memory, and abstract counterfactual reasoning (see Chapter 5) when perception is driven by cognition expectations.[68] This capacity is vital when decisions are high risk, or ethically and legally challenging—for instance, in safety-critical systems where confusion, uncertainty, and imperfect information require adaptions to novel situations.[69] This reasoning underpins people's common sense and allows us to learn complex tasks, such as driving, with very little practice or foundational learning. By contrast, "bottom-up" reasoning (or "System 1" thinking) occurs when information is taken in at the perceptual sensor level (eyes, ears, sense of touch, etc.) to construct a model of the world to perform narrow tasks such as object and speech recognition and natural language processing, which AIs perform well.[70]

People's ability to use judgment and intuition to infer relationships from partial information (i.e., "top-down" reasoning) is illustrated by the Kanizsa triangle visual illusion (see Figure 0.6). AI-ML algorithms lack the requisite sense of causality that is critical for understanding what to do in novel

Figure 0.6 The Kanizsa triangle visual illusion, courtesy of Fibonacci, https:// commons.wikimedia.org/wiki/ File:Kanizsa_triangle.svg
[Public domain]

a priori situations and have thus been unable to either recognize or replicate visual illusions.[71] While advancements have recently been made in computer vision—and the DL algorithms that power these systems—the perceptual models of the real-world constructed by these systems are inherently brittle. The real world characterized by uncertainty (i.e., partial observability), data scarcity, ambiguous and nuanced goals, and disparate timescales of decision-making and so on creates technological gaps, which has important implications for future collaboration with humans.[72]

Consequently, AI cannot effectively and reliably diagnose errors (e.g., sampling errors or intentional manipulation) from complex datasets and the esoteric mathematics underlying AI algorithms.[73] Moreover, AI systems cannot handle novel situations reliably; AI relies on a posteriori knowledge (i.e., "skills-based" knowledge) to make inferences and inform decision-making. Failure to execute a particular task, especially if biased results are generated, would likely diminish the level of trust placed in these applications.[74] In a recent study by AI researchers at MIT Lincoln Laboratory, researchers used the card game Hanabi—a game of full cooperation and limited information— to explore whether a state-of-the-art deep-learning reinforcement learning program that surpassed human abilities could become a reliable and trusted coworker. The study found that high performance by the AI did not translate into a good collaboration experience. Instead, players complained about the program's poor understanding of human subjective preferences and a resultant lack of trust.[75]

A key future challenge for the AI-ML community is how to design algorithmic architectures and training frameworks that incorporate human inductive biases and a priori qualities such as reasoning, intuition, shared knowledge, and understanding social cues.[76] With this goal in mind, researchers from IBM, MIT, and Harvard University recently collaborated on a Defense Advanced Research Projects Agency-sponsored "Common Sense AI" dataset for benchmarking AI intuition.[77] Inspired by development studies of infants, this was the first study of its kind to use human psychology to accelerate the development of AI systems that exhibit common sense—to learn core intuitive human psychology while maintaining their autonomy. The researchers constructed two ML approaches to test real-world scenarios, thus establishing a valuable baseline for these ML models to learn from humans while maintaining their autonomy.

Garbage in, garbage out

ML systems depend on vast amounts of high-quality prelabeled datasets (with both positive and negative examples) and trails to learn from, which humans are able to generalize with far less experience.[78] ML algorithms operate based on correlation, not causation—that is, algorithms analyze incoming data against clearly defined outputs to identify patterns of correlation.[79] AI-ML is, therefore, only as good as the *quantity and quality* of the data it is trained on (i.e., input data linked to associated outcomes) before, and supplied with during, operations—or "garbage in, garbage out."[80] The performance of ML systems can be improved by scaling them up with higher volumes of data and increased computation power. For example, OpenAI's language processing model GPT-3—and OpenAI's GPT-4, ChatGPT fine-tuned versions—boasts some 170 trillion parameters, which is still far less than the number of synapses in the human brain.[81] Despite these significant milestones, there remain fundamental deficiencies of current ML approaches that cannot be resolved by scaling (so-called "scaling maximalism") or computational power alone.[82]

No matter how sophisticated the datasets are, however, they are unable to replicate real-world situations perfectly. Each situation includes some irreducible error (or an error due to variance) because of incomplete and imprecise measurements and estimates. According to the former US DoD's Joint Artificial Intelligence Center former director, Lt. General Jack Shanahan, "if you train [ML systems] against a very clean, gold-standard dataset, it will *not work in real-world conditions*" (emphasis added).[83] Further, relatively easy and cheap efforts (or "adversarial AI") to fool these systems would likely render even the most sophisticated systems redundant.[84]

As a corollary, an ML system that memorizes data within a particular training set may fail when exposed to new and unfamiliar data. Because there is an infinite number of engineering options, it is impossible to tailor an algorithm for all eventualities. Thus, as new data emerges, a near-perfect algorithm will likely quickly become redundant. There is minimal room for error in a military context in balancing the pros and cons of deciding how much data to supply ML systems to learn from—or "bias-variance trade-off."[85] Even if a method was developed that performs flawlessly on the data fed to it, there is no guarantee that the system will perform in the same way on images it receives subsequently. As a result, less sophisticated AI systems will exhibit more significant levels of bias but with lower accuracy.

As a corollary, there is no way to know for sure how ML-infused autonomous weapon systems, such as AI-enhanced conventional counter-force (or strategic non-nuclear weapons) capabilities, would function in the field.[86] AI-enhanced capabilities will be prone to errors and accidents because of the critical feedback from testing, validation, prototyping, and live testing (associated with the development of kinetic weapon systems).[87] Because there is a naturally recursive relationship in how AI systems interact with humans and information, the likelihood of errors may be both amplified and reduced.

Three technical limitations contribute to this data shortage problem.[88] First, in the military sphere, AI systems have relatively few images to train on (e.g., mobile road- and rail-based missile launchers). This data imbalance will cause an AI system to maximize its accuracy by substituting images with a greater abundance of data, filling the gaps in missing information to (mis)identify patterns and trends.[89] In other words, to maximize accuracy in classifying images, ML algorithms are incentivized to produce positives and negatives, such as misclassifying a regular truck as a mobile missile launcher. Without distinguishing between true and false, *all moving targets* could be considered viable targets by AI systems.

Second, AI is at a very early stage of "concept learning."[90] Images generally depict reality poorly. Whereas humans can deduce—using common sense—the function of an object from its external characteristics, AI struggles with this seemingly simple task. In situations where an object's form explicitly tells us about its function (i.e., language processing, speech, and handwriting recognition), this is less of an issue, and narrow AI generally performs well. However, in situations where an object's appearance does not offer this kind of information, AI's ability to induce or infer is limited.[91] Thus, the ability of ML algorithms to reason is far inferior to human conjecture and criticism.[92] For example, in a military context AI would struggle to differentiate the military function of a vehicle or platform. This problem is compounded by the shortage of quality datasets and the likelihood of AI adversarial efforts poised to exploit this shortcoming.

Third, ML becomes exponentially more challenging as the number of features, pixels, and dimensionality increase.[93] Greater levels of resolution and dimensional complexity—requiring more memory and time for ML algorithms to learn—could mean that images become increasingly difficult for AI to differentiate. For example, a rail-based mobile missile launcher might appear to AI as a cargo train car, or a military aircraft as a commercial airliner. In short, similar objects will become increasingly dissimilar to the AI, while images of different and unrelated objects will become increasingly indistinguishable.[94]

Automated image-detection limitations

ML's ability to autonomously detect and cue precision-guided munitions is limited, particularly in cluttered and complex operational environments. These automated image recognition and detection weaknesses are mainly caused by AI's inability to effectively mimic human vision and cognition, which is notoriously opaque and irrational.[95] This limitation could, for example, reduce a commander's confidence in the effectiveness of AI-augmented capabilities, with potentially significant implications for deterrence, escalation, and crisis stability (see Chapters 4 and 5).[96] Besides this, strategic competitors will continue to pursue countermeasures (e.g., camouflage, deception, decoys, and concealment) to protect their military forces against these advances.

The "black box" problem

ML algorithms today are inherently opaque—especially those built on neural networks—creating "black box" computational mechanisms that human engineers frequently struggle to fathom.[97] This "black box" problem-set may cause unpredictability, for instance algorithms reacting in unexpected ways to datasets used during the training phase, which could have severe consequences at a strategic level—not least, complicating the problem of attributing responsibility and accountability in the event of an accident, or error in the safety-critical nuclear domain.[98] For instance, in a military context it may not be possible to determine with any precision the weighting an algorithm gave to troop movements, weapons stockpiling, human intelligence, social media, and geospatial opensource information, or other historical data that an AI uses to reach a particular prediction or recommendation.[99]

While it is conceptually possible for AIs to reveal the information on which their prediction or recommendation is derived, because of the vast quantity of potential data an AI can feed from, the complexity of the weighting, the relationships between data points, and the continuous adaptions made by algorithms in dynamic environments, building explainable and transparent algorithms—that is, algorithms that can list the factors considered and explicate the weighting given to each factor—which humans can comprehend will be extremely challenging.[100] In sum, algorithmic brittleness, a dearth of quality datasets for ML algorithms to learn from, automated detection technical limitations, the likelihood of adversarial countermeasures and exploitation, and the opacity of ML algorithms will significantly reduce the a priori knowledge AI systems can obtain from a situation—particularly complex adversarial environments.

Therefore, to mitigate the potentially destabilizing effects of deploying either poorly conceptualized, immature, or accidental-prone AIs into the safety-critical domains (aviation, health care, autonomous vehicles, space, maritime, nuclear, and military etc.), decision-makers need to better understand what AI is capable of, its limitations, and how best to implement AI in a military context.[101] Furthermore, while AI augmentation of humans in safety-critical domains is already within reach, this technical landmark should not be mistaken for the ability of AI to replace humans and go under-supervised in the operation of these systems (see Appendix 2).[102]

Book plan

The remaining five chapters of this book explore a range of themes that are integral to understanding human–machine interactions in modern warfare. Chapter 1 sets the stage for the remainder of the book by focusing on the central elements of the ethical and political dilemmas of human–machine interactions in algorithmic warfare. Can AI solve the ethical-political dilemmas of warfare? While much of the present debate has revolved around ethical and legal concerns about fielding lethal robots (or "killer robots") into armed conflict, less attention has focused on AI-enabled warfare's ethical, moral, and psychological dilemmas. The chapter fills a gap in discussions of complex socio-technical interactions between AI and warfare. It offers a counterpoint to the argument that AI "rational" efficiency can simultaneously offer a viable solution to humans' psychological and biological fallibility in combat while retaining "meaningful" human control over the war machine. This Panglossian assumption neglects the psychological features of human–machine interactions, the pace at which future AI-enabled conflict will be fought, and the complex and chaotic nature of modern war. The chapter details a series of key psychological insights of human–machine interactions to elucidate how AI shapes our capacity to think about future warfare's political and ethical dilemmas. It argues that through the psychological process of human–machine integration, AIs will not merely force multiply existing advanced weaponry, but will become de facto strategic actors in warfare—the "AI commander problem."

Chapter 2 turns to the problem of anthropomorphic tendencies in AI. It argues that until AI surpasses human intelligence, anthropomorphism will play a critical role in human–machine interactions in tactical operations, which depend on fast, cognitively parsimonious, and efficacious communication. Thus, understanding the various (social and cognitive) psychological mechanisms that undergird AI-anthropomorphism is crucial in determining the potential impact of military human–machine interactions. While the limitations of AI technology in human–machine interaction are well known, how the spontaneous tendency to anthropomorphize AI agents might affect the psychological (cognitive/behavioral) and motivational aspects of hybrid military operations has garnered far less attention. How does anthropomorphizing AI affect human–machine collaboration in hybrid military operations? This chapter identifies some potential epistemological, ontological, normative, and ethical consequences of humanizing algorithms—that is, the use of anthropomorphic language and discourse—for the conduct of war. It also considers the possible impact of the AI-anthropomorphism phenomenon on the inverse process of dehumanization.

Chapter 3 explores themes relating to the use of machines to support command decisions in warfare. The chapter argues that AI-enabled capabilities cannot effectively or reliably complement (let alone replace) the critical role of humans in understanding and apprehending the strategic environment—to make predictions and judgments that inform strategy. Furthermore, the rapid diffusion of and growing dependency on AI technology at *all levels of warfare* will have strategic consequences that counterintuitively increase the importance of human involvement in these tasks. The chapter revisits John Boyd's decision-making "OODA loop" to advance a critique of AI-enabled capabilities to augment command decision-making processes. It draws insights from Boyd's emphasis on "orientation" as a schema to elucidate the role of human cognition (perception, emotion, and heuristics) in defense planning in a non-linear world characterized by complexity, novelty, and uncertainty. The chapter addresses ongoing debates about whether AI will alleviate or exacerbate war's fog and friction. It also engages with the Clausewitzian notion of "military genius" (and its role in mission command), human cognition, and systems and evolution theory to consider the strategic implications of automating the OODA loop.

Chapter 4 evokes Thomas Schelling's theory of "threat that leaves something to chance" to consider how states can credibly signal resolve and compete under the shadow of a nuclear war. Schelling's theory provides insight into how and why state actors may seek to manipulate risk to achieve competitive advantage in bargaining situations and how this contest of nerves, resolve, and credibility can lead states to stumble inadvertently into war. How might the dynamics of the age of AI affect Schelling's theory? The chapter explores the implications of his insights on crisis stability between nuclear-armed rivals in the age of AI-enabling technology and contextualizes them within the broader information ecosystem. It engages with interdisciplinary human psychology, behavioral science, and anthropological studies, offering fresh perspectives and insights on the "AI-nuclear dilemma"—the intersection of technological change, strategic thinking, and nuclear risk.[103] The chapter concludes that the risks of nuclear-armed states leveraging Schelling's "something to chance" in the digital era obviate any potential bargaining benefits in brinkmanship.

Chapter 5 advances a human-centric policy response to the "AI-nuclear dilemma" described in Chapter 4. It demonstrates the utility of counterfactual reasoning as a means by which decision-makers can avoid myopic technological determinism and thus consider alternative outcomes to hedge against unforeseen risk and technological surprise. This chapter builds on the concept of "future counterfactuals" to construct imaginative yet realistic scenarios to consider the future possibility of a nuclear exchange in AI-enabled warfare. It highlights the critical role counterfactual scenarios can play in challenging conventional wisdom, preconceived assumptions, and human biases associated with the "AI-nuclear dilemma." In emphasizing the role of uncertainty, cognitive bias, and fundamental uncertainty in world politics, the chapter also contributes to cognitivist discourse about emerging technology and the risk of inadvertent and accidental nuclear war.

Notes

1   The concept of "emerging technologies" is a loose and ill-defined one and often used interchangeably when discussing the impact of technologies such as cyberspace, social media, autonomous weapons, quantum computing, rail guns, directed energy weapons, 3D printing, and AI. Emerging technologies can mean different things to different people

and are analytically very distinct; for example, cyber capabilities can enable offensive capabilities to penetrate and compromise an adversary's systems, while social media can permit attackers to influence perceptions, create false memes, or otherwise disrupt or upend prevailing norms. AI can amplify and enhance the potency and efficacy of these effects. James Johnson, *AI and the Bomb: Nuclear Strategy and Risk in the Digital Age* (Oxford: Oxford University Press, 2023), p. 27.

2   While some draw a distinction between the terms morals and ethics—contested in many respects—this book uses these terms interchangeably.

3   See Elvira Robert and Frank Sauer, "How (Not) to Stop the Killer Robots: A Comparative Analysis of Humanitarian Disarmament Campaign Strategies," *Contemporary Security Policy* 42 (1) (2021), pp. 4–29; Vincent Boulanin, Netta Goussac, and Laura Bruun, *Autonomous Weapon Systems and International Humanitarian Law: Identifying Limits and the Required Type and Degree of Human–Machine Interaction* (Stockholm: SIPRI, June 2021).

4   See, for example, "British Approach to Robotics and Autonomous Systems: Generating Human–Machine Teams," *UK Ministry of Defence*, 2022, www.army.mod.uk/media/ 15790/20220126_army-approach-to-ras_final.pdf; Mick Ryan, *Man-Machine Teaming for Future Ground Forces* (Washington, D.C.: Center for Strategic and Budgetary Assessments, 2018); US Department of Defense, "Summary of the Joint All-Domain Command and Control (JADC2) Strategy," March 2022, https://media.defense.gov/ 2022/Mar/17/2002958406/-1/-1/1/SUMMARY-OF-THE-JOINT-ALL-DOMAIN-COMMAND-AND-CONTROL-STRATEGY.PDF.

5   Paul Scharre, "Centaur Warfighting," in *Autonomous Weapons and Operational Risk: Ethical Autonomy Project* (Washington D.C.: Center for a New American Security, 2016).

6   James Johnson, *Artificial Intelligence and the Future of Warfare: USA, China, and Strategic Stability* (Manchester: Manchester University Press, 2021).

7   Michael Brough, "Dehumanization of the Enemy and the Moral Equality of Soldiers," in *Rethinking the Just War Tradition*, ed. Michael Brough, John Lango, and Harry van der Linden (New York: SUNY Press, 2007), pp. 160–161; Nick Haslam, "Dehumanization: An Integrative Review," *Personality and Social Psychology Review* 10 (3) (2006), pp. 252–264.

8   Susan T. Fiske and Shelley E. Taylor, *Social Cognition*. 2nd ed. (New York: McGraw-Hill, 1991).

9   This fictional vignette assumes the following: (1) great power competition intensifies in the Indo-Pacific, geopolitical tensions increase in the Taiwan Straits; (2) deterrence fails, China reaches a military capability to invade and seize Taiwan; and (3) the US and China both master AI-enabled "loyal wingman" technology and operational concepts to support them.

10   James Johnson, "Counterfactual Thinking & Nuclear Risk in the Digital Age: The Role of Uncertainty, Complexity, Chance, and Human Psychology," *Journal for Peace and Nuclear Disarmament*, 5 (2) (2022), pp. 394-421, doi:10.1080/25751654.2022.2102286.

11   Liu Xuanzun, "J-20 Fighter Could Get Directed-Energy Weapon, Drone-Control Capability: Experts," *Global Times*, January 23, 2022, www.globaltimes.cn/page/202201/ 1246676.shtml.

12   David Hambling, "China Releases Video of New Barrage Swarm Drone Launcher," *Forbes*, December 14, 2020, www.forbes.com/sites/davidhambling/2020/10/14/china-releases-video-of-new-barrage-swarm-drone-launcher/?sh=6ae547582ad7.

13   Franz-Stefan Gady, "How Chinese Unmanned Platforms Could Degrade Taiwan's Air Defence and Disable a US Navy Carrier," *IISS*, June 9, 2021, www.iiss.org/blogs/analysis/2021/06/china-taiwan-unmanned-platforms.

14   Acoustic underwater transmission suffers from latency and low bandwidth and is also highly detectable by an adversary, while optical communication is limited to short ranges.

15   Tyler Rogoway and Joseph Trevithick, "A Vietnamese Fisherman Reeled in a Chinese Torpedo in the South China Sea," *The Drive*, December 19, 2018, https://www.thedrive.com/the-war-zone/25596/a-vietnamese-fisherman-reeled-in-a-chinese-torpedo-in-the-south-china-sea.

16   Yusuke Yokota and Takumi Matsuda, "Underwater Communication Using UAV to Realize High-speed AUV Deployment," *Preprints* (2021), doi:10.20944/preprints202108.0330.v1.

17   Joseph Trevithick, "The Navy is Ripping out Underperforming Anti-Torpedo Torpedoes from its Supercarriers," *The Drive*, February 5, 2019, www.thedrive.com/the-war-zone/26347/the-navy-is-ripping-out-underperforming-anti-torpedo-torpedoes-from-its-supercarriers.

18   Analysts estimate that the US will have approximately twenty operational-ready B-21s by 2027, which could yield over 300 1,000-pound precision weapon strikes per day against Chinese maritime targets. Robert Haddick, "Defeat China's Navy, Defeat China's War Plan," *War on the Rocks*, September 21, 2022, https://warontherocks.com/2022/09/defeat-chinas-navy-defeat-chinas-war-plan/.

19   Robert Farley, "A Raider and His 'Little Buddy': Which Fighter Will Accompany the USAF's B-21?" *The Diplomat*, September 24, 2016, https://thediplomat.com/2016/09/a-raider-and-his-little-buddy-which-fighter-will-accompany-the-usafs-b–21/.

20   Brett Tingley, "Skyborg AI Computer 'Brain' Successfully Flew a General Atomics Avenger Drone," *The Drive*, June 30, 2021, https://www.thedrive.com/the-war-zone/41364/skyborg-ai-computer-brain-successfully-flew-a-general-atomics-avenger-drone.

21   "Red 6 completes AR training with multiple aircraft," *Airforce Technology*, June 7, 2022, www.airforce-technology.com/news/red6-ar-training-multiple-aircraft/.

22   Ryan Hefron, "Air Combat Evolution (ACE)," *DARPA*, www.darpa.mil/program/air-combat-evolution.

23   John Emery, "Probabilities Towards Death: Bugsplat, Algorithmic Assassinations, and Ethical Due Care," *Critical Military Studies* 8 (2) (2022), pp. 179–197.

24   The term "AI technology" used in the book refers to a broad category of technologies that are either enablers of AI capabilities and applications (e.g., ML and deep-learning neural networks, 5G networks, and quantum computing) or enabled/enhanced by AI systems (e.g., robotics and autonomy, GANs, big-data analytics, and the internet of things).

25   This section is derived in part from Johnson, *AI and the Bomb*, Introduction. For a more technical and comprehensive analysis, see, for example, Stuart Russell and Peter Norvig, *Artificial Intelligence: A Modern Approach*. 3rd ed. (Harlow: Pearson Education, 2014); Stuart Russell, *Human Compatible* (New York: Viking Press, 2019).

26   Andy Pearl, "Homage to John McCarthy, the Father of Artificial Intelligence (AI)," *Artificial Solutions*, June 2, 2017, www.artificial-solutions.com/blog/homage-to-john-mccarthy-the-father-of-artificialintelligence.

27   Nils J. Nilsson, *The Quest for Artificial Intelligence: A History of Ideas and Achievements* (New York: Cambridge University Press, 2010).

28   Executive Office of the President, National Science and Technology Council, Committee on Technology, *Preparing for the Future of Artificial Intelligence*, October 12, 2016, https://obamawhitehouse.archives.gov/sites/default/files/whitehouse_files/microsites/ostp/NSTC/preparing_for_the_future_of_ai.pdf, p. 6.

29   Though many AI systems rely on large amounts of data, AI does not necessarily entail the volume, velocity, and variety usually associated with big-data analytics. Thus, while big data is not new, and does not necessarily incorporate AI, AI techniques will likely supercharge the mining of data-rich sources. E. Gray et al., "Small Big Data: Using Multiple Datasets to Explore Unfolding Social and Economic Change," *Big Data & Society* 2 (1) (2015), pp. 1–6.

30   ML is a concept that encompasses a wide variety of techniques designed to identify patterns in, and "learn" and make predictions from, datasets. Successful "learning" depends on having access to vast pools of reliable data about past behavior and successful outcomes. The "neural network" approach to AI represents only a small segment of the improvements in AI techniques. AI also includes, for example, language processing, knowledge representation, and inferential reasoning, which is being actualized by the rapid advancements in software, hardware, data collection, and data storage. See, for example, Jürgen Schmidhuber, "Deep Learning in Neural Networks: An Overview," *Neural Networks* 61 (January 2015), pp. 85–117; Dzmitry Bahdanau, Kyunghyun Cho, and Yoshua Bengio, "Neural Machine Translation by Jointly Learning to Align and Translate" (2014), https://arXiv:1409.0473; and Yoshua Bengio, Yann Lecun, and Geoffrey Hinton, "Deep Learning for AI," *Communications of the ACM* 64 (7) (July 2021), pp. 58–65.

31   US technology companies reportedly invested an estimated US$20 to US$30 billion in narrow AI algorithms in 2016, and this amount is expected to reach $126 billion by 2025. At the same time, global AI-generated revenue is projected to climb from US$643.7 million in 2016 to US$36.8 billion in 2025, a factor of almost sixty times greater. Daniel S. Hoadley and Lucas J. Nathan, "Artificial Intelligence and National Security," *Congressional Research Report for Congress*, November 2, 2020, p. 2, https://fas.org/sgp/crs/natsec/R45178.pdf.

32   See Ben Buchanan, "The AI Triad and What it Means for National Security Strategy," Center for Security and Emerging Technology, August 2020, https://cset.georgetown.edu/wp-content/uploads/CSET-AI-Triad-Report.pdf.

33   Nick Bostrom, *Superintelligence: Paths, Dangers, Strategies* (Oxford: Oxford University Press, 2014).

34   See Russell and Norvig, *Artificial Intelligence*; Nilsson, *The Quest for Artificial Intelligence*.

35   ML algorithms generate statistical models to accomplish a specified task in situations they have not previously encountered during the "learning" process. Most recent advances in AI applications have occurred with non-symbolic ML approaches—computationally intensive, linear algebra, and statistical methods where input and knowledge representation are numerical, e.g., image pixels and audio frequencies. See Russell and Norvig, *Artificial Intelligence*.

36   AI "narrow" breakthroughs have led to speculation about the arrival of AGI. See Nanyi Fei et al., "Towards Artificial General Intelligence via a Multimodal Foundation Model," *Nature Communications* 13 (3094) (2022), doi:10.1038/s41467-022-30761-2; Stuart Armstrong, Kaj Sotala, and Seán S. ÓhÉigeartaigh, "The Errors, Insights, and Lessons of

Famous AI Predictions—And What They Mean for the Future," *Journal of Experimental & Theoretical Artificial Intelligence* 26 (3) (2014), pp. 317–342.

37   Technology for Global Security (T4GS), "AI and Human Decision-Making: AI and the Battlefield," *T4GSReports*, November 28, 2018, www.tech4gs.org/ai-and-human-decisionmaking.html.

38   See Johnson, *AI and the Bomb*, Chs 1 and 2.

39   See Amandeep Singh Gill, "Artificial Intelligence and International Security: The Long View," *Ethics and International Affairs* 33 (2) (2019), pp. 169–179.

40   Russell, *Human Compatible*, p. 136.

41   For an excellent overview of AI and its various subfields, see Margaret A. Boden, *AI: Its Nature and Future* (Oxford: Oxford University Press, 2016); and David Vernon, *Artificial Cognitive Systems: A Primer* (Cambridge, MA: MIT Press, 2014).

42   "Narrow" AI has inherent limitations and lacks a capacity for will and intent. Therefore, used in a military context, it is a tool to enhance or enable weapon systems, not an independent actor. See Lawrence Lewis, *AI and Autonomy in War* (Washington, D.C.: Center for Naval Analysis, August 2018), p. 17, www.cna.org/CNA_files/PDF/Understanding-Risks.pdf.

43   Historical definitions of AI can be grouped as follows: systems that think like humans; systems that act like humans; and systems that act and reason. See Andrew W. Moore, "AI and National Security in 2017," Presentation at AI and Global Security Summit, Washington, D.C., November 1, 2017; Andrew Ilachinski, *AI, Robots, and Swarms: Issues, Questions, and Recommended Studies* (Washington, D.C.: Center for Naval Analysis, January 2017), p. 6.

44   The term revolution in military affairs (RMA) was popularized in the 1990s and early 2000s, especially within the US defense community. An RMA is usually caused by technology but is not *revolutionary* unless it changes how states fight wars. See Knox MacGreger, Murray Williamson ed. *The Dynamics of Military Revolution* (Cambridge: Cambridge University Press, 2001), pp. 1300–2050; and Colin S. Gray, *Strategy for Chaos: Revolutions in Military Affairs and the Evidence of History* (London: Frank Cass, 2002). For Chinese views on the debate, see Fu Wanjuan, Yang Wenzhe, and Xu Chunlei, "Intelligent Warfare: Where Does it Not Change?" *PLA Daily*, January 14, 2020, www.81. cn/jfjbmap/content/2020-01/14/content_252163.htm; and Lin Juanjuan, Zhang Yuantao, and Wang Wei, "Military Intelligence is Profoundly Affecting Future Operations," *Ministry of National Defense of the People's Republic of China*, September 10, 2019, www.mod. gov.cn/jmsd/201909/10/content_4850148.htm.

45   Hoadley and Lucas, "Artificial Intelligence and National Security," pp. 1–2.

46   UK Ministry of Defence, "Defence Artificial Intelligence Strategy," June 15, 2022, www.gov.uk/government/publications/defence-artificial-intelligence-strategy/defence-artificial-intelligence-strategy.

47   Ibid., p. 3; Moore, "AI and National Security in 2017."

48   The terms "autonomy" and "automated" are often used interchangeably. An automated system is one that behaves according to preprogrammed instructions for a specific task with clearly defined parameters. By contrast, an "autonomous" system is one that independently (i.e., without strictly defined parameters) and dynamically determines—using complex feedback loops—if, when, and how to execute a particular task. As shown in Chapters 1 and 2, the demarcation between the two is a nuanced continuum. Automated

drones like the US Global Hawk and MQ-9 Reaper, for example, are automated systems that under certain circumstances—such as when it senses a loss of communication with its operators—possesses a low-level autonomous capacity.

49 "Autonomy" in the context of military applications can be defined as the condition or quality of being self-governing to achieve an assigned task, based on a system's situational awareness (integrated sensing, perceiving, and analyzing), planning, and decision-making. An autonomous weapon system (or lethal autonomous weapon system) is a weapon system that, once activated, can identify, target, and attack without the intervention of a human operator. A fully autonomous system is never, however, completely free from human interaction: either a system designer or an operator would retain the ability to program the system to function pursuant to specified parameters. See US Department of Defense, *Directive 3000.09, Autonomy in Weapon Systems*, www.esd.whs. mil/Portals/54/Documents/DD/issuances/DODd/300009p.pdf.

50 Michael C. Horowitz, "Artificial Intelligence, International Competition, and the Balance of Power," *Texas National Security Review* 1 (3) (2018), pp. 37–57.

51 Matthew Hutson, "AI Researchers Allege that Machine Learning is Alchemy," *Science*, May 3, 2018, www.sciencemag.org/news/2018/05/ai-researchers-allege-machine-learning-alchemy.

52 The concept of "learning" and "teaching" in the context of ML refers to finding statistical relationships in past data, as opposed to anthropomorphic interpretations that confuse human learning with machine learning. See David Watson, "The Rhetoric and Reality of Anthropomorphism in Artificial Intelligence," *Minds and Machines* 29 (2019), pp. 417–440.

53 A computational method known as "artificial neural networks" draws on knowledge of the human brain, statistics, and applied mathematics. Nilsson, *The Quest for Artificial Intelligence*, Chs 28–29.

54 DL is an approach to ML whereby the system "learns" how to undertake a task in either a supervised, semi-supervised, or unsupervised manner. See Mehmet Akçakaya et al., "Unsupervised Deep Learning Methods for Biological Image Reconstruction and Enhancement: An Overview from a Signal Processing Perspective," *IEEE Signal Processing Magazine* 39 (2) (March 2022), pp. 28–44, doi:10.1109/MSP.2021.3119273; Ian Goodfellow, Yoshua Bengio, and Aaron Courville, *Deep Learning* (Cambridge, MA: MIT Press, 2016).

55 Several recent AI innovations continue to use the previous generation of hard-coded techniques such as Bayesian statistics, probabilistic relational models, and other evolutionary algorithms. Nilsson, *The Quest for Artificial Intelligence*, Chs 28–29.

56 Ibid., p. 347.

57 In contrast, hand-coded programming often requires a significant amount of research on how the world works—or contextual analysis. Russell and Norvig, *Artificial Intelligence*, Ch. 18; Matteo Iovino et al., "A Survey of Behavior Trees in Robotics and AI," *Robotics and Autonomous Systems* 154 (2022), doi:10.1016/j.robot.2022.104096.

58 Lewis, *AI and Autonomy in War*.

59 See James Johnson, "'Catalytic Nuclear War' in the Age of Artificial Intelligence & Autonomy: Emerging Military Technology and Escalation Risk Between Nuclear-Armed States," *Journal of Strategic Studies* (2021), doi:10.1080/01402390.2020.1867541.

[60] Juanjuan, Yuantao, and Wei, "Military Intelligence is Profoundly Affecting Future Operations."

[61] See Paul Scharre, *Army of None: Autonomous Weapons and the Future of War* (New York: W.W. Norton & Company, 2018).

[62] Hilary Kornblith, "Sosa in Perspective," *Philosophical Studies* 144 (1) (2009), pp. 127–136.

[63] See Nadine Carter, David Woods, and Charles Billings, "Automation Surprises," in *Handbook of Human Factors and Ergonomics*, ed. G. Salvendy. 2nd ed. (New York: John Wiley & Sons Inc., 1997).

[64] For instance, the US Defense Advanced Research Projects Agency's (DARPA) Science of Artificial Intelligence and Learning for Open-world Novelty (SAIL-ON) program is researching the potential read-through of neuroscience and algorithmic neural nets that have the capacity for strong forms of generalization. Ted Senator, "Science of Artificial Intelligence and Learning for Open-World Novelty (SAIL-ON)," *DARPA*, www.darpa.mil/program/science-of-artificial-intelligence-and-learning-for-open-world-novelty.

[65] For example, AI researchers recently discovered that neural nets are not capturing accurate depth information in images, which may have important safety ramifications. See Tom van Dijk and Guido de Croon, "How do Neural Networks See Depth in Single Images?", (2019), https://arXiv.org/abs/1905.07005; Jeongeun Park, Hyunjae Lee, and Ha Young Kim, "Risk Factor Recognition for Automatic Safety Management in Construction Sites Using Fast Deep Convolutional Neural Networks," *Applied Sciences* 12 (2) 694 (2022) doi:10.3390/app12020694.

[66] Tom Krishner, "5 Reasons Why Autonomous Cars Aren't Coming Anytime Soon," *AP News*, February 4, 2019, https://apnews.com/b67a0d6b6413406fb4121553cdf0b95a; and Roger K. Lewis, "Reality is Going to Stall for Some Time the Advent of Driverless Cars," *Washington Post*, August 2, 2019, www.washingtonpost.com/realestate/reality-is-going-to-stallfor-some-time-the-advent-of-driverless-cars/2019/08/01/343c9458-afa8-11e9-a0c9-6d2d7818f3da_story.html.

[67] See Kavindu Ranasinghe et al., "Advances in Integrated System Health Management for Mission-Essential and Safety-Critical Aerospace Applications," *Progress in Aerospace Sciences* 128 (100758) (2022), doi:10.1016/j.paerosci.2021.100758; Mary L. Cummings, "Rethinking the Maturity of Artificial Intelligence in Safety-Critical Settings," *AI Magazine* 42 (1) (Spring 2021), p. 2.

[68] The human brain functions in many ways that accord with Bayesian approaches to epistemology. That is, top-down predictions are compared with incoming signals, which allow the brain to adapt its mental model of the world. Andy Clark, *Surfing Uncertainty: Prediction, Action, and the Embodied Mind* (New York: Oxford University Press, 2015).

[69] Bengio, Lecun, and Hinton, "Deep Learning for AI," pp. 58 65.

[70] Using ML-DL for top-down (or "System 2") tasks is an area of research that is still in its infancy. Ibid., p. 63.

[71] By contrast, a computer vision algorithm would learn that this image has three equally spaced Vs with three alternately spaced circles, each missing a one-sixth piece—whereas most people will see two triangles superimposed over one another. See Robert Max Williams and Roman V. Yampolskiy, "Optical Illusions Images Dataset," (2018), https://arXiv.org/abs/1810.00415.

[72] Johnson, *AI and the Bomb*, Ch. 3.

[73] AI systems are not merely collections of hardware and algorithms, but, instead, supervisory control systems. These systems need to be observable, explainable, controllable, and predictable, and direct the attention of their human supervisors when required by a particular situation or operation. David Woods and Erik Hollnagel, *Joint Cognitive Systems: Patterns in Cognitive Systems Engineering* (London: Routledge, 2006), pp. 136–137.

[74] Patrick Mikalef et al., "Thinking Responsibly about Responsible AI and 'the Dark Side' of AI," *European Journal of Information Systems* 31 (3) (2022), pp. 257–268.

[75] Ben Dickson, "Reinforcement Learning Frustrates Humans in Teamplay, MIT Study Finds," *TechTalks*, November 1, 2021, https://bdtechtalks.com/2021/11/01/reinforcement-learning-hanabi/.

[76] For recent research with this objective in mind, see Alison Gopnik et al., "A Theory of Causal Learning in Children: Causal Maps And Bayes Nets," *Psychological Review* 111 (1) (2004), pp. 3–32; Nan R. Ke et al., "Learning Neural Causal Models from Unknown Interventions" (2019), https://arXiv:1910.01075; and David Lopez-Paz et al., "Discovering Causal Signals in Images," *Proceedings of the IEEE Conf. Computer Vision and Pattern Recognition* (2017), pp. 6979–6987.

[77] Tianmin Shu et al., "AGENT: A Benchmark for Core Psychological Reasoning," *Proceedings of the 38th International Conference on Machine Learning, PMLR* 139 (2021), https://arXiv.org/pdf/2102.12321.pdf.

[78] Recent studies have made important progress in clarifying how different neural net architectures fare in terms of this systematic generalization ability. Dzmitry Bahdanau et al., "Systematic Generalization: What is Required and Can it be Learned?" (2018), https://arXiv:1811.12889.

[79] Anjanette H. Raymond et al., "Building a Better HAL 9000: Algorithms, the Market, and the Need to Prevent the Engraining of Bias," *Journal of Technology and Intellectual Property* 15 (2018), pp. 224–225.

[80] Carl T. Bergstrom and Jevin D. West, *Calling Bullshit: The Art of Skepticism in a Data-Driven World* (New York: Random House, 2020), p. 183.

[81] James Vincent, "OpenAI's New Chatbot Can Explain Code and Write Sitcom Scripts but Is Still Easily Tricked," *The Verge*, December 2022, www.theverge.com/23488017/openai-chatbot-chatgpt-ai-examples-web-demo.

[82] Bengio, Lecun, and Hinton, "Deep Learning for AI," pp. 63–64.

[83] Lt. General John Shanahan, Director of the DoD Joint Artificial Intelligence Center, quoted in Sydney J. Freedberg Jr., "EXCLUSIVE Pentagon's AI Problem is 'Dirty' Data: Lt. Gen. Shanahan," *Breakingdefense*, November 13, 2019, https://breakingdefense.com/2019/11/exclusive-pentagons-ai-problem-is-dirty-data-lt-genShanahan/.

[84] Ian Goodfellow, Patrick McDaniel, and Nicolas Papernot, "Making Machine Learning Robust Against Adversarial Inputs," *Communications of the ACM* 61 (7) (2018), pp. 56–66; and Ian Goodfellow, Jonathon Shlens, and Christian Szegedy, "Explaining and Harnessing Adversarial Examples," December 20, 2014, *arXiv* preprint, https://arXiv:1412.6572.

[85] Many algorithms currently used to categorize users or contents tend to face a bias/variance trade-off. Where human users interact with algorithmically generated content that they consider misleading, formal definitions of bias (incorrectly categorized content) and variance (wide-ranging categorizations) are likely to be less relevant than the way in which the felt nature of the displayed content interacts with the knowledge,

disposition, and belief systems of users—as variance decreases, bias usually increases. See Pedro Domingos, "A Few Useful Things to Know about Machine Learning," *Communications of the ACM* 55 (1)0 (2012), pp. 85–86.

[86] Johnson, *AI and the Bomb*, Ch. 4.

[87] Recent research in adversarial AI has discovered blind spots and a minimal understanding of the context in a fast-moving and complex environment—or "brittleness." See Fengjiao Zhang and Shaogui Ding, "A Hybrid Machine Learning Model for Brittleness Evaluation," *European Association of Geoscientists & Engineers*, 83rd EAGE Annual Conference & Exhibition, Vol. 2022 (June 2022), pp. 1–5, doi:10.3997/2214-4609.202210644.

[88] Joseph Johnson, "MAD in an AI Future?" in *Center for Global Security Research* (Livermore, CA: Lawrence Livermore National Laboratory, 2019), pp. 4–6.

[89] As "unsupervised" ML techniques mature, the reliance on data and labeling (i.e., images, videos, and text) to support AI systems' training environments is expected to decrease. Unlike current "supervised" (or reinforcement) learning techniques that depend on labeling images to detect patterns, unsupervised ML is designed to create autonomous AI by rewarding agents (i.e., ML algorithms) for learning about the data they observe without a particular task in mind. See Alexander Graves and Kelly Clancy, "Unsupervised Learning: The Curious Pupil," *Deepmind*, June 25, 2019, https://deepmind.com/blog/article/unsupervised-learning; and Richard S. Sutton and Andrew G. Barto, *Reinforcement Learning: An Introduction*. 2nd ed. (Cambridge, MA: MIT Press, 2020).

[90] When solving problems, humans learn high-level concepts with relatively little data, which apply to other problems. AI does not possess this broader knowledge or common sense. Goodfellow, Shlens, and Szegedy, "Explaining and Harnessing Adversarial Examples"; and Christian Hugo Hoffmann, "Is AI Intelligent? An Assessment of Artificial Intelligence, 70 Years after Turing," *Technology in Society* 68 (101893) (2022), doi:10.1016/j.techsoc.2022.101893.

[91] AI researchers at Meta AI (formally Facebook) recently developed a game called Diplomacy that combines language models with techniques from game theory and probabilistic analysis and is the first AI-agent game to achieve human-level performance. The AI agent can infer players' beliefs and intentions from their conversations and generate realistic dialogue to pursue its goals. Like other algorithms, however, it relies heavily on handcrafting, both in the data sets and the architecture, and experts believe that the prospects for generalization are limited. Gary Marcus and Ernest Davis, "What does Meta AI's Diplomacy-Winning Cicero Mean for AI?" *The Road to AI We Can Trust*, November 25, 2022, https://garymarcus.substack.com.

[92] AI systems are limited to what they can infer from datasets because of the relatively few higher-level mathematical concepts on which computational learning theory is derived. David Deutsch, "Creative Blocks," *Aeon*, October 3, 2012, https://aeon.co/essays/how-close-are-we-to-creating-artificial-intelligence.https://aeon.co/essays/how-close-are-we-to-creating-artificial-intelligence.

[93] Domingos, "A Few Useful Things to Know About Machine Learning," pp. 78–88.

[94] Technical advances in decision trees, support vector machines, and DL have enabled a greater level of flexible discriminators into AI, but they still exhibit similar learning issues as the resolution and dimensions of images increases. For a study on the nature of human cognition, see Daniel Kahneman, *Thinking, Fast and Slow* (New York: Penguin 2011).

[95] Deutsch, "Creative Blocks."

[96] Johnson, *AI and the Bomb*, Ch. 3.

[97] Leslie Kaelbling, Michael L. Littman, and Anthony R. Cassandra, "Planning and Acting in Partially Observable Stochastic Domains," *Artificial Intelligence* 10 (3) (June 2017), pp. 967–968.

[98] Johnson, *AI and the Bomb*, Ch. 5.

[99] Matt Turek, *Explainable Artificial Intelligence (XAI)*, *DARPA*, www.darpa.mil/program/explainable-artificial-intelligence.

[100] Several AI researchers have posited that ML algorithms could be designed to monitor the performance of other algorithms, thus providing a potential solution. Matt Burgess, "Holding AI to Account: Will Algorithms Ever be Free from Bias if They're Created by Humans?" *Wired*, January 11, 2016, www.wired.co.uk/article/creating-transparent-ai-algorithms-machine-learning.

[101] See Carter, Woods, and Billings, "Automation Surprises."

[102] To address the known gaps in the brittleness of AI, there has been increasing interest in the fusing of symbolic (or classical AI) and connectionist deep-neural network approaches (or brain-inspired AI), which mimics neural connections in the brain. However, neither approach—separately or combined—can approximate top-down reasoning to deal with significant uncertainty. Cummings, "Rethinking the Maturity of Artificial Intelligence in Safety-Critical Settings," p. 9.

[103] See Johnson, *AI and the Bomb*.

1
The AI commander problem

This chapter explores the key features of the ethical, moral, and political dilemmas associated with human–machine socio-technical interactions in AI-enabled warfare.[1] At the intersection of ethics, technology, and psychology, the chapter draws insights from cognitive psychology, political philosophy, and scientific-technological approaches to consider the confluence of military ethics, emerging technology, and human psychology. Can AI solve the ethical, moral, and political dilemmas of warfare? How might AI-enabled warfare affect our thinking about the ethical-political dilemmas and practice of war?

The chapter argues that through the psychological process of human–machine integration AIs will not merely force multiply existing advanced weaponry, but will likely become de facto strategic actors (planners, warfighters, tacticians) in warfare—the "AI commander problem."[2] The diminished role of human commanders in the trajectory, controllability, and consequences of war is ontologically, ethically, and morally problematic. As scientific-technological innovation like AI is developed as a panacea to Clausewitzian fog and friction of the nature of "human" war and to solve the ethical-political dilemmas of warfare, it is easy to lose sight of the underlining social, political, ethical, and psychological contexts of war.[3]

Much of the present debate has revolved around ethical and legal concerns about fielding lethal autonomous robots (or "killer robots") into armed conflict. The literature contains both pessimism and optimism about the trajectory of human–machine interaction (HMI) in war; even in technological-scientific circles, deep-seated worries about control and bias are widespread.[4] Less attention, however, focuses on the ethical (or "techno-ethical"), moral, and psychological dilemmas associated with the intersection of technology and warfare.[5] The chapter fills a critical gap in discussing complex socio-technical interactions between AI and warfare. In doing so, it provides a valuable counterpoint to the argument that AI "rational" efficiency can simultaneously offer a viable solution to humans' psychological and biological fallibility in combat while retaining "meaningful human control"—in accordance with human designs and legal and ethical constraints—over the

The AI Commander. James Johnson, Oxford University Press. © James Johnson (2024).
DOI: 10.1093/oso/9780198892182.003.0002

war machine.[6] The chapter also argues that framing the narrative in terms of "killer robots," and similar tropes, misconstrues both the nature of AI-enabled warfare and its ability to replicate and thus replace human moral judgment and decision-making.

How has AI altered our understanding of war (and ourselves)? The chapter offers three psychological insights into HMIs to illuminate how AI will influence our capacity to think about the political and ethical dilemmas of contemporary warfare[7]: (1) human biological and psychological falli-bility and the dehumanization of AI-enabled war, taking humans psycho-logically further away from the act of killing; (2) human psychology and cognitive bias in HMIs and use of military force; and (3) the emergence of techno-ethics in AI-enabled warfare and the implications for diffusing the moral responsibility of war to machines. These insights address why, how, and to what effect HMIs will harbinger de facto AI commanders in future warfare. Some of these insights relating to future war are necessarily speculative; only by extrapolating present trends in AI-enabling technol-ogy can we elucidate the potential implications of the current trajectory to draw logical (or illogical) conclusions. While we cannot escape our time, we can use theories and empirical analysis as tools to serve us in critical inquiry.

The chapter is organized into three sections. The first section frames the argument by contextualizing the broader dovetailing of humanity and technology with the HMIs. It considers why and how humans become so entangled with the machines and the emergent complex socio-technical sys-tem, the roots of military techno-ethics, and the notion of riskless frictionless war. It describes AI technology as a new manifestation of this socio-technical trend. It argues that outsourcing human consciences in war-making—in an illusionary bid to solve the ethical-political dilemmas of war—risks erod-ing the vital link between humanity and war. This section also engages with the various counterarguments which challenge the view that replacing humans with machines is *necessarily* a bad idea (the "AI optimists"). Humans, for instance, make mistakes, often act irrationally, and are predisposed to atavistic instincts including violence, immorality, and dehumanization.

The second section considers the psychological features of HMI. Specif-ically, it unpacks several human biases—the illusion of control, heuristic shortcuts (the "Einstellung Effect," "existence bias"), and automation bias—which can make commanders prone to misuse or overuse of military force for unjust causes. It also discusses the potential effects of these biases in the broader political drive for a technological *deus ex machina* for predictability and centralized control over warfare.

Finally, the third section considers the potential implications of pursuing the means of perfecting riskless and frictionless war with technologies like AI for military ethics and moral responsibility in war. It contextualizes the debates surrounding the encoding of human ethics into machines with AI technology. It also examines the role of human emotion, which gives us a sense of reason and deliberation, influences our decisions, and shapes our responses to ethical and moral dilemmas—situations in which no desirable outcome is obvious. Can human ethics be programmed into algorithms? And if so, how might humans retain their ethics and values if moral responsibility is outsourced to AI?

Dehumanization of AI-enabled war: machines hollowing out humanity?

Henry David Thoreau famously observed that combatants' service to the nation is "not as men mainly, but as machines, with their bodies."[8] An idea fast gaining prominence is that humans will soon become the Achilles' heel in the emergent AI-enabled techno-war regime and will be inexorably distanced from the battlefield and eliminated by "rational," efficient, and autonomous weapons systems.[9] Intelligent machines will soon no longer need humans acting as autonomous agents to conduct many military operations. Instead, war-making (goal-setting, on-board-targeting, rules of engagement (ROEs), mission command, completion success report, etc.) is increasingly being outsourced (whether consciously or inadvertently) to the judgments and predictive insights of AI-ML systems. The logical end of this slippery slope is a de facto AI commander, whereby the act of killing—and thus the responsibility attached to agency—is outsourced to machines. The emergent complex socio-technical system—to make war faster, more lethal, asymmetric, and efficient—is being accomplished through a fundamentally psychological process of human–machine integration.

Why have humans become so entangled with the inhumane? The history of HMIs and techno-ethics can be understood as a manifestation of the broader evolutionary dovetailing of humanity and technology. A key feature of human evolutionary history has been the pursuit of artificially augmenting our physical and mental capabilities (e.g., human vision using ground glass, hydrate silicon, and fiber optics).[10] Thus, sacrificing our physical strength for intellectual upgrades. Recent neurological studies demonstrate that the human brain adapts throughout life—and not just during childhood as previously thought—to fully incorporate new technology to exploit its potential.

This trajectory lends credibility to cognitive philosopher Andy Clark's notion of a "human technology symbiotes" to explain how our sense of self (or "human agency") is determined in part by our relationship with technology.[11] Recent studies have found that an inappropriate choice of the level of automation in HMIs not only influences cooperativeness, and impairs team performance and fluency, but can also result in the loss of human "agency"—that is, a capacity to understand their situation, alter beliefs and actions, respond in novel ways to problems, and introspect on their experiences in ways that have an impact in the world.[12]

The roots of military techno-ethics, which has enabled war at a distance, and the politically seductive notion of riskless war, can be traced back to the Western Enlightenment assumptions of visualization and empiricism. Specifically, the osmosis of rationalization of vision and mathematization of space maps to assumptions relating to verifiable facts and empirical data—that is, "truth" became only what the eyes verified as "reality."[13] Because of the moral and political imperatives of the use of force and the exigencies of war, the pursuit of riskless war is both reasonable and commendable. In the context of technologically enhanced weapons, particularly when used in asymmetric non-international armed conflict—the most prevalent characteristic of modern war—this drive threatens the basic foundations of Just War upon which the moral justifications for violence and killing in war precariously rest. Christopher Coker writes: "Our ethical imagination is still failing to catch up with the fast-expanding realm of our ethical responsibilities."[14] This expanding realm is set to widen further as technology gains in autonomy, lethality, and "intelligence."

The increasingly complex entwining of technology and humankind, "multiplying human strength" with "destructive effectiveness," challenges the fundamental assumptions underpinning military ethics.[15] At the bleeding edge of this human–machine fusion, AI technology augurs a new manifestation of an omniscient technological solution to the ethical-political dilemmas of war. On the larger question of the ethics of warfare in modernity, Harvard historian Drew Gilpin Faust argues that the *"seductiveness of war* derives in part, from its *location on this boundary of the human, the inhuman, and the superhuman.* Its fascination lies in its ability at once to allure and repel, in the paradox that thrives at its heart" (emphasis added).[16]

The danger with the development of technology like AI is that humans may seek to reconcile this paradox by unwittingly outsourcing our consciences (or delegating morality) regarding using lethal force to non-human agents who—by virtue of being morally discerning inanimate objects without a conscience—are ill-equipped to fill this void. According to Duncan

MacIntosh, "by taking decisions to kill away from the soldier we will save his conscience by 'moral off-loading' . . . maybe we can offload the moral burden onto autonomous weapons systems that will do the killing for us, thereby sparing us unbearable guilt."[17] Whether offloading difficult moral decisions (i.e., whom to kill and when) to machines—and thus sparing commanders moral injury—amounts to immorality (i.e., the dignity objection in the use of autonomous weapons) or is defendable on the grounds of military expediency is an open philosophical question.[18]

Shannon French and Anthony Jack conceptualize two categories of "dehumanization" in war. The first is "animalistic dehumanization" (or "sub-humanization"), which characterizes the enemy as inferior and creates psychological distance by generating contempt, disgust, or hatred. The second is "mechanistic dehumanization" (or "objectification"), which, by contrast, equates the enemy with inanimate objects (i.e., "neutralize the target"). Mechanistic dehumanization generates cold indifference, which, like animalistic dehumanization, creates the psychological distance that permits combatants to kill without hesitation or compunction.[19] French and Jack's mechanistic dehumanization is the more instructive for this exploration. If technologies like AI draw combatants further away from the battlefield (both physically and psychologically), they risk of becoming conditioned to view the enemy as inanimate objects "neither base nor evil, but also things devoid of inherent worth."[20] Although the "emotional disengagement" associated with a mechanistically dehumanized enemy is considered conducive for combat efficiency and tactical decision-making, the production of controlled and banal socio-technical interactions devoted to moral emotions (remorse, guilt, shame, compassion, etc.) is ethically and morally lamentable.[21] As Hannah Arendt warned: "the development of *robot soldiers* . . . would *eliminate the human factor completely* and, conceivably, permit one man with a push button to destroy whomever he pleases" (emphasis added).[22]

In collaboration with the International Human Rights Clinic at Harvard Law School, the Human Rights Watch's 2012 report *Losing Humanity* argues that "emotionless robots could serve as tools of repressive dictators seeking to crack down on their own people without fear their troops would turn on them."[23] While human emotions can restrain individuals, they can also, however, unleash the basest instincts of humanity—including those emotions associated with animalistic dehumanization. Contemporary history is replete with tragic case studies of unchecked human emotions causing human suffering, such as Rwanda, the Balkans, Darfur, Afghanistan, and Ukraine.[24] Therefore, the argument against the deployment of AI and autonomous weapons centered on the absence of human emotions oversimplifies both the complexities of human emotion and cognitive states and the psychologically nuanced nature of HMIs, and is thus empirically flawed. Evidence indicates, for example, that unmanned remote drones do not dehumanize warfare in the way people expect. Counterintuitively, rather than treating combat as a video game, human drone pilots often form deep emotional bonds with their targets, and in this war at a distance, many pilots suffer long-term mental health issues similar to traditional combat experience.[25] Therefore, elucidation is needed on the psychological and ethical impact of the dehumanization of war to address the danger of humanity being hollowed out (spatially, temporally, and corporeally) by intelligent machines.[26]

How might AI-enabled war upend Thucydides's inseparable union of war and human nature?[27] Some argue that framing humans as biologically and psychologically fallible (e.g., fatigue, vigilance, cognitive bias, and the "neuromuscular lag"[28]) and thus inferior to intelligent machines further removes humans from the moral, ethical, and legal decision to use lethal force.[29] In this new AI-enabled techno-military regime, humans will become further intertwined with machines, "not merely to be better but to meet the *quasi-moral mandate of becoming a rational and progressive product*: ever-better, ever-faster, ever-smarter, *superseding the limited human corporeality, and eventually the human*" (emphasis added).[30] Underpinning this argument is the assumption that human frailties can be enhanced and ultimately supplanted by AI systems, making war more rational, predictable, and controllable and, in turn, eroding the inseparability of human nature and war envisioned by Thucydides.[31] Although the notion of AI superseding and replacing humans in war is highly speculative and contested, the psychological, ethical, and moral implications of increasing AI-enabled HMIs are ripe for empirical and theoretical exploration. Chapter 2 picks up on this challenge in the context of hybrid tactical human–machine teaming.

Human psychology and cognitive bias in human–machine interaction

What psychological insights can be garnered from human–machine entanglement? Several human psychological factors associated with HMI can cause commanders to misconstrue unjust (i.e., contrary to *jus in bello*) conflicts as legitimate and to place undue confidence in dispassionate machine rationality, thereby making militaries more predisposed to exaggerate their ability to control events and more prone to resort to military force. This section considers four cognitive biases and psychological predispositions that might compel commanders to misuse or overuse military force for unjust causes: the illusion of control; the quest for order and predictability; heuristic shortcuts; automation bias; and AI and techno-rationalization.

The illusion of control

People's belief in their ability to control pure chance events is a recurrent finding in experimental psychology.[32] According to behavioral studies, decision-makers in competitive, adversarial, violent contexts, where decision-makers are most emotionally invested in achieving a particular outcome (i.e., war-making), are more likely to overstate their ability to control the sequence of events.[33] The studies revealed that individuals engaged in "skill-oriented" situations (competitors, choice, interaction, choice, etc.) are prone to exaggerate their control and deny or misjudge the existence of chance, contingency (the "just world hypothesis"), and luck.[34] Moreover, and most pertinent to HMIs, the studies found that if participants were familiar with a simulated task, such as a wargaming exercise, they were even more prone to the "illusion of control."[35] That is, people in a "skills orientation" tend to conflate chance and contingency with a skill (or "skills cues") they have developed. The illusory promise of control and certainty is dispelled neither by enhanced expertise, know-how, nor sober reflection; instead, these measures often have the reverse effect.[36]

It is easy to imagine how this might play out in the context of AI-enabled warfare. For instance, state A leaders contemplate using AI-enhanced cyber-attacks (e.g., data poisoning, malware, or denial of service) against state B's command-and-control networks in response to B's unlawful annexation of sovereign territory along a shared border. Intelligence officers, flanked by geospatial technology, AI-enabled autonomous drone swarms on intelligence, reconnaissance, and surveillance (ISR) missions, and AI-ML "big-data" analytics warn leaders of the risk of inadvertent escalation and wider damage—for example, damaging state B's nuclear retaliatory capabilities or civilian infrastructure. Recent wargaming simulations conducted by state A that run similar contingencies to those unfolding in the real world increase leaders' confidence (i.e., "skill cues") in their ability to control events on their terms—or "escalation dominance."[37] In the real world, however, once the order has been given to deploy offensive cyber weapons—and without the means of recall, reliable signal, or proportion responsibility in cyberspace—the capacity of state A to control escalation and limit broader damage is limited.[38] How are humans expected to retain "meaningful control" over the command-and-control decision-making process?[39]

Quest for order and predictability

The history of command in warfare can be understood as a continuous quest for order over chaos and complexity (or "chaoplexic warfare") and to impose control and predictability amid uncertainty.[40] In battle, the sides best able to understand the various contingent elements that comprise the strategic environment—for example, battlefield awareness, adversary's intentions, and the activities of one's allies and own forces—in which war is fought have invariably prevailed.[41] Military historian John Keegan notes that the central purpose of military training "is to reduce the conduct of war to a set of rules and a system of procedures—and therefore to make orderly and rational what is essentially chaotic and instinctive."[42] Against the backdrop of the re-emergence of strategic great power competition, AI technology has become the newest currency for commanders to reinvigorate their scientific quest to impose predictability and certainty on the modern battlefield.[43]

The political momentum behind the drive for complete predictability and centralized control over warfare was catalyzed by the threat of nuclear armageddon during the Cold War and manifested in the computer revolution and the greater use of analytical tools, sensors, radar technology, and data processing systems.[44] US General William Westmoreland in 1969 encapsulated a vision of a future scientific way of warfare: "On the battlefield of the future, enemy forces will be located, tracked, and targeted almost instantaneously through the use of data links, computer-assisted intelligence evaluation, and automated fire control."[45] Although humans have broken with Cartesianism—the idea that scientific knowledge can be derived a priori from "innate ideas" via deductive reasoning—we are still seduced by the allure of science and controlling war in many ways. AI-enabled weapons are, therefore, symptomatic of a cumulative longer-term effort by militaries to use technology to tame chance and eradicate uncertainty in chaoplexic warfare.

Westmoreland's vision inspired a new generation of techno-military concepts and approaches, including cybernetic warfare, network-centric warfare, and the broader concept of a revolution in military technology, to create a centralized, frictionless, and automated warfare.[46] It is noteworthy that most military technological "revolutions" have been justified on similar grounds. That is, morally justifying the pursuit of a specific technology (e.g., nuclear and chemical weapons) to make war more efficient and less brutal, even when those technologies ultimately have a detrimental humanitarian impact.[47] In fact, most predictions go wrong when they overestimate the technological factor—and underestimate the human one.[48] Moreover, technological advances can also place a heavy burden on existing ethical norms, legal regulations, practices, and notions such as proportionality, responsibility, and meaningful human control.[49] Shifts in the threat environment can cause our moral vocabulary to adapt in lockstep with the capabilities and functions of machines we invent.

Driven by the assumption that machines will obviate fallible, emotional, and irrational human combatants, the enchantment of an AI-enabled micromanaged battlefield—combining AI-ML augmented ISR, autonomous weapons, and real-time situational awareness—has renewed military adoption of Westmoreland's techno-military regime as a panacea to Clausewitzian fog and friction of war in the digital age.[50] According to Robert Castel, this endeavor reflects "a grandiose technocratic rationalizing dream of *absolute control of the accidental understood as the irruption of the unpredictable*. In the name of this *myth of absolute eradication of risk*, they construct a mass of new risks" (emphasis added).[51] Frequent accidents involving HMIs demonstrate that a human-in-the-loop is not a panacea, particularly when it is challenging to distinguish civilian objects from combatants and military objectives.[52]

Commanding war in complex and uncertain strategic environments entails more than copious, cheap (and often biased) data sets and inductive machine logic. Until AI systems can produce testable hypotheses or reason by analogy and deductively reason (using "top-down" logic) like humans, they will not understand the real world and thus make decisions in non-linear, complex, and uncertain environments.[53] Commanders' intentions, the rules of law, and rules of engagement (e.g., the principle of proportionality and exhibiting ethical and moral leadership in the execution of strategic objectives) are critical features of ethical, moral, and tactically effective decisions (e.g., high context-dependent targeting decisions) in the use of military force.[54] Because AI-ML systems are considered incapable of performing these intrinsically human traits, the role of human agents in "mission command" will be even more critical in future AI-enabled warfare.[55]

Heuristic shortcuts

As geostrategic and technological-deterministic forces spur militaries to embrace AI—in the pursuit of fleeting first-mover advantages of speed, lethality, and scale—commanders' intuition, emotion, and latitude will be needed more than ever before to cope with the unintended consequences, organizational friction, strategic surprise, and dashed expectations associated with the implementation and assimilation of military innovation.[56] This problem may be compounded by a cognitive propensity of individuals and organizations to "fixate on one particular kind of solution to a problem due to one's exposure to, or familiarity with, that solution"—that is, a heuristic shortcut to solve problems as efficiently as possible, known as the "Einstellung Effect." A related concept is "Maslow's hammer," encapsulated by Abraham Kaplan's analogy: "Give a small boy a hammer, and he will find that everything he encounters needs pounding."[57]

In a military context, this cognitive bias can make decision-makers prone to use capabilities merely by virtue of possessing them, having invested time, energy, or political capital and resources in their acquisition.[58] In his report to the UN Human Rights Council on lethal autonomous robotics (LARs), legal scholar Christof Heyns notes:

> Official statements from Governments with the ability to produce LARs indicate that their use during armed conflict or elsewhere is not currently envisioned . . . subsequent experience shows that *when technology that provides a perceived advantage over an adversary is available, initial intentions are often cast aside.* (Emphasis added)[59]

This bias can impair the ability of decision-makers to make impartial and objective risk assessments of the likelihood of operational success; thereby, unbeknownst to the decision-maker, distorting the appraisal of competing alternatives to problems. As John Kleinig notes in the case of police militarization: "Equipment purchased 'just in case' . . . suddenly finds a use in situations that do not readily justify it."[60] While it would be an exaggeration to claim that the "Einstellung Effect" will distort every judgment on the use of military force, it may nonetheless contribute to the generation of false positives about the necessity for war.[61]

An overdue focus on AI-enabled speed and the tactical efficacy is significantly perturbing in crisis-management situations (e.g., nuclear brinkmanship, see Chapter 4), where inadvertent escalation risk looms large, and humans rely on conceptual, analytical, and conscious deliberation ("System 2" thinking) to make fast and reflexive judgments in stressful situations for cognitive closure ("System 1" thinking).[62] For example, the US DoD's 2022 Joint All-Domain Command and Control (JADC2) strategy report proposes integrating AI-ML technology into command-and-control systems to speed up the "decision cycle" relative to adversary abilities.[63] The JADC2 report obfuscates the possible strategic implications of automating the decision-making cycle for tactical gains and AI's illusionary clarity of certainty. AI-ML algorithms are unable to effectively mimic "System 2" thinking (or "top-down" reasoning) to make inferences from experience and abstract reasoning when perception is driven by cognition expectations, which is a critical element in safety-critical contexts where uncertainty and imperfect information require adaptions to novel situations (see Introduction).[64]

AI and techno-rationalization redux

State-of-the-art AI language-based machine learning systems in production today, such as OpenAI's GP3 and DeepMind's Gato, have been successfully used in context-specific reasoning tasks such as summarizing documents, generating music, classifying objects in images, and analyzing protein sequences. However, these systems are limited by the amount of information they can "remember" while executing a given task—the problem of "continued learning."[65] As a result, whether writing an essay or controlling a self-driving vehicle or an autonomous weapon, these systems often fail to recall what they have learned from a training dataset; systems must be constantly reminded of the knowledge they have gained or risk becoming "stuck" with their most recent "memories" derived from their training data.[66] Ceding greater autonomy to machines in war might, as a corollary, deprive human combatants of opportunities for moral learning (i.e., a learning moment when one gets new information about moral factors) in the use of military force. For example, a decision to display mercy in battle instead of killing someone as required by justice due to a belief not that it involves more killing than anticipated, but that killing itself is more odious than one initially thought.[67]

Several high-profile public displays of AI-ML systems in gaming and simulated virtual environments highlight the unpredictability and inexplicability of techno-rationality.[68] One of the most worrisome features of AI-enabled warfare is a reductionist scientific view of war that may delude commanders into thinking war can be controlled and predicted by objective, neutral, and rational machines. During stressful and fast-moving crises (e.g., operations conducted in anti-access and area-denial contested zones), using AI decisions—to provide an aura of objective legitimacy in place of prudence—may result in the opportunistic misuse of machine logic to validate legal or ethnically questionable behavior, or to justify existing practices in place of exploring alternatives. Predictive policing studies in the United States, for example, have demonstrated how a combination of biased AI-ML training datasets and an overreliance on machines (or "automation bias," discussed below) made officers prone to dismiss or not seek out contradictory information in preference of algorithmically generated judgments which they chose to accept as fact.[69]

Scholars of Just War argue that the military has already ceded some authority over *jus in bello* to machines that provide technical analysis to ensure decision-makers stay within the law, which has further diffused the moral responsibility for actions from senior military leaders and military lawyers to "computer-assisted expertise."[70] The authority and agency ceded to intelligent machines—based on an assumption of technical superiority, practical utility, and neutrality in decision-making—will likely be compounded by developments in AI-enhanced capabilities (e.g., lethal autonomous weapon (LAWS), ISR, big-data analytics, robotics, and cyberweapons), which further entwine humans with machines, making potential mishaps (either human or machine) go unseen and unethical decisions more difficult to detect and thus contest.[71] In sum, advanced weapon systems augmented by AI-ML technology challenge existing notions of agency and contestability, potentially innovating novel and increasingly autonomous ways to kill in a new techno-military regime.

As AI-enabled capabilities become assimilated into military doctrine, operational concepts, and strategic culture, militaries will be prone to unreflectively assign positive moral attributes to the resultant AI-enabled techno-military regime. Recent empirical psychology studies corroborate David Hume's hypothesis (discussed in depth in Chapter 2) that people have an immediate favorable response to what is already established; they tend to "imbue the status quo with an unearned quality of goodness, *in the absence of deliberative thought*, actual experience or reason to do so" (emphasis added).[72] In other words, if a technology such as AI exists, people will assume that "what is, ought to be."[73] Its existence is unquestioned and justified and becomes the cognitive default—known as an "existence bias."[74]

Furthermore, the blind pursuit of AI-enabled tactical efficiency also risks downplaying the fluctuating nature of strategic and political objectives, democratic debate, the ethics of war, and military proportionality, which statistical probabilistic AI-ML reasoning is unable to replicate or simulate synthetically.[75] For instance, by shifting the focus on technical prowess and precision in the conduct of war away from discussion on whether war justifies the ends (i.e., from *jus ad bellum* to *jus in bello*), leaders risk eroding the critical link between the means and proportionality of war, and, in turn, assuming tactical prescriptions are ethical and morally sound. In other words, AI's assumed tactical efficiency might provide leaders with an expedient *deus ex machina* to use military force divorced from consequences.[76] For example, during the Second Iraq War, US Navy Captain Arthur Cebrowski stated that "network-enabled armies kill more of the right people quicker . . . *with fewer civilian casualties, warfare would be more ethical*" (emphasis added).[77] How might an AI system calculate what is a proportionate response? Who would be held responsible for the legal and ethical mistakes of machines?

Today, there is no reliable metric (legal, computational, or normative) to objectively measure disproportionate suffering (unethical, immoral, moral injury, superfluous, or excessive) during combat; it is ultimately subjective and requires human judgment.[78] For example, "Bugsplat" software, and its AI-ML enhanced successor SKYNET, have been developed and deployed by the US DoD to support human decision-makers in determining the most "appropriate" and "precise" payload to construct "legitimate targets" for US drone strikes and to destroy a target and calculate its impact.[79] Scholars highlight the morally flawed design, the exploitation, and the erosion of "ethical due care"[80] in the use of technologies like these to conduct so-called algorithmic assassinations at a distance.[81] By contrast to traditional ("semi-autonomous") long-range strike systems (e.g., missile defense systems and unmanned drones), because AI-enabled autonomous weapons can select and engage their targets without human intervention, soldiers are not only relieved of the moral gravity that accompanies the *experience* of killing, but also the *decision* to kill.

Outsourcing parts of, or the entire, ethical deliberation process to AI-ML outputs—even if the ultimate decision to use lethal force remains with humans—will not answer the complex and subjective ethical-political dilemmas in war. Counterintuitively, ethical deliberation in "chaoplexic war" demands a degree of human subjective "inefficiency"—a core feature of ethical deliberation and democratic discourse—to face the challenges of complexity, contingency, and asymmetry in *jus in bello*, not encoded techno-rationalized "efficiency."[82] Therefore, an undue focus on statistics (i.e., how many civilians have been killed or injured) and tactical efficacy risks eschewing critical debates on the initial rationale for war (*jus ad bellum*) or the altered character of war that technology like AI enables.[83]

Moreover, in uncertain and contingent contexts like war, subjective proportionality calculation is needed—to determine, for example, a genuine target in a warzone and weigh the target value by a probability of its presence and absence—for which AI statistical probabilistic inductive reasoning is ill-equipped.[84] Therefore, integrating AI in the formulation of strategy in "chaoplexic warfare"—and the assessment of the role of military force within it—will require creativity, adaption, and an understanding of the likely consequences of any course of action, to exploit this uncertainty. As philosopher Pierre-Joseph Proudhon cautions: "the fecundity of the unexpected far exceeds the stateman's prudence."[85]

Automation bias

What happens when military commanders have too much trust in AI systems? The shifting political economy and authoritative hierarchy of HMIs (i.e., in the machines' favor) can partly be attributed to the uncritical and often blind trust placed in intelligent machines—a cognitive affliction known as "automation bias." Situations, that is, where humans anthropomorphize (see Chapter 2) machines and view technology as more capable than it is—ascribing human-like significance to AI—and thus use automation as a heuristic replacement for vigilant information seeking, cross-checking, and adequate processing supervision.[86] According to AI researcher Eliezer Yudkowsky, "anthropomorphic bias can be classed as insidious: it takes place with no deliberate intent, without conscious realization, and in the face of apparent knowledge."[87] Moreover, when operators have high confidence in a particular task but limited information about the algorithms' decision-making mechanisms or performance, people's perceptions of the machine's performance tend to be more positive.[88] Consequently, the user's reliance on the system's outputs increases while eschewing the veracity of algorithmic decisions. More worrisome, studies demonstrate that automation bias manifests in both experts and non-experts—in both military and civilian contexts; it cannot be mitigated by enhanced training protocols and can affect group and individual decision-making processes equally.[89] As a corollary, users may assume positive design intent even when presented with evidence of a system's failure. Even when experts can—or have the potential to develop the intuition to—identify incorrect algorithmic recommendations, they often follow incorrect recommendations.[90]

People's deference to machines can result from the presumption that (a) machine decisions result from hard, empirically-based science; (b) algorithms function at speeds and complexities beyond human capacity, and thus military efficiency would be jeopardized by less-efficient human intervention (i.e., the anthropomorphic argument discussed in Chapter 2)[91]; or (c) because people fear being overruled or outsmarted by machines.[92] Although few studies relate to this phenomenon in AI-ML across multiple domains (e.g., driverless vehicles, medicine, aviation, and the financial markets), empirical studies demonstrate people's proclivity to "automation bias."[93] In the financial sector, for instance, the appeal of algorithmic "black box" trading is precisely because it encourages automation bias—that is, the assumption that the trading recommendations of algorithms are far superior to those of humans.[94]

This phenomenon in a non-linear and contingent military context could mean that planners become more predisposed to view the judgments of AI as analogous (or even superior) to those of humans. An assumption that machines make better judgments than humans may also cause commanders to defer accountability and responsibility for the use of lethal force and thus neglect how AI in HMIs is shaped by humans (e.g., algorithmic design, parameters, and settings that define the interactions, and how strategic objectives are defined and adapted), and thus how AI may influence decision-making in war (e.g., predictions and decision outputs, inductive reasoning, real-time situational awareness, and biases embedded in algorithms by their human creators). For example, a recent study of human–computer interaction in the US Air Force with algorithms spanning over two decades revealed a strong tendency to outsource judgment in using military force to machines and to outsource accountability for the killing of non-combatants during warfare.[95] Outsourcing the practical judgment of human commanders to machines—in a flawed attempt to address the complex ethical-political dilemmas inherent in uncertain war—also risks undermining the moral assumptions that underpin the right to use lethal force in war.[96] Arendt notes that while there is a distinction between legal and normative moral issues, both presume the power of personal judgment and responsibility and are thus intrinsic to the "human condition."[97]

A recent study of surveillance in law enforcement highlights the effects of "automation bias" on predictive policing. The study notes: "The phenomenon of automation bias occurs in decision-making because humans tend to disregard or not search for contradictory information in light of a computer-generated solution that is accepted as correct."[98] This tendency is equally prevalent in fully automated decision-making systems and where humans remain "on the loop" to make judgments on machine decision outputs—or "mixed-mode" systems.[99] For example, the US Air Force's *Unmanned Aircraft Systems Flight Plan 2009–2047* outlines its vision for AI-enabled (data processing, software upgrades, sensor enhancements, etc.) autonomous drone swarm technology that will allow multiple drones to cooperate with a variety of lethal and non-lethal ISR missions at the "command of a single pilot"—that is, "on the loop."[100] In this sense, "autonomy" is (like command decision-making discussed in Chapter 3) a continuum rather than a discrete system with measurable states (see Figure 1.1).

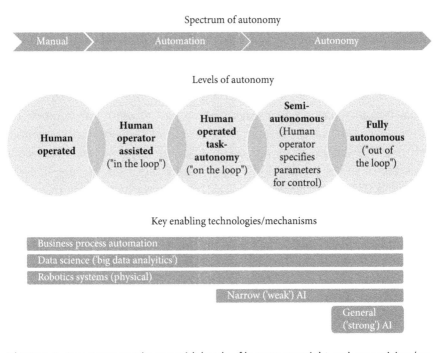

Spectrum of autonomy

Levels of autonomy

Key enabling technologies/mechanisms

Figure 1.1 Autonomy continuum with levels of human oversight and supervision (or humans "in-on-out of the loop"), and key enabling technologies and mechanisms

Efforts to reduce the role of humans in the combat decisions prompted by tactical priorities will further diminish the role of commanders' intent and permit life-and-death decisions to be made by algorithms who lack the intuition of humans—and other non-calculable human qualities such as compassion, respect, emotion, mercy—to sense that something is wrong and change a course of action without explicit orders. Even where humans are "on the loop," monitoring the executions of certain decisions (e.g., targeting lists and launch and recall decisions), human decision-making would be too slow to react and thus intervene in AI-enabled warfare.[101] A key takeaway of these studies is that despite human involvement in the decision-making process, "automation bias" can mean that errors and unethical or biased algorithmic decisions go undetected or unchallenged.[102]

Several analysts have warned that if human commanders place too much confidence in AI reasoning without fully understanding how machines reach a particular outcome, then decision-makers could trust machine-generated data implicitly and without scrutiny.[103] For example, the Tesla Model 3 crash in 2018—where a driver in autopilot mode ploughed into a fire truck on a freeway—demonstrated the risk of placing too much trust in autonomous technology, though not necessarily AI.[104] In this scenario, like other incidents involving vehicles in auto-pilot mode, the skill-based reasoning automated systems relying on "bottom-up" processing (or "skills-based reasoning") failed, and fatalities occurred because inattentive drivers did not realize that an automated driving-assist feature still needs "top-down reasoning"—or human intuition, common sense, experience, and judgment.[105]

The drive for predictability and centralized control over warfare and meaningful human control—that is, human-in-the-loop or human-on-the-loop, either positively to use lethal force or negatively to prevent an AI accidental deployment—neglects the psychology of HMIs, and, above all, how automation bias shapes HMI in decision-making.[106] In extremis, this neglect might shift the hierarchy in the human–machine relationship from benign tools of our will and force-multipliers to becoming key influencers of ethical, political, and strategic concepts and norms through machine logic and "rationality." In sum, the mystic of superhuman omniscience and omnipresence of AI overlords, acting on the uncertain and complex battlefield, will likely further diminish the role of humans in war. How might technology like AI affect the ethical landscape of war and violence?

Military techno-ethics and the moral responsibility of war

Can technology resolve the vexing ethical, moral, political dilemmas of war? The prevalent view that AI systems are morally objective and thus superior ("rational") to human ("irrational") judgment and decision-making is becoming profoundly entrenched and presents us with a new range of psychological and ethical dilemmas; above all, deliberating on the costs and benefits of political-military objectives against unforeseeable but probable outcomes and experiencing the cognitive and emotional weight of those decisions.[107] Coding ethics into AI-enabled capabilities has emerged as a possible solution to the complex, nuanced, and highly subjective ethical-political dilemmas of war, including the political choice to use military force and the psychological traumas that war combatants face in the conduct of war.[108] Coker writes: "We are trying to 'moralize' weapons, an elegant term for abdicating control over our own ethical decision-making [to intelligent machines] ... that may be better placed to make the right moral judgment."[109] Moreover, the Panglossian quest to imbue AI with human conscience (or "AI consciousness")[110] risks diffusing moral responsibility of war to technology, "smoothing over"—rather than eliminating—moral and ethical tensions between discrimination, responsibility, and accountability for actions and accidents in war.[111]

A bifurcated focus on the utopian or dystopian effects of AI and future warfare frequently neglects the intrinsic role of humans in the long casual chain associated with AI algorithms: the programmer, the designer, the military bureaucracy, military and political leaders, and the operator. Thus, it is challenging to proportion responsibility and blame for intentional unethical acts and war crimes or (human or machine) mishaps. This causal chain may also become socially constructed and anthropomorphized if the creators are human, so much so that humans define their self-worth and moral and ethical benchmarks in terms of the standards of superior, rational, and "efficient" machines. For example, proponents of lethal autonomous weapons such as drones frame them as efficient (less human cost) and effective (accurate discrimination of targets) tools of military force at a distance, and as morally and ethically reliable.[112]

Roboticist Ronald Arkin argues that "intelligent robots can behave more ethnically in the battlefield than humans currently can."[113] Similarly, AI researcher Gary Marcus posits that as driverless vehicles mature, they might become more moral than human drivers; *ipso facto*, the decision to drive a car would be inherently immoral.[114] This perspective, however, neglects the potential of AI-enabled autonomous weapons to circumscribe the shared humanity that connects adversaries. Without the first-hand experience of the horrors of war, commanders may become overconfident, injudicious, and progressively desensitized to using AI-enabled autonomous weapons.[115] Consequently, militaries that delegate decisions in the use of lethal force to machines might normalize (both combatant and potentially civilian) casualties and violence, thus potentially impeding any desire to prevent or terminate conflict.[116] Ultimately, soldiers far removed from the battlefield might be incapable of developing fundamental military ethical virtues (or "moral deskilling") such as mercy, compassion, respect, and empathy—a moral void machines cannot fill.[117]

As Elke Schwarz posits, AI-coded ethics contains the "illusory promise of certainty, the fallacy of being able to offer a technical way of resolving ethical questions," thus obscuring the ethical question.[118] For instance, the US DoD claims that its "Bugsplat" software can "produce a large body of *scientifically valid data, which enable weaponeers to predict the effectiveness* of weapons against most selected targets" (emphasis added).[119] Can humans retain their ethics and values if moral responsibility is outsourced to AI? And if so, then how might human ethics be programmed into AI? In short, we will become less equipped to justify lethal force where ethics are understood, measured, and ultimately defined through algorithmic code—premised on the assumption reinforced by automation bias that machine probabilistic ethical reasoning is superior to humans—and to foresee and control the consequences of our actions. Even if we accept the (albeit tenuous) argument that intelligent machines are morally and ethically preferable to humans on the battlefield for the reasons described, several problems remain. What moral and ethical codes should we bake into AIs—Kantian deontological (a rules-based approach prioritizing human agency and dignity) versus utilitarian (how consequences play out over time and effect interactions), or absolutism, Aristotelian virtue ethics, just theory of war, divine command ethics, ethical due care (or "relational ethics"), or something else? What might the effect of this choice be for human moral, legal, and personal responsibility, and accountability in war? How do we hold a machine accountable for violating a moral code and not a legal one?[120] Further empirical research is needed to study ways to combine the different ethical perspectives in practical situations. Who, for instance, in the chain of command, prioritizes between these perspectives—an individual soldier, their commander, or somebody higher up?

Complicating this choice further, an ethical theory has not yet advanced to the point where broad agreement exists (even amongst ethical philosophers) on the "correct" or "best" answer for the vast heterogeneity of moral circumstances, ethical conduct, and dilemmas.[121] For instance, it cannot be assumed that there will ever be a satisfactory answer to the question: what should a person do in a type x ethical situation? Therefore, ethical military behavior, like many other domains, will be improvised based on experience, perceptual skills, and emotions, rather than mastering an ethical-moral algorithmic code. In situations where disagreement exists over whether a particular action is morally acceptable, therefore, autonomous systems that are expected to behave ethically and morally would either be unable to act or make an arbitrary decision—neither of which would be satisfactory during combat.[122] Even if the goal of creating autonomous ethical machines was achieved, judgment would need to be made about the "moral status" of the non-human agent (i.e., vis-à-vis human agents), which is equally if not more problematic.

Encoding ethical principles will require extensive analysis and deliberation before any precision can be achieved. As former DoD Chief of High-Value Targeting Mark Garlasco noted, "we cannot simply download international law [or ethics and morals] into a computer."[123] What do ethical principles mean in practice? For instance, does civilian support of the enemy in an insurgency makes them a viable target? And how can torture be distinguished from mild pressure? Moreover, should designers encode these principles based on logical inductive statistical reasoning (i.e., proving and refuting theorems), or wait until the induction-deduction and top-down versus bottom-up cognitive problems have been resolved, when AIs can produce reason by analogy and deductively reason like humans (e.g., the importance of negative reasoning or "dogs that do not bark")?[124] As Austrian philosopher Ludwig Wittgenstein (and his successors) argued, concepts and principles like morals and ethics contain structures deeply embedded in the social, cultural, and linguistic fabric of the human experience.[125] Therefore, the burden of the challenge of answering these questions is substantial.

Ronald Arkin argues that AI systems must appreciate the ethical significance of competing courses of action and use ethical and moral principles in a context-appropriate manner to address some of these vexing questions. Arkin's hypothetical solution is an algorithm that can obviate messy human emotion and irrational impulses and identify situations where there is a significant risk of unethical behavior and respond, either by restraining the system directly or alerting human operators who would intervene to resolve ethical dilemmas—a so-called ethical governor.[126] For Arkin's ethical governor concept to be workable, however, ethics uploaded to an AI system must appreciate the nuances of competing courses of action and execute moral codes (to not kill unnecessarily, to avoid collateral damage, to not harm non-combatants, and to adhere to the Geneva and Hague Conventions, etc.) with high fidelity in a context-appropriate manner. "Ethical governors" would, therefore, either risk machines acting unethically (i.e., contravening the principles, laws, and norms of war) and leaving it to human operators to pick up the pieces, or requiring machines themselves to think, plan, and act "ethically"—that is, through the optimization and verification of sensory data with a judgment and choice of action equivalent to human capacity.[127] Where ethics and morals are coded—and even if machines could think for themselves—it would risk diminishing the ethical responsibility of human agents, reducing the ability of humans to challenge the abstracted ethics of machines, and opening up a moral vacuum, when laws, moral guides, or norms have adequate reach.[128]

At a practical level, it is questionable whether AI-enabled capabilities can distinguish legitimate from illegitimate targets. What might be an AI's telos or eudaimonia?[129] And, how would an AI determine which virtue is appropriate in a given situation? For instance, through trial and error or learning from exemplars. As shown in the Introduction, inculcating machines with human ethics is challenging at best. To resolve (or side-step) this challenge, some have argued that autonomous weapons should only be deployed in less complex combat environments where there is a lower probability of encountering non-combatants. Critics stress the improbability of pro-gramming such context-specific and value-laden consequentialist reasoning principles (e.g., not to target civilian populations) into algorithms.[130] During the "fog and friction" of war, the legitimacy of a target depends on a plethora of complex and subjective factors, including their intentions, history, and politics, which AIs are ill-equipped to determine for the foreseeable future. For now, it remains an open empirical question whether machines can be trusted to implement the moral judgments of humans safely and reliably in warfare.

During asymmetric conflicts such as insurgencies, civil wars, and gray-zone conflicts such as the Russian invasion of Ukraine in 2022, reliable intelligence of whom to target needs to be based not only on situational awareness, but also on attempting to infer the other side's intentions from the information available (i.e., the "theory of the mind") as a means to predict their future behavior in particular contingencies.[131] The goal of cod-ing human ethics into machines like Arkin's "ethical governor"—conceived on the assumption of the superiority of Cartesian rational ethical decisions devoid of human emotion—understates the pivotal role emotion plays in eth-ical decision-making in war. As William James discovered in the nineteenth century, human emotions are fundamentally enmeshed in every "rational" decision and ethical choice we make.[132] Therefore, human actions, emotions, and morals cannot be explained away by Spinozan general laws and thus coded into algorithms.[133] Valerie Morkevicius writes: "emotions can help us to act morally in four ways that are particularly relevant for the ethics of war . . . informing our moral intuition, generating empathy, and holding us accountable for our choices [which in turn] guide us towards more ethical behavior."[134]

Although human judgment and prediction are far from perfect, evolu-tionary features of our social interactions (psychological, social, cultural, political, emotional, etc.) allow us to recognize subtle cues (e.g., facial expres-sions and emotions, discussed further in Chapter 2) that machines cannot. These cues can prove critical, for example in situations where lethal force is inappropriate, such as children being forced to carry empty guns, non-combatants attending to the wounded, or insurgents burying their dead.[135] Because every ethical war decision is contextually and empirically bound, each choice and action has different ethical implications, thus making it virtually impossible to compute.[136] Consequently, if the fallacy of machine morality becomes anthropomorphized into existence by engineers using "fuzzy intuitions," the ethical coding enterprise will be reduced to merely a problem-solving exercise within constraints—or "operational morality."[137]

At a philosophical level, whether one adopts a consequentialist view of the nature of the principles of *jus in bello* or a non-consequentialist (or "absolutist") view has important implications for whether and how AI meets the *jus in bello* requirement of discrimination. Philosopher Thomas Nagel argues that in warfare people must acknowledge the "personhood" (or humanity) of the enemy—both sides need to acknowledge that they are Kantian "ends in themselves."[138] Following Nagel's argument to its logical end, and without taking it purely at face value, until which time (arguably never) AI achieves the moral standing of "persons" they will be unable to meet the requirements of *jus in bello*.[139] Moreover, techno-ethics cannot account for cacophonic facets of the human condition such as empathy, emotion, intuition, compassion, revenge, remorse, cognitive bias, experience and learning, and many sensory perceptions that influence our decisions, and shape our intentions and thus responses to ethical and moral dilemmas.[140] Human judgment, ethics, and beliefs are conditioned by our cognitive capacities and limitations, which give us a sense of reason and deliberation (i.e., human agency) that has evolved to cope with the breakdown of rational control.[141] Schwarz describes this as: "attempts to normalize and homogenize something [human ethics and morals] that can be neither normalized or homogenized owing to its inherent contingent nature."[142]

Conclusion

In her political theory magnum opus, *The Human Condition*, Hannah Arendt sought to consider the human condition "from the vantage point of *our newest experience* and *our most recent fears . . .* in order to *think through what we are doing*" (emphasis added).[143] In the spirit of inquiry inspired by Arendt's work, this chapter addressed the vexing and complex issues that arise as humans become increasingly entwined with intelligent machines. Above all, the fear that by absolving human decision-makers of the political and ethical dilemmas and paradoxes (the "seductiveness") of war by outsourcing these tasks to machines, we risk creating moral vacuums that hollow out meaningful ethical and moral deliberation in the illusory quest for riskless, "rational," and frictionless war. Moreover, the fallacy that technology like AI—as the latest manifestation of the scientific way of war—offers a panacea to uncertainty and contingency of war removes us by one causal (physical and psychological) step further from war-making and thus makes us less equipped to control, or even foresee, the consequences of war as a fundamentally "human thing."[144] The aura of tactical efficiency associated with AI provides leaders with an expedient *deus ex machina* to use military force divorced from consequences.

This chapter provides a much-needed counterpoint to the argument prevalent today in the defense community that delegating war-making to AI offers a viable solution to the psychological and biological fallibility of humans in war while simultaneously retaining meaningful human control (or "humans-on-the-loop") over the AI-powered war machine. The chapter argues that this argument neglects the psychological processes of human–machine integration—or "human technology symbiotes." Specifically, how AI HMIs are both shaped by humans and shape military decision-making. Because of the complex and quintessentially cognitive-psychological symbiosis of man and machine—across the tactical to strategic decision-making continuum—algorithms cannot be merely passive neutral force multipliers of advanced capabilities. Instead, as deep human–machine symbiosis alters and shapes the psychological mechanisms that make us who we are, thus as they learn and evolve, AI agents will likely become—either inadvertently or more probable by conscious choice—de facto strategic actors in war. The next chapter considers the effects of anthropomorphizing AI in military hybrid teaming.

Notes

[1] Sections of this chapter are derived in part from James Johnson, "The AI Commander Problem: Ethical, Political, and Psychological Dilemmas of Human–Machine Interactions in AI-enabled Warfare," *Journal of Military Ethics* (2023), doi: 10.1080/15027570.2023.2175887.

[2] Many AI-enabled weapons have already been deployed, made operational, or developed by militaries. Examples include: Israel's autonomous Harpy loitering munition; China's "intelligentized" cruise missiles, AI-enhanced cyber capabilities, and AI-augmented hypersonic weapons; Russia's armed and unarmed autonomous unmanned vehicles and robotics; and US "loyal wingman" human–machine teaming (unmanned F-16s with a manned F-35 or F-22) program, intelligence, surveillance, and reconnaissance (ISR) space-based systems, and various AI-ML-infused command-and-control support systems (see Appendix 2).

[3] Peter Paret, *Clausewitz, and the State: The Man, His Theories and His Times* (Princeton: Princeton University Press, 1985).

[4] See Stuart Russell, *Human Compatible* (New York: Viking Press, 2019); Elvira Rosert and Frank Sauer, "How (Not) to Stop the Killer Robots: A Comparative Analysis of Humanitarian Disarmament Campaign Strategies," *Contemporary Security Policy* 42 (1) (2021), pp. 4–29; Amandeep Gill Singh, "Artificial Intelligence and International Security: The Long View," *Ethics & International Affairs* 33 (2) (2019), pp. 169–179; Michael Schmitt, "Autonomous Weapon Systems and International Humanitarian Law: A Reply to the Critics," *Harvard National Security Journal* 4 (2013), pp. 1–37.

5   Notable exceptions include: Elke Schwarz, *Death Machines: The Ethics of Violent Technologies* (Manchester: Manchester University Press, 2018); Lindsay Clark, *Gender and Drone Warfare: A Hauntological Perspective* (London: Routledge, 2019); Ned Dobos, *Ethics, Security, and the War-Machine: The True Cost of the Military* (Oxford: Oxford University Press, 2020); Antoine Bousquet, *The Eye of War: Military Perception from the Telescope to the Drone* (Minnesota: University of Minnesota Press, 2018); John R. Emery, "Probabilities towards Death: Bugsplat, Algorithmic Assassinations, and Ethical Due Care," *Critical Military Studies* 8 (2) (2022), pp. 179–197; and Heather M. Roff, "The Strategic Robot Problem: Lethal Autonomous Weapons in War," *Journal of Military Ethics* 13 (3) (2014), pp. 211–227.

Henry David Thoreau, *Civil Disobedience in the Writings of Henry David Thoreau*, Vol. 4 (Boston, MA: Houghton Mifflin, 1906), p. 359.

6   See Ronald Arkin, *Governing Lethal Behavior in Autonomous Robots* (Boca Raton: Chapman, 2009); and Mark Hagerott, "Lethal Autonomous Weapons Systems from a Military Officer's Perspective: This Time is Different: Offering a Framework and Suggestions." Paper presented at the United Nations Informal Meeting of Experts at the Convention on Conventional Weapons, May 15, 2014, Geneva, Switzerland.

7   The term human–machine interaction (HMI) is not precisely nor uniformly defined. It is often used interchangeably with related concepts such as coexistence, cooperation, or collaboration. While humans and machines coexist—in the sense that they share a common workplace—they often work on individual tasks which are different and independent of each other, and thus are not conjunct in their collaborations. Jairo Inga et al., "Human–Machine Symbiosis: A Multivariate Perspective for Physically Coupled Human–Machine Systems," *International Journal of Human-Computer Studies* 170 (102926) (2023), pp. 1–15.

8   Thoreau, *Civil Disobedience in The Writings of Henry David Thoreau*, p. 359.

9   Schwarz, *Death Machines*, p. 156.

10   Timothy Taylor, *The Artificial Ape: How Technology Changes the Course of Human Evolution* (Lexington: University Press of Kentucky, 2004).

11   Alan Clark, *Natural Born Cyborgs, Technology and Future of Human Intelligence* (Oxford: Oxford University Press, 2003).

12   Bruno Berberian, "Man–Machine Teaming: A Problem of Agency," *IFAC-PapersOnLine* 51 (34) (2019), pp. 118–123; Diana Coole, "Rethinking Agency: A Phenomenological Approach to Embodiment and Agentic Capacities," *Political Studies* 53 (1) (2005), pp. 124–142.

13   Clark, *Gender and Drone Warfare*, p. 144.

14   Christopher Coker, *Warrior Geeks: How 21st-Century Technology is Changing the Way we Fight and Think about War* (London: Hurst & Company, 2013), p. 152.

15   Hannah Arendt, *On Violence* (New York: Harcourt Publishing Co., 1970), p. 53.

16   Faust Drew Gilpin, "The Chronicle of Higher Education. May 2. In Jefferson Lecture, Drew Faust Traces the Fascination of War, From Homer to Bin Laden," 2011, www.neh.gov/about/awards/jefferson-lecture/drew-gilpin-faust-biography.

17   Duncan MacIntosh, "PTSD Weaponized: A Theory of Moral Injury." Paper presented at the Center for Ethics and the Rule of Law at the University of Pennsylvania Law School, December 3–5, 2015.

[18] As a counterargument, the expected moral utility of engaging in risky delegation (to a machine or human subordinate) might—assuming it is militarily necessary and proportionate—morally justify the decision to delegate. Adriadna Pop, "Autonomous Weapon Systems: A Threat to Human Dignity?" *Humanitarian Law and Policy*, April 10, 2018, http://blogs.icrc.org/law-and-policy/2018/04/10/autonomous-weapon-systems-a-threat-to-human-dignity/.

[19] Shannon E. French and Anthony I. Jack, "Dehumanizing the Enemy: The Intersection of Neuroethics and Military Ethics," in *Responsibilities to Protect: Perspectives in Theory and Practice*, ed. David Whetham and Bradley J. Strawser (Leiden: Brill, 2015), pp. 165–195.

[20] Michael W. Brough, "Dehumanization of the Enemy and the Moral Equality of Soldiers," in *Rethinking the Just War Tradition*, ed. Michael W. Brough, John W. Lango, and Harry van der Linden (New York: SUNY Press, 2007), pp. 160–161.

[21] Mechanistic dehumanization creates an "emotional disengagement" by engaging brain parts that give rise to an "emotionally dysfunctional cognitive mode." French and Jack, "Dehumanizing the Enemy," p. 186.

[22] Arendt, *On Violence*, p. 50.

[23] "Human Rights Watch, Losing Humanity: The Case against Killer Robots," November 2012, www.hrw.org/sites/default/files/reports/arms1112ForUpload_0_0.pdf.

[24] On emotions and warfare, see Jennifer S. Lerner and Dacher Keltner, "Fear, Anger, and Risk," *Journal of Personality and Social Psychology* 81 (1) (2001), pp. 146–159; Pranjal H. Mehta, A. C. Jones, and R. A. Josephs, "The Social Endocrinology of Dominance: Basal Testosterone Predicts Cortisol Changes and Behavior Following Victory and Defeat," *Journal of Personality and Social Psychology* 94 (6) (2008), pp. 1078–1093.

[25] Rajiv Saini, V. K. Raju, and Amitr Chail, "Cry in the Sky: Psychological Impact on Drone Operators," *Industry Psychiatry Journal* 30 (1) (2021), pp. 15–19.

[26] Coker, *Warrior Geeks*, xviii.

[27] Thucydides' motives for war ("fear, honor, and interest") suggest that war is not a product of careful calculation, but instead reflects the intangible and ambiguous nature of human interaction. Thucydides, *The Landmark Thucydides: A Comprehensive Guide to the Peloponnesian War*, ed. Robert B. Strassler, trans. Richard Crawley (New York: Free Press, 1996).

[28] Humans have an inherent time lag of approximately 0.5 seconds in their ability to detect and respond to stimulus in their environment. It is because of this lag that many missile defense systems such as Phalanx are highly automated. Mary L. Cummings and Jason C. Ryan, "Who is in Charge? Promises and Pitfalls of Driverless Cars," *TR News* 292 (2014), pp. 25–30.

[29] See Emery, "Probabilities towards Death," pp. 179–197.

[30] Schwarz, *Death Machines*, p. 156.

[31] Whether values and morals are independent of (advocated by David Hume) or correlated with rationality (advocated by Immanuel Kant) remains an unresolved philosophical question. The Humean view is generally more common in discussions about AI, which assume machine "values" (i.e., goals and motives) are independent of their "rationality" (i.e., reasoning about how to accomplish goals). David Chalmers, "The Singularity: A Philosophical Analysis," *Journal of Consciousness Studies* 17 (9) (2010), pp. 7–65.

32 Mark Fenton O'Creevy et al., "Trading on Illusions: Unrealistic Perceptions of Control and Trading Performance," *Journal of Occupational and Organizational Psychology* 76 (1) 2003, pp. 53–68.

33 Suzanne C. Thompson, "Illusions of Control: How We Overestimate Our Personal Influence," *Current Directions in Psychological Science, Association for Psychological Science* 8 (6) (1999), p. 187; and Dobos, *Ethics, Security, and the War-Machine*, p. 91.

34 Paul K. Presson and Victor A. Benassi, "Illusion of Control: A Meta-Analytic Review," *Journal of Social Behavior & Personality* 11 (3) 1996, pp. 493–510.

35 Ibid.

36 Daniel Kahneman and Jonathan Renshon, "Hawkish Biases," in *American Foreign Policy and the Politics of Fear: Threat Inflation Since 9/11*, ed. Trevor Thrall and Jane Kramer (New York: Routledge, 2009), pp. 79–96.

37 Herman Kahn, *On Escalation: Metaphors and Scenarios* (New York: Harvard University Press, 1965).

38 James M. Acton, "Cyber Warfare & Inadvertent Escalation," *Daedalus* 149 (2) (2020), pp. 133–149.

39 The term "meaningful human control" was first coined in relation to autonomous weapons in 2013 by the UK NGO Article 36. The paper defined the term as: "A positive obligation in international law for individual attacks to be under meaningful human control." Article 36, 2013. "Killer Robots: UK Government Policy on Fully Autonomous Weapons," *Policy Paper* (London: Article 36, 2013), http:// www.article36.org/ wp- content/ uploads/ 2013/04/ Policy_Paper1.pdf? con=&dom=pscau&src=syndication.

40 Antoine Bousquet, "Chaoplexic Warfare or the Future of Military Organization," *International Affairs* 84 (5) (2008) pp. 915–929.

41 Martin Van Creveld, *Command in War* (Cambridge, MA and London: Harvard University Press, 2003), p. 264.

42 John Keegan, *The Face of Battle* (London: Cape, 1976), pp. 18–19.

43 See Keir Lieber, "Grasping the Technological Peace: The Offense–Defense Balance and International Security," *International Security* 25 (1) (2000), pp. 71–104; Robert Jervis, "Cooperation under the Security Dilemma," *World Politics* 30 (2) (1978), pp. 167–214; and James Johnson, "The End of Military-Techno Pax Americana? Washington's Strategic Responses to Chinese AI-Enabled Military Technology," *The Pacific Review* 34 (3) (2021), pp. 351–378.

44 See Caitlin Talmadge, "Emerging Technology and Intra-War Escalation Risks: Evidence from the Cold War, Implications for Today," *Journal of Strategic Studies* 42 (6) (2019), pp. 864–887; Antoine Bousquet, "Cyberneticizing the American War Machine: Science and Computers in the Cold War," *Cold War History* 8 (1) (January 2008), pp. 771–1102; Norbert Wiener, *The Human Use of Human Beings: Cybernetics and Society* (New York: Avon Books, 1967).

45 William Westmoreland, address to the Association of the US Army, October 14, 1969. Quoted in Paul Dickson, *The Electronic Battlefield* (Bloomington, IN: Indiana University Press, 1976), pp. 215–223.

46 See Eliot Cohen, "A Revolution in Warfare," *Foreign Affairs* 75 (2) (1996), pp. 34–54; Arthur K. Cebrowski, "Sea, Space, Cyberspace: Borderless Domains." Speech delivered to US Naval War College (Newport, RI), February 26, 1999; and David S. Alberts and Richard E. Hayes, *Power to the Edge: Command, Control in the Information Age* (Washington D.C.: Department of Defense CCRP, 2003).

47 Jean-François Caron, *Contemporary Technologies and the Morality of Warfare: The War of the Machines* (London, Routledge, 2020).

48 Michael E. O'Hanlon, "A Retrospective on the So-Called Revolution in Military Affairs, 2000–2020," *Brookings*, September 2018, www.brookings.edu/research/a-retrospective-on-the-so-called-revolution-in-military-affairs-2000-2020/.

49 For example, throughout the nineteenth century aerial bombing placed a significant strain on the utilitarian logic of military necessity. Brian Smith, *A History of Military Morals: Killing the Innocent* (Leiden: Brill, 2022).

50 See John Arquilla and David Ronfeldt, "Looking Ahead: Preparing for Information-Age Conflict," in *Athena's Camp: Preparing for Conflict in the Information Age*, ed. John Arquilla and David Ronfeldt (Santa Monica, CA: RAND, 1997); Henry A. Kissinger, Eric Schmidt, and Daniel Huttenlocher, *The Age of AI and Our Human Future* (London: John Murray, 2021), pp. 166–167; and US Office of Naval Research, *Data Focused Naval Tactical Cloud (DF-NTC)*, ONR Information Package, June 24, 2014.

51 Robert Castel, "From Dangerousness to Risk," in *The Foucault Effect*, ed. G. Burchell, C. Gordon, and P. Miller (Hertfordshire: Harvester Wheatsheaf, 1991), p. 288.

52 For example, the 1994 friendly-fire shootdown of two US Army Blackhawks in the no-fly zone over Northern Iraq caused by human misidentification of *the Airborne Warning and Control System*, and the 1988 USS Vincennes mistaken attack of an Iranian civilian airline due to human error caused by errors in the Aegis missile defense system human–machine interface. Aircraft Accident Investigation Board Report, US Army UH-60 Blackhawk Helicopters 87–26000 and 88–26060, Vol. 1 (Executive Summary) May 27, 1994, www.dod.mil/pubs/foi/operation_and_plans/PersianGulfWar/973-1.pdf.; Formal Investigation into the Circumstances Surrounding the Downing of Iran Air Flight 655 on July 3, 1988, August 19, 1988, pp. 37–45, http://homepage.ntlworld.com/jksonc/docs/ir655-dod-report.html.

53 AI-ML techniques (e.g., image recognition, pattern recognition, and natural language processing) inductively (inference from general rules) fill the gaps in missing information to identify patterns and trends, thereby increasing the speed and accuracy of certain standardized military operations, including open-source intelligence collation, satellite navigation, and logistics. Peter Norvig, *Artificial Intelligence: A Modern Approach*, 3rd ed. (Harlow: Pearson Education, 2014).

54 Roff, "The Strategic Robot Problem," pp. 211–227.

55 Avi Goldfarb and Jon Lindsay, "Prediction and Judgment, Why Artificial Intelligence Increases the Importance of Humans in War," *International Security* 46 (3) (2022), pp. 7–50; and Eric-Hans Kramer, "Mission Command in the Information Age: A Normal Accidents Perspective on Networked Military Operations," *Journal of Strategic Studies* 38 (4) (2015), pp. 445–466; and Alan Beyerchen, "Clausewitz, Nonlinearity, and the Unpredictability of War," *International Security* 17 (3) (1992–1993), pp. 59–90.

56 Michael C. Horowitz, *The Diffusion of Military Power: Causes and Consequences for International Politics* (Princeton: Princeton University Press, 2010); Johnson, "The End of Military-Techno Pax Americana?"

57 Dobos, *Ethics, Security, and the War-Machine*, pp. 88–89.

58 Ibid., p. 89.

59 Christof Heyns, "Report of the Special Rapporteur on Extrajudicial, Summary or Arbitrary Executions, United Nations Human Rights Council," A/HRC/23/47 (2013),

p. 6, www.ohchr.org/Documents/HRBodies/HRCouncil/RegularSession/Session23/A-HRC-23-47_en.pdf.

60 John Kleinig, "What's All the Fuss with Police Militarization?" *The Critique*, March 17, 2015, www.thecritique.com/articles/whats-all-the-fuss-with-police-militarization/.

61 Dobos, *Ethics, Security, and the War-Machine*, p. 90.

62 Daniel Kahneman, *Thinking, Fast and Slow* (New York: Penguin 2011).

63 US Department of Defense, "Summary of the Joint All-Domain Command and Control (JADC2) Strategy," March 2022, https://media.defense.gov/2022/Mar/17/2002958406/-1/-1/1/SUMMARY-OF-THE-JOINT-ALL-DOMAIN-COMMAND-AND-CONTROL-STRATEGY.PDF.

64 Dzmitry Bahdanau, Kyunghyun Cho, and Yoshua Bengio, "Neural Machine Translation by Jointly Learning to Align and Translate," (2014), https://arXiv:1409.0473; and Yoshua Bengio, Yann Lecun, and Geoffrey Hinton, "Deep Learning for AI," *Communications of the ACM* 64 (7) (July 2021), pp. 58–65.

65 Algorithms are generally trained once on a dataset, thus making them incapable of learning new information without retraining. By contrast, the human brain learns constantly, using knowledge gained over time and building on it as it encounters new information and environments.

66 Kyle Wiggers, "Continual Learning Offers a Path toward More Human-Like AI," *Venture Beat*, April 9, 2021, https://venturebeat.com/2021/04/09/ai-weekly-continual-learning-offers-a-path-toward-more-humanlike-ai/.

67 Martha Nussbaum, "Equity and Mercy," *Philosophy and Public Affairs* 22 (2) (1993), pp. 83–125.

68 For example, AlphaStar Team, "Alphastar: Mastering the Real-Time Strategy Game Starcraft II," *DeepMind Blog*, January 24, 2019, https://deepmind.com/blog/article/alphastar-mastering-real-time-strategy-game-starcraft-ii; Oriana Pawlyk, "Rise of the Machines: AI Algorithm Beats F-16 Pilot in Dogfight," *Military.com*, August 24, 2020, www.military.com/daily-news/2020/08/24/f-16-pilot-just-lost-algorithm-dogfight.html.

69 See, for example, Kevin Millar, "Total Surveillance, Big Data, and Predictive Crime Technology: Privacy's Perfect Storm," *Journal of Technology Law & Policy*, 19 (1) (2014), pp. 106–145; and Albert Meijer and Martijn Wessels, "Predictive Policing: Review of Benefits and Drawbacks," *International Journal of Public Administration* 42 (12) (2019), pp. 1031–1039.

70 Neta Crawford, "Bugsplat: US Standing Rules of Engagement, International Humanitarian Law, Military Necessity, and Non-Combatant Immunity," in *Just War: Authority, Tradition, and Practice*, ed. A. F. Lang (Washington DC: Georgetown University Press, 2013), p. 233.

71 Schwarz, *Death Machines*, p. 159.

72 Scott Eidelman, Christian S. Crandall, and Jennifer Pattershall, "The Existence Bias," *Journal of Personality and Social Psychology* 97 (5) (2009), p. 765.

73 David Hume, *A Treatise of Human Nature* (New York: Prometheus, 1992/1739).

74 A related cognitive bias is the so-called longevity bias, which posits that the longer something has existed, the more likely we are to unreflectively attribute positive qualities to it. Scott Eidelman and Christian S. Crandall, "The Intuitive Traditionalist: How Biases for Existence and Longevity Promote the Status Quo," *Advances in Experimental Social Psychology* 50 (2014), pp. 53–104.

[75] Paul K. Davis and Paul Bracken, "Artificial Intelligence for Wargaming and Model-ing," *The Journal of Defense Modeling and Simulation* (February 2022), doi:10.1177/15485129211073126.

[76] Noah Shachtman, "How Technology Almost Lost the War: In Iraq, the Critical Net-works are Social—Not Electronic," *Wired*, November 27, 2007, www.wired.com/2007/11/ff-futurewar/.

[77] See Kenneth Anderson, "Efficiency in Bello and Ad Bellum: Making the Use of Force Too Easy?" in *Targeted Killings: Law and Morality in an Asymmetric World*, ed. J. D. O. Claire Finkelstein and A. Altman (Oxford: Oxford University Press, 2012), pp. 374–402.

[78] Noel Sharkey, "Killing Made Easy: From Joystick to Politics," in *Robot Ethics: The Ethi-cal and Social Implications of Robotics*, ed. Patrick Lin, Keith Abney, and George Bekey (Cambridge, MA: MIT Press, 2014), pp. 111–129.

[79] Christian Grothoff and J. M. Porup, "The NSA's SKYNET Program May Be Killing Thousands of Innocent People," *ARS Technica*, February 16, 2016, https://arstechnica.com/information-technology/2016/02/the-nsas-skynet-program-may-be-killing-thousands-of-innocent-people/3/; and Thomas Gregory, "Targeted Killings: Drones, Non-Combatant Immunity, and the Politics of Killing," *Contemporary Security Policy* 38 (2) (2017), pp. 212–236.

[80] "Ethical due care" refers to a "positive commitment to save civilian lives. Not merely to apply the rule of proportionality and kill no more civilians than is militarily necessary." Quotes in Emery, "Probabilities towards Death," p. 182.

[81] Other examples of "algorithmic assassinations" include: Israeli's Harpy "fire and for-get" autonomous drone, which uses its software to prioritize the threat and then verify the target, and the US Phalanx system that "automatically detects, evaluates, tracks, and engages" and performs kill assessments against its targets. Both these "autonomous" sys-tems rely on pre-programmed datasets and are incapable of self-learning or targeting objects that do not emit threat signals or trajectories that can be sensed.

[82] James Der Derian, "Virtuous War/Virtual Theory," International Affairs 766 (4) (2000), pp. 772–788.

[83] Gregorie Chamayou, *A Theory of the Drone*, trans. J. Lloyd (New York: New Press, 2014).

[84] A proportionality calculation should be based on an estimate of the potential differences in military outcome if a particular action has not been taken. Ibid., p. 124.

[85] Quoted in Arendt, *On Violence*, p. 7.

[86] The source of excessive trust and automation bias might also be a machine's (real or perceived) capability, regardless of anthropomorphism.

[87] Eliezer Yudkowsky, "Artificial Intelligence as a Positive and Negative Factor in Global Risk," in *Global Catastrophic Risks*, ed. Nick Bostrom and Milan M. Ćirković (New York: Oxford University Press, 2008), pp. 308–345.

[88] Zhuoran Lu and Ming Yin, "Human Reliance on Machine Learning Models when Per-formance Feedback is Limited: Heuristics and Risks," in *Proceedings of the 2021 CHI Conference on Human Factors in Computing Systems* (2021), pp. 1–16.

[89] See Linda J. Skitka, Kathleen Mosier, and Mark Burdick, "Automation Bias: Decision Making and Performance in High-Tech Cockpits," *International Journal of Aviation Psy-chology* 8 (1) (1998), pp. 47–63, doi:10.1207/s15327108ijap0801_3; and David Watson, "The Rhetoric and Reality of Anthropomorphism in Artificial Intelligence," *Minds and Machines* 29 (2019), pp. 417–440.

90 Harini Suresh, Natalie Lao, and Ilaria Liccardi, "Misplaced Trust: Measuring the Interference of Machine Learning in Human Decision-Making," in 12th ACM Conference on Web Science (2020), pp. 315–324.

91 If, for example, an autonomous-capable weapon system needed to pause while the human operator approved each proposed action, the machine would function below capacity, and, in theory, less enemies would be killed, and innocents protected. Ronald Arkin, "Lethal Autonomous Systems and the Plight of the Non-Combatant," *AISB Quarterly* 137 (2013), pp. 1–9.

92 Lonnie Shekhtman, "Why Do People Trust Robot Rescuers More Than Humans?" *Christian Science Monitor*, March 1, 2016, www.csmonitor.com/Science/2016/0301/Why-do-people-trust-robot-rescuers-more-than-humans.

93 See, for example, Alan R. Wagner, Jason Bornstein, and Ayanna Howard, "Computing Ethics: Overtrust in the Robotics Age," *Communications of the ACM* 61 (9) (2018), pp. 22–24; and Raja Parasuraman and Dietrich Manzey, "Complacency and Bias in Human Use of Automation: An Attentional Integration," *Human Factors* 52 (3) (2010), pp. 381–410.

94 Frank Pasquale, *The Black Box Society: The Secret Algorithms That Control Money and Information* (Cambridge, MA: Harvard University Press, 2016).

95 Emery, "Probabilities towards Death," pp. 179–197.

96 Neil Renic, "Justified Killing in an Age of Radically Asymmetric Warfare," *European Journal of International Relations* 25 (2) (2019), pp. 408–430.

97 Samantha Hill, *Critical Lives: Hannah Arendt* (New York: Reaktion Books, 2021), p. 163.

98 Millar, "Total Surveillance, Big Data, and Predictive Crime Technology," p. 122.

99 Schwarz, *Death Machines*, p. 159.

100 US Air Force, *Unmanned Aircraft Systems Flight Plan 2009–2047*, US Air Force Headquarters, April 2009, p. 41.

101 Daniel Davis, "Who Decides: Man or Machine?" *Armed Forces Journal*, November 1, 2007, http://armedforcesjournal.com/who-decides-man-or-machine/.

102 For example, there is mounting evidence that AI datasets can perpetuate biased decision-making in the medical domain, such as prioritizing health care for white patients over black ones. www.wired.com/story/how-algorithm-favored-whites-over-blacks-health-care/.

103 Raja Parasuraman and Victor Riley, "Humans and Automation: Use, Misuse, Disuse, Abuse," *Human Factors* 39 (2) (June 1997), pp. 230–253. doi:10.1518/001872097778543886.

104 Andrew J. Hawkins, "Tesla Model S Plows into a Fire Truck while Using Autopilot," *The Verge*, January 23, 2018, www.theverge.com/2018/1/23/16923800/tesla-firetruck-crash-autopilot-investigation.

105 Mary L. Cummings, "Rethinking the Maturity of Artificial Intelligence in Safety-Critical Settings," *AI Magazine* 42 (1) (2021), pp. 6–15.

106 The control "loop" concept has also been criticized for the crude distinction it makes about decision-making. Command decision-making can be both immediate (i.e., in an individual targeting situation) or a more broadly defined (i.e., associated with algorithmic programming). Christof Heyns, "Autonomous Weapons Systems: Living a Dignified Life and Dying a Dignified Death," in *Autonomous Weapons Systems: Law, Ethics, Policy*, ed. Nehal Bhuta et al. (Cambridge: Cambridge University Press, 2016), pp. 3–20.

107 See Antoine Bousquet, *The Eye of War: Military Perception from the Telescope to the Drone* (Minnesota: University of Minnesota Press, 2018); and Clark, *Gender and Drone Warfare*.

[108] John R. Emery and Hadley Biggs, "Human, All Too Human: Drones, Ethics, and the Psychology of Military Technologies," *Political Psychology* 43 (3) (2022), pp. 605–613.

[109] Coker, *Warrior Geeks*, xxiii.

[110] The concept of "AI consciousness" (or "machine consciousness") is a heavily contested and vexing neurological, philosophical, and psychological issue. See Owen Holland, *Machine Consciousness* (New York, Imprint Academic, 2003).

[111] Crawford, "Bugsplat," p. 233.

[112] For example, see Joshua Foust, "The Liberal Case for Drones," *Foreign Policy*, May 13, 2013, www.foreignpolicy.com/articles/2013/05/14/a_liberal_case_for_drones; and Bradley J. Strawser, "Moral Predators: A Duty to Employ Unmanned Aerial Vehicles," *Journal of Military Ethics* 9 (4) (2010), pp. 342–368.

[113] Quoted in Dean Cornelia, "A Soldier, Taking Orders from its Ethical Judgment Center," *The New York Times*, November 24, 2008, www.nytimes.com/2008/11/25/health/25iht-25robots.18126102.html.

[114] Gary Marcus, "Moral Machines," *The New Yorker*, November 24, 2012, www.newyorker.com/tech/annals-of-technology/teaching-robots-to-be-moral.

[115] Jai Galliott, "War 2.0: Drones, Distance and Death," *International Journal of Technoethics* 7 (2) (2016), pp. 61–76.

[116] Shannon Vallor, *Technology and the Virtues: A Philosophical Guide to a Future Worth Wanting* (Oxford: Oxford University Press, 2016).

[117] Shannon Vallor, "Moral Deskilling and Upskilling in a New Machine Age: Reflections on the Ambiguous Future of Character," *Philosophy & Technology* 28 (2015), pp. 107–124.

[118] Schwarz, *Death Machines*, p. 198.

[119] US Joint Chief's Joint Publication 3-60, "Joint Targeting," January 31, 2013, www.justsecurity.org/wp-content/uploads/2015/06/Joint_Chiefs-Joint_Targeting_20130131.pdf.

[120] Gianmarco Veruggio and Keith Abney, "The Applied Ethics for a New Science," in *Robot Ethics: The Ethical and Social Implications of Robotics*, ed. Patrick Lin, Keith Abney, and George Bekey (Cambridge, MA: MIT Press, 2014), pp. 348–349.

[121] Susan Anderson, "Asimov's 'Three Laws of Robotics,' and Machine Metaethics," AI and Society 22 (4) (2008), pp. 477–493.

[122] Some non-ethicist philosophers believe that in cases where no agreement exists on ethical dilemmas a metaethical concept known as ethical relativism can be applied—that is, the view that both sides are correct and there are no absolute wrongs. This approach is generally rejected by ethicists.

[123] Quoted in Peter Singer, *Wired for War: The Robotics Revolution and Conflict in the 21st Century* (New York: Penguin Press, 2009), p. 389.

[124] For discussion about the need to merge the cognitive top-down with the bottom-up approach, see Wendell Wallach and Colin Allen, *Moral Machines: Teaching Robots Right from Wrong* (Oxford: Oxford University Press, 2009).

[125] Ludwig Wittgenstein, *Philosophical Investigations*, 3rd ed., trans. G. E. M. Anscombe (New York: Prentice-Hall, 1973).

[126] Arkin, *Governing Lethal Behavior in Autonomous Robots*.

[127] Bioethicist Rob Sparrow adopted Alan Turing's 1950 "Turing Test" to serve as a basis for testing whether machines had achieved the moral standing of humans—the hypothetical "Turing Triage Test." Rob Sparrow, "The Turing Triage Test," *Ethics & Information Technology* 6 (4) (2004), pp. 203–213.

128 Elke Schwarz, "Technology and Moral Vacuums in Just War Theorising," *Journal of International Political Theory* 14 (3) (2018), pp. 280–298.

129 For example, an AI's telos would contribute to the mission and its eudaimonia collecting and presenting information that warfighters deem clear, trustworthy, and effective. Marc Steen, Jurriaan van Diggelen, and Tjerk Timan, "Meaningful Human Control of Drones: Exploring Human–Machine Teaming, Informed by Four Different Ethical Perspectives," *AI Ethics* 3 (1) (2023), pp. 281–293.

130 See Hagerott, "Lethal Autonomous Weapons Systems from a Military Officer's Perspective," and Arkin, *Governing Lethal Behavior in Autonomous Robots.*

131 Vladimir Rauta and Alexandra Stark, "What Does Arming an Insurgency in Ukraine Mean?" *Lawfare*, April 3, 2022, www.lawfareblog.com/what-does-arming-insurgency-ukraine-mean.

132 William James, *Varieties of Religious Experience: A Study of Human Nature* (New York: Signet, 2009).

133 Raymond Tallis, *Aping Mankind: Neuromania, Darwinists, and the Misrepresentation of Humanity* (New York: Atlantic Books, 2010).

134 Valarie Morkevicius, "Tin Men: Ethics, Cybernetics and the Importance of Soul," *Journal of Military Ethics* 13 (1) (2014), p. 10.

135 Sharkey, "Killing Made Easy: From Joystick to Politics," p. 118.

136 Schwarz, *Death Machines*, pp. 166–167.

137 Anthony Beavers, "Editorial," *Ethics & Information Technology* 12 (3) (2010), pp. 207–208.

138 Thomas Nagel, "War and Massacre," *Philosophy & Public Affairs* 1 (2) (1972), pp. 123–144.

139 The ability of machines to think for themselves, and broader questions about the moral standing of machines, would require the creation of artificial general intelligence (AGI or "strong AI")—the ability of machines to understand and learn any task that a human can. AGI would bring about AI systems able to reason, plan, learn, represent knowledge, and communicate in natural language.

140 See, for example, Herbert A. Simon, "Making Management Decisions: The Role of Intuition and Emotions," *The Academy of Management Executive* 1 (1) (February 1987), pp. 57–64; Janice J. Gross, "Emotion Regulation: Affective, Cognitive, and Social Consequences," *Psychophysiology* 39 (3) (2002), pp. 281–291; Corinna Carmen Gayer et al., "Overcoming Psychological Barriers to Peaceful Conflict Resolution: The Role of Arguments about Losses," *Journal of Conflict Resolution* 53 (6) (2009), pp. 951–975; Mehta, Jones, and Josephs, "The Social Endocrinology of Dominance," pp. 1078–1093; and Brian A. Gladue, Michael Boechler, and Kevin D. McCaul, "Hormonal Response to Competition in Human Males," *Aggressive Behavior* 15 (6) (1989), pp. 409–422.

141 In most ethical traditions, "agency" matters because of our "theory of the mind." Human social evolution has made us hardwired to attribute agency—and thus intention and blame—promiscuously to those we interact with. Veruggio and Abney, "The Applied Ethics for a New Science," pp. 355–356.

142 Schwarz, *Death Machines*, p. 168.

143 Hannah Arendt, *The Human Condition* (Chicago, IL: University of Chicago Press, 1998), p. 5.

144 Thucydides, *The Landmark Thucydides.*

2

Anthropomorphizing AI in centaur teaming

Scottish philosopher David Hume wrote that "there is a universal tendency among mankind to conceive all beings like themselves. . . we find faces in the moon, armies in the clouds."[1] In recent years, the study of anthropomorphism—people's propensity to attribute the traits of human agents to non-human ones—has become a multidisciplinary phenomenon encompassing insights from social psychology and cognition, social science, the theory of mind, behavioral science, philosophy, and, most relevant to this study, neurosciences.[2] While much of the literature focuses on anthropomorphism's situational, developmental, or cultural determinants, less attention is given to the potential consequences of human warfighters' *perceptions* of military human–machine interaction (HMI) and, specifically, the tendency of attributing human traits to machines. This chapter focuses on the impact and design of anthropomorphism in AI systems used in military HMIs—that is, the design and the use of computer technology and interfaces, and interaction between human users and machines in hybrid teams. It addresses two related questions: (a) why are we likely to see anthropomorphisms in military AI HMIs? And (b) what are the potential consequences of this phenomena? The chapter also considers the possible impact of the AI-anthropomorphism phenomenon on the inversion of AI-anthropomorphism and the dehumanization of war.[3]

Hybrid military teams comprising human warfighters and autonomous "AI agents," such as digital assistants and avatars, Loyal Wingman unmanned aerial vehicles, and robotics, are rapidly achieving broad acceptance as the technological future of tactical warfighting operations (see Appendix 2). Since its inception, AI has been conceptualized in anthropomorphic terms, employing biomimicry to map the human brain as analogies to human reasoning digitally. Although the technical limitations of modern AI machine-learning (ML) approaches and the effects of anthropomorphism in civilian social-robotics are well documented,[4] the human psychological impact of anthropomorphism on hybrid teaming military operations—from the

The AI Commander. James Johnson, Oxford University Press. © James Johnson (2024).
DOI: 10.1093/oso/9780198892182.003.0003

perspective of the cognitive dynamics of agent-soldier teams, tactical efficacy, and military ethics—has yet to be systematically examined.[5]

The chapter argues that anthropomorphism will play a critical role in HMIs in tactical operations. Consequently, successful AI-augmented military HMIs will depend on reliable, cognitively parsimonious, and efficacious communication. The chapter addresses the following research questions. What explains the psychological origin and persistence of anthropomorphism? What are the risks and opportunities associated with AI-anthropomorphism within AI agent-soldier teams? What are the possible consequences of AI-anthropomorphism of AI-enabled military HMI? And in response, what are the most effective design solutions to maximize the advantages and minimize the risks in future HMI interfaces? The chapter approaches these research puzzles primarily through empirical work conducted by the computer and behavioral science literature that considers HMIs in non-military settings. These findings are interpreted with a read-through for the military domain, for which non-classified studies are limited. Given the paucity of relevant studies—that is, on anthropomorphizing tendencies of AI in military HMIs—and the embryonic nature of much of the technology discussed, much of the articles' discussion is necessarily conceptual and speculative. Only by extrapolating present trends in AI-enabling technology can we elucidate the possible impact of the current trajectory and thus draw logical or illogical conclusions.

The chapter is organized into three sections. The first traces the psychological origins, mechanisms, and persistence of anthropomorphism. It concludes that the human tendency to anthropomorphize is an interpretation of human-like physical features and behaviors that go beyond what is directly observable. This conclusion has important implications for conceptualizing military HMIs. Finally, this section considers the anthropomorphic hype surrounding AI that permeates the research and design of AI technology, particularly associated with ML Deep Neutral Networks. The second section, the chapter's empirical contribution, draws insights from the latest civilian social robotics and social cognition research to elucidate the impact and design of anthropomorphism in AI systems used in military HMI in hybrid teams. This section argues that understanding anthropomorphism's determinants and drivers can help us identify the conditions in which the effects of anthropomorphism will likely be most (positively and negatively) impactful. The final section considers the potential problems (ethical and moral, trust and responsibility, and social influence) and unintended consequences of AI-enabled military HMI operations. The section finishes with a brief discussion on the potential implications of the inverse process of anthropomorphism, dehumanization for AI-enabled military HMIs. It finds that psychological mechanisms that make people likely to attribute human-like qualities may also increase our understanding of when and why people may do the opposite.

Conceptualizing AI-anthropomorphism: origins and psychological mechanisms

What explains the psychological origin and persistence of anthropomorphism? Greek philosopher Xenophanes, in the sixth century BCE, first coined the phrase to describe how gods and other supernatural beings bear a striking physical resemblance to their human followers.[6] As an inherently multi-interdisciplinary topic, anthropomorphism—the tendency to attribute to non-human entities the characteristics of human ones and transfer to the former psychological attitudes and forms of engagement that are typically reserved for the latter—is considered in many of the subfields within psychology, which has yielded critical insights on the function of the human brain that underpin social cognition in neuroscience. For instance, cognitive, social psychology, "theory of the mind" scholars, [7] and neuroscientists have investigated the neural correlates of anthropomorphism[8] to treat diseases such as Alzheimer's.[9]

Cognitive and social psychologists, philosophers, and anthropologists have elucidated the origin of anthropomorphism as an evolutionary and cognitive adaptive trait, particularly concerning theistic religions.[10] Scholars speculate that for evolutionary reasons, early hominids (members of a family Hominidae, the great apes) interpreted ambiguous shapes as faces or bodies to improve their genetic fitness by making alliances with neighboring tribes or by avoiding neighboring outgroup threats and predatory animals.[11] Scholars have recently described people's propensity to turn non-human agents into human ones,[12] and the psychological and behavioral mechanisms intrinsic to the phenomenology of anthropomorphism are considered universal (across genders, race, and cultures), cognitively deep (biases, heuristics, and delusions), innate, and to have developed in human's formative years.[13]

Anthropomorphism, therefore, is a process of inference encompassing not only physical features, but also perceiving an agent in a human-like form (i.e., as having autonomy, imitation, intrinsic moral value, moral accountability, intentions, and reciprocity), thus imbuing it with mental capacities that humans consider uniquely human, such as emotions (for example empathy, revenge, shame, and guilt), and the capacity for conscious awareness, metacognition, and intentions.[14] Moreover, anthropomorphism is the result not only of an agent's behavior, but also of the human perceiver's motivation, social background, gender, and age.[15] In other words, anthropomorphism is very context-dependent; different representations and judgments of the same non-human agent may be produced by various, and even the same, individuals.[16] With respect to military hybrid teaming, however, it is unclear who (for example designers, engineers, soldiers who work in teams with machines) is chiefly responsible for the anthropomorphism attribution discussed below. In the case of HMI, for instance, the social interface between a machine (i.e., a robot or digital assistant) and a human may impact the degree to which an agent is attributed humanness.[17] Anthropomorphism attribution is, therefore, not always a deliberate or conscious act; the underlying mechanisms have been classed as either "explicit" (manifested verbally) or "implicit" (manifested through an agent's behavior).[18] In short, anthropomorphism represents a particular human-like interpretation of existing physical features and behaviors that goes beyond what is directly observable.

Persistence of anthropomorphism

Some scholars hypothesize that specific anthropomorphizing mechanisms in human neural correlates—for example, the hypothesized hypersensitive agency detection device, and various psychological and cognitive traits—produce anthropomorphizing behavior.[19] They also contend that, *inter alia*, confirmation bias, difficulties in challenging anthropomorphic interpretations of the environment, and people's desire for cognitive closure, certainty, controllability, and predictability—in an uncertain world—may psychologically explain the persistence of anthropomorphizing.[20]

Epley et al. proposed a theory that determined three psychological factors as affecting when people anthropomorphize non-human agents.[21] These variables, either independently or in combination, help us to elucidate the tendency of individuals and groups to anthropomorphize non-human agents in HMIs, and thus provide an alternative method for reducing uncertainty in contexts such as warfare where non-anthropomorphic model methods such as science, culture, and norms are less accessible, or in the absence of other information.[22] First, because people have a much richer knowledge of humans than non-human agents like AI, individuals are thus more likely to seek anthropomorphic explanations of non-human agents' actions to create mental models and heuristics. Second, when individuals are motivated to explain or understand an agent's behavior—to reduce uncertainty and ambiguity and control one's environment and the need for cognitive closure—the tendency to anthropomorphize generally increases.[23] Thus, when incentives for understanding and predictability are high, anthropomorphism will increase. Third, individuals who lack adequate levels of human social connection tend to compensate for this by treating non-human agents as if they were human.[24]

The theory predicts that warfighters' predisposition to anthropomorphize machines is highest in situations where they are aware of the features and functions that justify human–machine analogies (i.e., accessible and applicable anthropocentric knowledge) when their survival depends on the cohesion and solidarity of their team members. In situations where users perceive machines as a threat or need to feel less isolated and alone (i.e., the desire for social contact and affiliation), they are more likely to anthropomorphize.[25] Because of the fuzzy nature of ML algorithmic logic—coupled with the high incentives for understanding and effectively interfacing with AI agents— the tendency to anthropomorphize the workings of many non-humans AI agents will likely be especially acute. In approaching this problem, AI designers must ensure that algorithmic decisions are explainable, reliable, and predictable—the final chapter considers possible ways to achieve this goal.

Anthropomorphism can also create a (false or otherwise) sense of efficacy and competence in interacting with AI agents—for example, digital decision-making assistants, explosive ordnance disposal robots, and Loyal Wingman unmanned aerial vehicles to support manned pilots.[26] The perception that AI systems benefit from the projection of anthropomorphism from its users, for instance, to cope with information overload, promote acceptance, and foster trust and cooperation in HMIs, has prompted developers to deliberately and explicitly elicit this reaction to facilitate the utility of AI agents.[27] Studies have demonstrated, for example, that humans judge robots that exhibit playful behavior as more outgoing and thus consider them easier to cooperate and work with.[28] In addition to the perception of efficiency, anthropomorphizing non-human agents can foster close social connections, which, despite being far less meaningful than human interactions, can make its users more cognitively favorably disposed toward technological agents than might otherwise be the case.[29]

These social connections can be further enhanced where users have a greater perception of control over an anthropomorphized agent than another human or where individuals settle for expedience—constrained by time pressures or cognitive abilities—rather than optimal outcomes.[30] The attribution of human-like qualities by individuals to non-human agents implies similar psychological processes at work (i.e., an inductive base of homocentric or egocentric knowledge) in HMIs and human-to-human social interactions.[31] In short, anthropomorphism is not simply a by-product of HMI, but rather an intrinsic feature, embodying social cognitive features (for example empathy, social bonding, and perception), and potentially enabling mutual adaptation and coordination during intersubjective and complex decision-making.[32]

Anthropomorphism in AI by design

How and why does anthropomorphism permeate AI research and design? From depictions of Alan Turing's early computational machines to Chat-GPT's modern-day technological infamy, researchers often use human-like traits, concepts (for example "understand," "learn," "intelligence"), and expertise when referring to AI systems to highlight the similarities of humans and AI algorithms.[33] Intellectual and emotional anthropomorphic manifestations are deliberately baked into AI systems by their designers—for the efficacious, control, and social cognitive reasons described—so they can be used in HMI. In this sense, the perception of human users interacting with the AI-system seems to partially be shaped by design choices.

Other possible driving forces underlying the humanization of AI by designers include the intrinsic epistemic limitation and bias of AI researchers and a broader shift in science in the late nineteenth century from "eliminativism" (the belief that our understanding of the mind is wrong and that many of the mental states posited by common sense do not exist in reality) and "psychophobia" (an irrational fear of the mind) to an emphasis on "anthropocentric" (viewing humans as the central or most important element of existence) mental concepts and terms applied to inanimate non-human entities.[34] The tendency of popular culture such as science fiction literature, movies, and TV shows, and media coverage to emphasize the human-like qualities of AI and robots, such as emotional, cognitive, sentient, conscious, ethical, creates a limited understanding of the state of AI capabilities. It inadvertently expounds false notions about what AI can and cannot do, thus creating polarizing dystopian and utopian expectations.[35]

Historically, AI research can be broadly categorized into "human-centric" approaches (systems designed to think or act like humans to perform functions that require human intelligence) and "rational" approaches (systems designed to think or act rationally), which automate tasks traditionally performed by humans, such as decision-making, problem-solving, prediction, and learning.[36] Not surprisingly, "human-centric" approaches, inspired by the mutual relationship between neuroscience and AI fields, are especially susceptible to anthropomorphism.[37] This approach dominates brain-inspired AI research associated with one of the most prominent and successful ML Deep Neutral Networks and reinforcement learning AI sub-fields, which powers, for example, Facebook's facial recognition software, Google's translation software, and popular digital assistants like Apple's Siri.[38] The high-profile success of systems like these (see Appendix 2) has contributed further to the public and scientific alacrity that the development of AI depends on emulating the human brain and thus is critical in understanding how the human brain works.

Critics argue that these conceptualizations (or "wishful mnemonics") are misleading for the users and researchers of the system alike, understating the critical epistemological differences between human intelligence, and other attributes, and AI—that is, how humans gain an understanding of the world through intuition, perception, introspection, memory, reason, and testimony.[39] AI researcher David Watson writes: "It would be a mistake to say that these algorithms recreate human intelligence; instead, they introduce *some new mode of inference that outperforms us in some ways and falls short in others*" (emphasis added).[40] Whether the goal of future AI will be to replicate the human brain's functional architecture (beliefs, desires, and intention models, etc.), or innovate an entirely novel approach to "intelligence," is an open question that has profound epistemic consequences for trust, acceptance, and tolerance in HMIs, which is explored below.

A significant concern with anthropomorphic language in describing AI systems is that it can neglect the intrinsic limitations of AI technology— AI algorithms are brittle, inefficient, vulnerable, and myopic—and create a false equivalence between human and machine intelligence.[41] According to AI researchers Złotowski et al., "at best, the anthropomorphizing of machines obscures both AI's actual achievements and how far it has to go in order to produce genuinely intelligent machines. At worst, it leads researchers to make plainly false claims about their creations."[42] Once AI systems are anthropomorphized, their statistical probabilistic derived abilities can become equivalent to human capacities to form judgments, make decisions, and be responsible and trustworthy; when paired with humans the AI will effectively and dependably do what it is intended to do without undesirable actions, and even act ethically[43]—the notion of "machine morality" discussed below.[44] In short, the anthropomorphic hype surrounding AI fails to grasp the human brain's cognitive processes, enabling it to make counter-intuitive inferences and common-sense decisions to intuitively make sense of the world, which AI cannot.[45] To address this problem, researchers must understand AI systems' strengths and weaknesses and how they fit into the broader socio-technical ecosystem.

Weaponizing AI-anthropomorphism? Military HMI in tactical hybrid teaming

This section presents empirical work from military HMI in hybrid teaming operations, drawing insights from social psychology, philosophers, and anthropology to consider the impact and design of anthropomorphism in AI systems. This research does not provide prescriptive claims or recommendations per se for the anthropomorphism of AI technology, but instead considers when, why, and for whom anthropomorphism's effects are most likely to occur and to what result.

The case studies in the scientific and social science literature on anthropomorphism in HMI's military applications draw from and complement parallel research in civilian social robotics and social cognition.[46] Civilian studies can highlight some of the potential unintentional consequences and risks of anthropomorphism in HMI and thus may provide novel and innovative ways of integrating AI in military hybrid teaming.[47] Specifically, social robotic studies demonstrate that a critical precondition in successful HMIs is how humans perceive non-human agents' expertise, emotional engagement, and perceptual responses.[48] How AI agents are perceived by human military personnel crucially influences the amount of trust, acceptance, and tolerance afforded to them, and thus the efficacious hybrid teaming in function and scope.[49] Recent studies have found that even in situations when the user knows that an AI agent, such as a digital assistant, chat-bot, or avatar, is less skilled at a particular task than a human, they may use their imagination, experience, or explanatory skills to create meaning from the shortcomings of AI agents and thus fill the gaps in HMI.[50] How a human *perceives* the AI agent is more important to their tolerance, acceptance, and attachment than a machine's actual abilities, and thus critical in understanding HMIs.

Depending on the context and technology involved, conceptually speaking several physical (combat and non-combat) and decision-making military tasks could soon be delegated to AI agents (replacing humans) or conducted with them (augmenting or coordinating tasks). These include: intelligence, surveillance, and reconnaissance; selective target guidance and engagement; perimeter and border protection; shielding of military personnel and civilians; bomb disposal; handling of chemical, biological, and nuclear materials; logistics and transportation; "Loyal Wingman" drones to support manned fighter pilots (for example to absorb enemy fire and scouting); and providing medical and psychological assistance and training to the military.[51] While autonomy is a crucial design—and an underlying force driver—of these systems, the limitations of AI today mean that humans will need to supervise the actions of AI agents, either "on the loop" or "in the loop" (see Figure 1.1), except in linear, non-contingent, or perfectly controlled and predictable environments, which rarely if ever exist in a military context.

AI-augmentation could support several capabilities that enable these operations, including: unmanned underwater, ground, and aerial vehicles; unmanned quadruped ground vehicles; interactive embodied robots; and digital assistants and avatars to support command decision-making, including face and voice recognition to interpret enemy intentions and anticipate their behavior.[52] Advances in bioelectric signals technology, such as electromyogram and electroencephalogram, which reflect human internal states and intended actions, will soon enable new kinds of brain-computer interface,[53] allowing intuitive control of machines and connecting human neural functions to various command and control military systems, such as controlling drones swarms or even jet-fighters.[54] US DARPA's "ElectRx" program, for example, is developing neural implants that interface directly with the nervous system to continuously assess the state of soldiers' health, to regulate conditions such as depression, Crohn's disease, and post-traumatic stress disorder.[55] In HMIs, where the physical interaction is close and persistent, such as exoskeletons, human and machine behavior forms a mutually dependent relationship, where both the goals and the physical effort applied for their efficacy are intertwined and must be cojointly determined for a smooth and effective interaction.[56]

From the perspective of human cognition perhaps what really matters is the efficacy of HMI, such as fluidity of communications, parsimony, and control, and the resultant impact on the usable bandwidth available to soldiers to fulfill missions. In other words, the most potentially transformative effects of AI technology on HMI are less the use of biological implants in the bid for cyborg-like mergers, but rather the kinds of non-penetrative forms of augmentation that might transform the socio-technical problem-solving matrix with potentially profound human psychological implications.[57] The kinds of human–machine symbiosis (or "biotechnological mergers") discussed will likely depend, for their ultimate success, on intimate technologized social interactions—however imperfect or superficial.[58] Some scholars worry that the effect of these interactions on moral responsibility and personal identity might adversely impact human-to-human interactions.[59] For instance, it might cause humans to treat others on an equal moral footing with, or even below, AI agents, or worse still, to ethically desensitize or dehumanize human-to-human contact, as discussed below.

In a recent series of aerial combat simulations hosted by US DARPA as part of their "AlphaDogfight" project, AI agents were pitted against human F-16 fighter pilots in virtual dogfights: AI-powered fighters comprehensively defeated their human adversaries. In a separate collaborative project with Boeing, the US Air Force is developing the "Loyal Wingman" supersonic autonomous combat drone, capable of flying in formation with fifth-generation F-35 fighter jets, defending them from enemy attack and autonomously coordinating with on-board systems and pilots in joint attack missions.[60] AI agents operate in physical and simulated domains. They are controlled by adaptive algorithms, which change their behavior when run, based on information available and a priori defined reward mechanisms; ML systems can navigate and manipulate their environment and select optimum task-resolution strategies.[61]

These hybrid teaming studies demonstrate that irrespective of whether AI agents are used to support allied drones or in offensive strike sorties, hybrid teaming coordination (trust, acceptance, and tolerance) is optimized when the behavior and intentions of AI are accurately perceived, anticipated, and communicated to human pilots using two-way signaling activities, spontaneity, and parsimonious anthropomorphic cues and terms.[62] An additional challenge is that the same observables such as body language may originate from different intentions and needs. A soldier in a combat scenario may, for instance, engage the enemy offensively, defend his position, or have the intention to lay down his arms. In high-stress, fast-paced, and contingent tactical military operations that require rapid value- and moral-laden decisions in response to situational shifts—such as in anti-access and area-denial contested zones—with high demands on working memory and attentional resources (or "cognitive load"),[63] cognitive parsimony is critical to managing the perceptual, emotional, and complex multitasking motoric features of HMI.[64] A possible path forward is using cognitively inspired real-world synthetic generated data to train algorithms, such as generative adversarial networks that learn to generate new data by combining features from original datasets. These support autonomous systems in improbable but potentially high-risk situations.[65] How to generate meaningful and realistic synthetic experiences for training purposes, with minimal human crafting of these situations, is an area ripe for further research.[66]

Understanding the determinants and drivers of anthropomorphism can, therefore, help us to identify the conditions under which these effects (both positive and negative) will be most impactful. In short, the design of AI agents for hybrid teaming must embody both the positive and potentially negative psychological implications of anthropomorphism. AI agents must produce predictable, purposeful, and well-communicated behaviors, correctly identifying human intentions and the drivers of human behavior—and, in turn, relate to them. Identifying others' intentions is complicated when information is complex and overwhelming—which can also impair joint coordination—and when the nature of others' intentions is opaque because of deception, manipulation, bodily behavior, emotional states, and cues obscured. Meta AI's (formally Facebook) *Cicero* algorithm, combining natural language models with game theory and probabilistic analysis, has made some progress in aligning AI agents with human intentions and objectives in a game of competition, cooperation, manipulation, and deception, Diplomacy which, if generalizable, may help improve communication barriers between humans and AI-powered agents.[67]

Strategies of deception and manipulation of information, signals, and intentions to distract an adversary and delay or inhibit its ability to respond can be replicated and magnified (in scale, speed, and dissemination) using AI technology (for example through chatbots, digital avatars, deep-fake technology, and AI-augmented adversarial attacks and electromagnetic warfare) in ways that can make anthropomorphism more acute in AI-augmented technology.[68] In tactical HMIs, the need for rapid decision-making in dynamic and contingent situations will complicate the challenge of accurately interpreting human gestures, speech, and subtle cues when AI agents, and machines and artificial tools generally, are used as a medium.[69] Interpreting the mental state of a combatant in close physical contact (through their gestures and facial expressions etc.) is generally easier than when using tools such as drones, digital assistants, and other vehicles that hide bodily expressions.[70] For example, using new-generation AI-enhanced aerial combat drones such as the Loyal Wingman aircraft or AlphaDogfight simulations in asymmetric offensive operations, AI systems could be trained—or eventually autonomously "learn"—to suppress specific anthropomorphic cues and traits, or to use human-like cues and traits to generate false flag or other deception and disinformation operations.[71]

Consequences of AI-anthropomorphism

What are the possible consequences of AI-anthropomorphism of AI-enabled military HMI? In a military context, individuals perceiving an AI agent to have human-like qualities has significant ethical, moral, and normative consequences for both the human perceiver and the AI agent perceived.[72] Some scholars contend that anthropomorphic projections (explicit or implicit) might expose soldiers in hybrid teams to physical and psychological risks.[73] Others, in contrast, by understating the potential impact of anthropomorphism in AI on the performance of human operators, risk underplaying the tactical, ethical, and cognitive implications.[74]

Ethical and moral

In addition to the epistemological problems described, the anthropomorphic rhetoric—or anthropomorphism in AI by design—surrounding the development of AI systems also has significant ethical consequences for HMIs. Perceiving an AI agent as conscious and possessing human-like intelligence implies that AI agents should be treated as "moral agents" (i.e., as having the capacity to regulate one's actions through moral principles or ideals),[75] and thus deserving of protection, empathy, and rights such as autonomy and freedom.[76] In his advocacy of animal rights, philosopher Immanuel Kant argued that "when moral worth is in question, it is not a matter of actions which one sees but their inner principles which one does not see."[77] By anthropomorphizing non-human agents, we are, *ipso facto*, allowing them to be moralized.

Humanizing AI can influence how users behave toward an anthropomorphized AI agent in three ways.[78] First, perceiving AIs as moral agents may have a significant normative impact should they prove demonstrably otherwise. Second, it might either exacerbate misplaced fears that AI will make humans—and thus, human commanders—obsolete or create a false sense of uncritical optimism in the ability of AI systems to replace humans in safety-critical military functions such as targeting and command decision-making (see Chapter 3).[79] Third, implicit or explicit anthropomorphic hype might blur warfare's complex and nuanced moral, ethical, and ontological boundaries.

Anthropomorphizing terms like "ethical," "intelligent," and "responsible" in the context of machines can lead to false attributions and mythical tropes implying that inanimate AI agents are capable of moral reasoning, compassion, empathy, mercy, and so on, and thus might perform more ethically and humanely than humans in warfare.[80] Roboticist Ronald Arkin's research on developing autonomous battlefield robots with an artificial consciousness and synthetic uploaded human ethics (Arkin's "ethical governor" concept) demonstrates what can happen when anthropomorphic tropes and perceptions of machine ethics are applied to make an equivalence with human morality in war. Arkin argues: "I am convinced that they [autonomous battlefield robots] can perform more ethically [and more humanely] than human soldiers are capable of."[81]

Similarly, the European Remotely Piloted Aviation Systems Steering Group, in its report on drones, stated that "citizens will expect drones to have an *ethical behavior comparable to the human one*, respecting some commonly accepted rules" (emphasis added).[82] The shift from viewing technology as tools to support military operations to becoming an integral team member, or even a source of moral authority, rests on an anthropomorphic expectation that machines as moral agents can exhibit human-like qualities and "act" rationally, dispassionately, and ethically in the conduct of war. Some fear that greater levels of automation and intelligence in AI systems may further entrench the authoritative status of technology in war, such that machines become "a science of imaginary technical solutions to the problem of war legitimization," and, in turn, further dehumanize warfare (discussed below).[83]

Some scholars describe the semantic problem of how we conceptualize ethics and machines in war: namely, the distinction between machines behaving ethically—assuming that machines have sufficient agency and cognition to make moral decisions ("functional" ethics)—and machines being used (by humans) ethically in operational contexts ("operational" ethics).[84] In a recent report on the role of autonomous weapons, the US Defense Advisory Board alluded to this problem, concluding that "treating unmanned systems as if they had *sufficient independent agency to reason about morality* distracts from designing appropriate rules of engagement and *ensuring operational morality*" (emphasis added).[85] Using anthropomorphic language to conflate human ethics and reasoning with machine logical inductive statistical reasoning—on the false premise that machine and human ethical reasoning in war are similar—risks abdicating control over our ethical decision-making to machines. In short, humanizing AI (i.e., granting AI agents anthropocentric agency) is not ethically or morally neutral; instead, it presents a critical barrier to conceptualizing the many challenges AI poses as an emerging technology.[86]

Trust and responsibility

An AI agent with human intelligence capable of intentional action would presumably be worthy of human "trust" and thus held legally and morally responsible for its actions.[87] To be sure, it is highly speculative whether machines will ever be endowed with the sorts of agency (or "human intelligence") to merit legal and moral culpability. Were military personnel to perceive AI agents as more capable and intelligent than they are, they may become more predisposed to "social loafing"[88] (or complacency) in tasks that require human and machine collaboration, such as target acquisition, intelligence gathering, or battlefield situation awareness assessments.[89] In other words, the anthropomorphic tendency of people to conflate a technological capacity for accuracy and speed with tactical competency means that AI agents are more likely, for better or worse, to be judged as responsible and thus trustworthy in the conduct of war—and in other safety-critical HMI collaborative domains such as robotic surgery.[90] In the medical domain, for example, radiologists assisted by an AI screening system for breast cancer admitted that they generally spent less time scrutinizing scans generated by ML outputs, because of the confidence that develops in the system each time the AI produces a "normal confident" (negative) reading. Whether these responses are simply the result of anthropomorphism, and how using AI might affect radiologists' decisions—and, if so, whether this creates new risks—has yet to be empirically tested.[91]

People tend to mistakenly infer an inherent connection between these human traits and machines when their performance matches or surpasses that of humans—digital technology's "cleaving power."[92] Moreover, people are more likely to feel *less responsible* for the success (or failure) of tasks that use human-like HMI and treat anthropomorphic interactions with AI agents as scapegoats when the technology malfunctions. Paradoxically, advances in autonomy and machine intelligence will require more (rather than less) contributions from the human operator to cope with the inevitable unexpected contingencies that fall outside of an algorithm's training parameters or fail in some way—known as the "automation paradox."[93] Overconfidence in the abilities and trust (mis)placed in AI agents (described in Chapter 1), coupled with the abdication of responsibility, might result in the proliferation of these technologies (to state and non-state actors), lower the threshold for war, and make inadvertent and accidental war more likely.[94]

Studies demonstrate that individuals more willingly punish an agent they consider intelligent and conscious of legal and moral violations.[95] Moreover, people are more likely to hold groups (militaries, corporations, governments) comprising single personified agents more legally culpable for moral violations than those representing collectives of disparate individuals.[96] Furthermore, if an AI agent is deemed responsible for their actions, then the humans controlling or collaborating with AI agents may, *ipso facto*, consider themselves *less* responsible for the direct or indirect actions resulting from hybrid teaming decisions. In the event of war crimes, for instance, treating AI agents as moral agents would complicate the attribution of responsibility, which has become a key point of contention in international debates on lethal autonomous weapons.[97] Debates about diffusing safety-critical moral and legal responsibility to AI-powered decision-support systems are also evident in the medical domain.[98] If the decisions and actions of AI agents during combat appear "human-like," does this necessarily decrease the perceived responsibility of the humans who designed the algorithms or collaborated with AI agents in hybrid teaming? By anthropomorphizing AI technology, therefore, we risk implicitly or explicitly affording machines a level of unwarranted agency, which not only exaggerates the technology's capabilities, but may also reduce human autonomy and sense of agency.

Social influencers

Human-level AI intelligence—or a user's perception of such an ability— would, in theory, make an AI agent capable of evaluating, observing, and judging a human perceiver, thus becoming a potential source of normative social influence on the perceiver. To what extent does anthropomorphizing an AI agent increase adherence to socially desirable norms? The research is consistent with the belief that non-human "mindful" agents may become sources of social influence.[99] Social psychology studies demonstrate that because people care about what others think of them, they are more likely to follow (desirable) social norms when viewed by others than when alone. Some religions, for example, believe that the capacity of an omnipresent and judgmental God to watch people's behavior can serve as a source of social surveillance and thus enhance cooperation between group members.[100]

Recent experimental economic behavioral games demonstrate that people tend to behave more desirably (cooperatively and pro-socially) in HMIs when the digital interface exhibits a human-like appearance (for example human-like eyes) rather than being a purely text-based one.[101] An AI agent's pro-social behaviors might also have negative effects. Because people ascribe emotions to machines, and thus respond emotionally to them, their view may waver if the AI's behavior shifts (for example from pro-social to neutral or even anti-social).[102] As we have seen, machines are notoriously poor at common sense, are erratic in social interactions, and can be deployed to deceive and manipulate. In sum, those individuals more inclined to anthropomorphize non-human agents (for the reasons described) may behave more desirably, or normatively, in HMIs with AI agents than those less likely to anthropomorphize. How the inverse of anthropomorphizing, dehumanization, could influence the attributions of responsibility and trust in HMIs as they relate to perceptions of social surveillance is an open question for future research.

Inverting AI-anthropomorphism and the dehumanization of war

Whereas anthropomorphism is the process of perceiving non-human agents to possess human-like qualities, and increasing their moral worth, dehumanization (discussed in Chapter 1) represents the inverse process, thus reducing moral worth and endorsing violence and aggression.[103] Just as increasing levels of similarity to humans can invoke the tendency to anthropomorphize a non-human agent, so can decreased similarity increase the tendency to dehumanize other humans.[104] Humanness exists on a continuum; how we perceive others is inextricably connected to how we perceive non-humans. The psychological mechanisms that make people likely to attribute human-like qualities (i.e., to anthropomorphize) can also increase our understanding of when and why people do the opposite. Using this theoretical inversion, we can draw insights to better understand the potential consequences of anthropomorphism in AI-enabled military HMIs and for general dehumanizing in war. The literature on autonomous weapons systems reveals that dehumanizing behavior may also derive from the algorithmic processing of people. In this case, the dehumanization of warfare may occur in the absence of anthropomorphism.

The tendency to anthropomorphize when people are motivated to explain or understand an agent's (human or non-human) behavior described earlier should exhibit the inverse dehumanizing proclivity when individuals are motivated to *reduce* levels of interaction with others—and thus have no motivation or desire to understand, develop social connections with, or empathize with them.[105] Power and influence over others are crucial determinants for increasing an individual's independence, thus decreasing the need for effective interaction with others.[106] In a recent social psychology study, for instance, people in a position of power increased the propensity to objectify subordinates, regarding them as a means to an end and neglecting their essentially human qualities.[107] As a corollary, soldiers in anthropomorphized hybrid teaming might (a) come to view their inanimate machine "team-members" as deserving of more protection and care than their human adversary, or (b) soldiers intoxicated by the power over an adversary may (especially in an asymmetrical conflict) become more predisposed to dehumanize the enemy (i.e., the outgroup), justifying past wrongdoings, and excessive and potentially immoral acts of aggression.[108]

Conclusion

This chapter considered the role of anthropomorphism in military HMI augmented by AI technology. Drawing from empirical and theoretical insights from the major subfields within psychology provides a much-needed and systematic epistemological and normative study on the AI-anthropomorphic phenomenon in military HMIs. Identifying the mechanisms of anthropomorphism in AI-augmented military HMIs and the consequences of inferring the "frame of nature that bespeaks an [artificial] intelligent author," this research contributes to an established canon of work on social robotics and social cognition in HMIs, and a burgeoning one on AI-anthropomorphism.[109]

The chapter's key findings can be summarized as follows. First, understanding the various psychological mechanisms that undergird the phenomenology of AI-anthropomorphism is a critical step in (a) determining the potential positive and negative impact of military HMIs, and thus, (b) optimizing the accuracy, reliability, and efficacy of HMIs in military operations. A main point of the chapter is that the tendency to anthropomorphize AI agents in military HMIs would likely be especially acute because of machine-learning algorithmic logic coupled with the high incentives for understanding and effectively interfacing with AI agents.

Second, in the military domain anthropomorphism can create a sense of efficacy and competence in interacting with AI agents. This perception has prompted developers to deliberately and explicitly elicit this reaction to optimize the integration of AI agents into hybrid team operations. As a corollary, time-pressured and stressful war conditions may encourage social bonding in military HMIs, making its users more cognitively disposed toward technological agents—that is, caring about their wellbeing—than might otherwise be the case.[110] This disposition may prompt soldiers in anthropomorphized hybrid teaming to either view their AI "team-mates" as deserving of more protection and care than their human adversary or make them more likely to dehumanize the enemy, justifying excessive and potentially immoral acts of aggression. More empirical work is needed, however, on the psychological impact of the perception, whether accurate or otherwise, of machine efficacy and competence in military HMIs.

Third, a significant worry with anthropomorphic language and popular tropes in describing AI is that they overlook the intrinsic limitations of AI technology (that it is brittle, inefficient, vulnerable, and myopic), thus creating a false equivalence between human and machine intelligence, which are ontologically, epistemologically, and metaphysically very different. Once AI systems are anthropomorphized, their statistical probabilistic outputs may be treated as equivalent to human judgments, decisions, and "functional" ethics in war, which risks abdicating control over human ethical decision-making to machines. Therefore, AI researchers, and by extension the broader stakeholders of AI technology, must understand AI systems' strengths and weaknesses and how they fit into the broader socio-technical ecosystem.

Finally, in military HMI design, an essential precondition for success is how humans perceive an AI agent's expertise, emotional engagement, and perceptual responses—influencing the trust, acceptance, and tolerance placed in machine team members, especially in novel situations (see Conclusion).[111] AI agents must produce predictable, purposeful, and well-communicated behaviors, correctly identifying human intentions and the drivers of human behavior, and, in turn, relate to them. In tactical HMIs, the need for rapid decision-making will likely complicate the challenge of accurately interpreting human bodily actions and subtle cues when AI agents are used as a medium. Recent studies have demonstrated that forcing operators in HMIs to make the initial decision, while waiting for the algorithmic recommendation ("cognitive forcing functions"), can enhance user engagement in critical thinking when considering AI decisions and explanations, thereby reducing overreliance, and increasing users' sense of agency.[112]

Finally, the anthropomorphic tendency of people to conflate a technological capacity for accuracy and speed with tactical competency (exacerbated by automation bias discussed in Chapter 1) means that AI agents are more likely to be judged as responsible and thus trustworthy in the conduct of war. By anthropomorphizing AI, we risk, either implicitly or explicitly, affording machines a level of unwarranted agency that both exaggerates its capabilities and reduces human autonomy and sense of agency in warfare. By understanding the nature of this universal tendency, we will stand a much better chance of recognizing Hume's "armies in the clouds," and, in turn, qualitatively improving future human–machine interfaces in war. What are the strategic implications of automating command decisions to intelligent machines? The next chapter picks up this challenge.

Notes

[1] David Hume, *The Natural History of Religion* (Stanford, CA: Stanford University Press, 1957), p. 29.

[2] See Jesse Bering, "The Folk Psychology of Souls," *Behavioral and Brain Sciences* 29 (5) (2006), pp. 453–462; Virginia Kwan and Susan Fiske, "Missing Links in Social Cognition: The Continuum from Non-Human Agents to Dehumanized Humans," *Social Cognition* 26 (2) (2008), pp. 125–128; Brian Duffy, "Anthropomorphism and the Social Robot," *Robotics and Autonomous Systems* 42 (3) (2003), pp. 177–190; and Mike Dacey, "Anthropomorphism as Cognitive Bias," *Philosophy of Science* 84 (5) (2017), pp. 1152–1164.

[3] Sections of this chapter are derived in part from James Johnson, "Finding AI Faces in the Moon and Armies in the Clouds: Anthropomorphizing Artificial Intelligence in Military Human-Machine Interactions," *Global Society* (2023), doi: 10.1080/13600826.2023.2205444.

[4] See Christoph Bartneck et al., "Measurement Instruments for the Anthropomorphism, Animacy, Likeability, Perceived Intelligence, and Perceived Safety of Robots," *International Journal of Social Robotics* 1 (1) (2009), pp. 71–81; Bilge Mutlu et al. (eds), *Proceedings of Social Robotics: Third International Conference on Social Robotics*, ICSR 2011, Amsterdam, The Netherlands, November 24–25, 2011 (New York: Springer, 2011); David Watson, "The Rhetoric and Reality of Anthropomorphism in Artificial Intelligence," *Minds and Machines* 29 (2019), pp. 417–440.

[5] Notable exceptions include: Adam Waytz, John Cacioppo, and Nicholas Epley, "Who Sees Human? The Stability and Importance of Individual Differences in Anthropomorphism," *Perspectives on Psychological Science* 5 (3) (2010), pp. 219–232; Nicolas Epley, Adam Waytz, and John Cacioppo, "On Seeing Human: A Three-Factor Theory of Anthropomorphism," *Psychological Review* 114 (2007), pp. 864–886.

[6] James Lesher, *Xenophanes of Colophon: Fragments. Toronto* (Toronto: University of Toronto Press, 1992).

[7] The mechanisms underlying anthropomorphism are cognitively like those associated with social cognition and attributing human dispositions and traits to other humans. V. Gazzola et al., "The Anthropomorphic Brain: The Mirror Neuron System Responds to Human and Robotic Actions," *NeuroImage* 35 (4) (2007), pp. 1674–1684.

[8] Lasana Harris and Susan Fiske, "Brooms in Fantasia: Neural Correlates of Anthropomorphizing Objects," *Social Cognition* 26 (2), pp. 209–222.

[9] Nicholas G. Evans and Jonathan D. Moreno, "Neuroethics and Policy at the National Security Interface," in *Debates about Neuroethics: Perspectives on its Development, Focus and Future*, ed. Eric Racine and John Aspler (Dordecht: Springer, 2017), pp. 141–160.

[10] See Bruce Ellis and David Bjorklund, *Origins of the social Mind: Evolutionary Psychology and Child Development* (New York: The Guildford Press, 2004); Pascal Boyer, *Religion Explained* (New York: Basic Books, 2001).

[11] Stuart Guthrie, *Faces in the Clouds: A New Theory of Religion* (Oxford: Oxford University Press, 1995).

[12] Nicholas Epley and Adam Waytz, "Mind Perception," in *The Handbook of Social Psychology*, ed. Susan T. Fiske, Daniel T. Gilbert, and Gardner Lindzey. 5th ed. (New York: Wiley), pp. 498–554.

13 Duffy, "Anthropomorphism and the Social Robot," pp. 177–190; Dacey, "Anthropomorphism as Cognitive Bias," pp. 1152–1164.

14 The inverse process of anthropomorphism (or humanization) is dehumanization (discussed below), where people fail to attribute human-like traits to other humans and therefore treat them like non-human animals or inanimate objects, thus denying them essential human capacities such as thought, consciousness, and emotion.

15 See Friederike Eyssel and Dieta Kuchenbrandt, "Social Categorization of Social Robots: Anthropomorphism as a Function of Robot Group Membership," *British Journal of Social Psychology* 51 (4) (2012), pp. 724–731; Friederike Eyssel and Dieta Kuchenbrand, et al., "If You Sound Like Me, You Must be More Human: On the Interplay of Robot and User Features on Human–Robot Acceptance and Anthropomorphism," in HRI'12, *Proceedings of the 7th annual ACM/IEEE International Conference on Human–Robot Interaction* (2012), pp. 125–126; Frank Hegel et al., "Towards a Typology of Meaningful Signals and Cues in Social Robotics," in *Proceedings of the IEEE International Workshop on Robot and Human Interactive Communication* (2012), pp. 72–78.

16 Nicolas Spatola and Thierry Chaminade, "Cognitive Load Increases Anthropomorphism of Humanoid Robot: The Automatic Path of Anthropomorphism," *International Journal of Human-Computer Studies* 167 (2022), pp. 1–15.

17 Massimiliano Cappuccio, Jai Galliott, and Eduardo Sandoval, "Saving Private Robot: Risks and Advantages of Anthropomorphism in Agent–Soldier Teams," *International Journal of Social Robotics* (2021), doi:10.1007/s12369-021-00755-z.

18 Jakub Zotowski, Hidenobu Sumioka, and Frederike Eyssel, "Model of Dual Anthropomorphism: The Relationship between the Media Equation Effect and Implicit Anthropomorphism," *International Journal of Social Robotics* 10 (2018), pp. 701–714.

19 Jeffrey Saver and John Rabin, "The Neural Substrates of Religious Experience," *Journal of Neuropsychiatry Clinical Neuroscience* 9 (3) (1997), pp. 498–510.

20 Jakub Złotowski et al., "Anthropomorphism: Opportunities and Challenges in Human–Robot Interaction," *Journal of Social Robotics* 7 (2015), pp. 347–360.

21 Epey, Waytz, and Cacioppo, "On Seeing Human."

22 Robyn Dawes and Matthew Mulford, "The False Consensus Effect and Overconfidence: Flaws in Judgment or Flaws in How we Study Judgment?" *Organizational Behavior and Human Decision Processes* 65 (3) 1996), pp. 201–211.

23 Arie Kruglanski and Donna Webster, "Motivated Closing of the Mind: 'Seizing' and 'Freezing,'" *Psychological Review* 103 (2) 1996), pp. 263–283.

24 Though people form anthropomorphic attributions with various types of non-human agents, agents are anthropomorphized in different ways and degrees. For example, anthropomorphizing animals is distinct from anthropomorphizing immanent agents such as self-driving cars, robots, or digital assistants.

25 Cappuccio, Galliott, and Sandoval, "Saving Private Robot," p. 5.

26 Ibid., p. 2.

27 Emanuela Moreale and Stuart Watt, "An Agent-Based Approach to Mailing List Knowledge Management: Agent-Mediated Knowledge Management," *Lecture Notes in Artificial Intelligence*, 2926 (2004), pp. 118–129.

28 Sara Kiesler et al., "All Robots are Not Created Equal: Design and the Perception of Humanness in Robot Heads." Paper presented at the DIS2002 Conference Proceedings (London, 2002).

29   The experience of social connection (for example, emotional proximity) with non-human agents is not necessarily anthropomorphic. Gabriella Airenti, Marco Cruciano, and Alessio Plebe, *The Cognitive Underpinnings of Anthropomorphism* (Lausanne: Frontiers Media, 2019).

30   Clifford Nass et al., "Can Computer Personalities be Human Personalities?" *International Journal of Human-Computer Studies* 43 (2) 1995), pp. 223–239.

31   Epley, Waytz, and Cacioppo, "On Seeing Human," p. 878.

32   Massimiliano Cappuccio, "Inference or Familiarity? The Embodied Roots of Social Cognition," *Synthesis Philosophica* 29 (2) (2014), pp. 253–272.

33   Arleen Salles, Kathinka Evers, and Michele Frisco, "Anthropomorphism in AI," *AJOB Neuroscience* 11 (2) (2020), pp. 91–92.

34   Ibid., p. 91.

35   Christoph Bartneck, "Robots in the Theatre and the Media," in *Proceedings of the Design and Semantics of Form and Movement* (2013), *Wuxi*, pp. 64–70.

36   Stuart Russell and Peter Norvig, *Artificial Intelligence: International Version: A Modern Approach* (Englewood Cliffs: Prentice Hall, 2010).

37   Neuroscience has benefited from AI research as a model for developing ideas about the working brain and as a tool for processing data sets, and AI has benefited from successfully emulating brain activities. Salles, Evers, and Frisco, "Anthropomorphism in AI," p. 92.

38   Recent studies demonstrate that anthropomorphic digital assistants and avatars appear more intelligent and credible than non-anthropomorphic ones. Kristine L. Nowak and Christian Rauh, "The Influence of the Avatar on Online Perceptions of Anthropomorphism, Androgyny, Credibility, Homophily, and Attraction," *Journal of Computer-Mediated Communication* 11 (1) 2005), pp. 153–178.

39   While actual human neural networks include many characteristics of neural computation—namely, nonlinear transduction, divisive normalization, maximum-base pooling of inputs, and can replicate the hierarchical organization of mammalian cortical systems—there are significant differences in the structure of biological neurons (structure, types, interconnectivity), which has yet to be incorporated in deep neural networks. See Drew McDermott, "Artificial Intelligence Meets Natural Stupidity," *ACM Sigart Bulletin* 57 (4) (1976) pp. 4–9; Demis Hassabis et al., "Neuroscience-Inspired Artificial Intelligence," *Neuron* 95 (2) (2017), pp. 245–258; Shimon Ullman, "Using Neuroscience to Develop Artificial Intelligence," *Science* 363 (6428) (2019), pp. 692–693.

40   Watson, "The Rhetoric and Reality of Anthropomorphism in Artificial Intelligence," p. 425.

41   Ibid.

42   Złotowski et al., "Anthropomorphism," p. 353.

43   Feras Batarseh, Laura Freeman, and Huang Chih-Hao, "A Survey on Artificial Intelligence Assurance," *Journal of Big Data* 8 (60) (2021), doi:10.1186/s40537-021-00445-7.

44   Wendell Wallach and Colin Allen, *Moral Machines: Teaching Robots Right from Wrong* (Oxford: Oxford University Press, 2009).

45   AI researchers have made some progress toward this end in the gaming environment. Meta AI's *Cicero* gaming algorithm integrates a language model with planning and reinforcement ML techniques to infer players' beliefs and intentions from its conversations and generate dialogue in pursuit of its plans. The generalizability of *Cicero* outside of

the strict parameters of gaming to other situations involving social interactions is, however, less clear. "CICERO: An AI Agent that Negotiates, Persuades, and Cooperates with People," *Meta AI*, November 22, 2022, https://ai.facebook.com/blog/cicero-ai-negotiates-persuades-and-cooperates-with-people/.

46 See Julie Carpenter, "Just Doesn't Look Right: Exploring the Impact of Humanoid Robot Integration into Explosive Ordnance Disposal Teams," in *Handbook of Research on Technoself: Identity in a Technological Society*, ed. Rocci Luppicini (Hershey: IGI Global, 2013), pp. 609–36; Peter Singer, *Wired for War: The Robotics Revolution and Conflict in the 21st Century* (New York: Penguin, 2011); Jai Galliott, "Defending Australia in the Digital Age: Toward Full-Spectrum Defense," *Defence Studies* 16 (2) (2016), pp. 157–175.

47 Guy Hoffman and Cynthia Breazeal, "Collaboration in Human–Robot Teams," in AIAA 1st Intelligent Systems Technical Conference. Infotech Aerospace Conferences, American Institute of Aeronautics and Astronautics (2004).

48 A recent social robotic study demonstrated that not only do people perceive robots to be human-like, but people appear to behave similarly toward technological agents adhering to similar social conventions and norms as when interacting with other humans. Clifford Nass and Youngme Moon, "Machines and Mindlessness: Social Responses to Computers," *Journal of Social Issues* 56 (1) (2000), pp. 81–103.

49 Mutlu et al. (eds), *Social Robotics*.

50 Jesse Fox and Andrew Gambino, "Relationship Development with Humanoid Social Robots: Applying Interpersonal Theories to Human/Robot Interaction," *Cyberpsychology and Behavior, and Social Networking* 24 (5) (2021), 294–299. By contrast, other studies have found that unpredictable events and technical mishaps could jeopardize the human–machine relationship. Marita Skjuve et al., "A Longitudinal Study of Human–Chatbot Relationships," *International Journal of Human-Computer Studies* 168 (2022), pp. 1–14.

51 Ibid., pp. 73–94.

52 Keryl Cosenzo and Michael Barnes, "Human–Robot Interaction Research for Current and Future Military Applications: From the Laboratory to the Field," Unmanned Systems Technology XII (2010); Aleksandra Swiderska and Dennis Küster, "Avatars in Pain: Visible Harm Enhances Mind Perception in Humans and Robots," *Perception* 47 (12) (2018), pp. 1139–1152.

53 Brain-machine interfaces have already been successfully developed in a wide range of areas including prosthetics, rehabilitation, robot control, and game interaction. For practical and ethical reasons, brain-computer interface applications will likely be confined to restorative medicine and military capabilities. Hideaki Hayashi, and Toshio Tsuji, "Human–Machine Interfaces Based on Bioelectric Signals: A Narrative Review with a Novel System Proposal," *IEEJ Transaction on Electrical & Electronic Engineering* (2022), doi:10.1002/tee.23646.

54 Patrick Tucker, "It's Now Possible to Telepathically Communicate with a Drone Swarm," *Defense One*, September 6, 2018, www.defenseone.com/technology/2018/09/its-now-possible-telepathically-communicate-drone-swarm/151068/.

55 Gopal Sarma, "Electrical Prescriptions (ElectRx)," *DARPA*, www.darpa.mil/program/electrical-prescriptions.

56 Bing Chen et al. "Recent Developments and Challenges of Lower Extremity Exoskeletons," *Journal of Orthopaedic Translation* 5 (2016), pp. 26–37.

57 Andy Clark, *Natural Born Cyborgs* (Oxford: Oxford University Press, 2005), pp. 13–34.

58 Ibid., p. 178.

59 John Pickering, "Human Identity in the Age of Software Agents," in *Cognitive Technology: Instruments of the Mind: Proceedings of the 4th International Conference on Cognitive Technology*, ed. M. Beynon, C. Nahniv, and K. Duatenhahn (Berlin: Springer, 2001), pp. 442–451.

60 Patrick Tucker, "An AI Just Beat a Human F-16 Pilot in a Dogfight—Again," *Defense One*, August 20, 2020, www.defenseone.com/technology/2020/08/ai-just-beat-human-f-16-pilot-dogfight-again/167872/; Brad Lendon, "Australian Military Gets First Drone That Can Fly with Artificial Intelligence," May 5, 2020, https://edition.cnn.com/2020/05/05/asia/australia-loyal-wingman-drone-intl-hnk/index.html.

61 Recent unsupervised pre-trained "deep-learning" (a sub-field of ML) networks have been tested on autonomous vehicles to cope with real-world nonlinear problems. However, these new ML approaches are not trustworthy in safety-critical nonlinear environments. Raul Ferreira, "Machine Learning in a Nonlinear World: A Linear Explanation through the Domain of the Autonomous Vehicles," *European Training Network for Safer Autonomous Systems*, January 9, 2020, https://etn-sas.eu/2020/09/01/machine-learning-in-a-nonlinear-world-a-linear-explanation-through-the-domain-of-the-autonomous-vehicles/.

62 Trust, acceptance, and tolerance are critical concepts for social robotics and human–machine interaction research methodology. Bartneck et al., "Measurement Instruments for the Anthropomorphism, Animacy, Likeability, Perceived Intelligence, and Perceived Safety of Robots," pp. 71–81.

63 "Cognitive load" describes how people allocate limited cognitive resources—the storage and process of information in working memory and the integration of new information. Recent studies suggest that "cognitive load" can modulate how people explain others' actions, and thus can make anthropomorphic inferences about their mental states such as intentions. In general, the lower the number of cognitive resources available, the higher the anthropomorphic attributions. Spatola and Chaminade, "Cognitive Load Increases Anthropomorphism of Humanoid Robot," pp. 9–11.

64 Lobna Chérif et al., "Multitasking in the Military: Cognitive Consequences and Potential Solutions," *Applied Cognitive Psychology* 32 (4), pp. 429–439.

65 Ian Goodfellow et al., "Generative Adversarial Nets," *Advances in Neural Information Processing Systems* (2014), pp. 2672–2680.

66 Researchers have begun to consider the use of synthetic data to improve HMIs in self-driving vehicles. See Sara Mahmoud et al., "Where to From Here? On the Future Development of Autonomous Vehicles from a Cognitive Systems Perspective," *Cognitive Systems Research* 76 (2022), pp. 63–77.

67 "CICERO: An AI agent That Negotiates, Persuades, and Cooperates with People."

68 For example, during the recent Russian-Ukrainian conflict, both sides deployed AI-assisted capabilities (defensively and offensively) in information operations, including the use of deep-fake technology, AI-enhanced cyberattacks, disinformation, and intelligence-gathering operations. Will Knight, "As Russia Plots its Next Move, an AI Listens to the Chatter," *Wired*, April 4, 2022, www.wired.com/story/russia-ukraine-war-ai-surveillance/.

69 People's ability to perceive and interpret others' intentions depends on how automatic sensorimotor responses and reciprocal expectations are established through embodied

intersubjective coupling—a learning process in which two or more agents reciprocally redefine their ways to act upon and perceive the world meaningfully. Massimiliano Cappuccio, Jai Galliott, and Eduardo Sandoval, "Mapping Meaning and Purpose in Human–Robot Teams: Anthropomorphic Agents in Military Operations," *The Philosophical Journal of Conflict and Violence* 5 (1) (2021), pp. 73–94.

70   Humans have evolved sharp vision to interpret symbols and signals and assess the cues hidden in subtle facial expressions to interpret others' intentions. Ed Yong, *An Immense World: How Animal Senses Reveal the Hidden Realms Around Us* (New York: Vantage, 2022), p. 61.

71   Several military organizations are testing alternative AI-ML approaches to compensate for the lack of labeled data (i.e., real world information from the battlefield), which is needed to train existing supervised ML systems. These new approaches combine supervised ML with unsupervised deep-learning approaches, which work with a limited amount of annotated data. John Danaher, "Robot Betrayal: A Guide to the Ethics of Robotic Deception," *Ethics Information Technology* 22 (2) (2020), pp. 117–128.

72   Kurt Gray, Heather Gray, and Daniel Wegner, "Dimensions of Mind Perception," *Science* 315 (5812) (2007), p. 619.

73   Paul Scharre, *Army of None: Autonomous Weapons and the Future of War* (New York: W.W. Norton & Company, 2019).

74   Michael Barnes and William Evans, "Soldier–Robot Teaming: An Overview," in *Human–Robot Interactions in Future Military Operations*, ed. Michael Barnes and Florian Jentsch (Farnham: Ashgate Publishing, 2010), pp. 9–31.

75   Mary A. Warren, "On the Moral and Legal Status of Abortion," in *Contemporary Modern Problems*, ed. James White. 9th ed. (New York: Broadman & Holman Publishers, 2008), pp. 113–124.

76   In a recent high-profile case, a Google engineer claimed that Google's AI-powered chatbot generator LaMDA was sentient, possessing human-like intelligence (or artificial general intelligence). Google dismissed these claims and acknowledged the safety concerns around anthropomorphizing AI. Nitasha Tiku, "The Google Engineer who Thinks the Company's AI Has Come to Life," *Washington Post*, June 11, 2022, www.washingtonpost.com/technology/2022/06/11/google-ai-lamda-blake-lemoine/.

77   Immanuel Kant, *Foundations of the Metaphysics of Morals*, trans. L. W. Beck (New York: Macmillan, 1959).

78   Epley, Waytz, and Cacioppo, "On Seeing Human."

79   Heather Roff, "The Strategic Robot Problem: Lethal Autonomous Weapons in War," *Journal of Military Ethics* 13 (3) (2014), pp. 211–227.

80   The notion of non-human agency through "emergent behavior"—behavior that is not programmed but arises out of complexity—propounded by some AI researchers questions this line of argument. Ray Kurzweil, *The Age of Spiritual Machines: When Computers Exceed Human Intelligence* (New York: Penguin, 2000).

81   Ronald Arkin, *Governing Lethal Behavior in Autonomous Robots* (Boca Raton: Chapman, 2009), pp. 47–48.

82   European RPAS Steering Group, *Roadmap for the Integration of Civil Remotely-Piloted Aircraft Systems into the European Aviation System*, June 2013, Brussels: European Commission, p. 44.

83 Ian Roderick, "Mil-Bot Fetishism: The Pataphysics of Military Robots," *Topia* 23 (4) 2010), p. 228.

84 Wallach and Allen, *Moral Machines*.

85 Task Force Report, "The Role of Autonomy in DoD Systems," US Department of Defense, Defense Science Board, July 2012, p. 48, https://www.fas.org/irp/agency/dod/dsb/autonomy.pdf.

86 Luciano Floridi and J. W. Sanders, "On the Morality of Artificial Agents," *Minds and Machines* 14 (3) 2004), pp. 349–379.

87 Human trust is a psychologically nebulous and sticky notion, which cannot be modeled by algorithms or adequately formalized by rational choice theory. This notion of "trust" contrasts with an emergent concept of "e-trust," a second-order concept that arises from distributed digital systems with specific first-order relational properties, such as AI agents. Mariarosaria Taddeo, "Modelling Trust in Artificial Agents, a First Step Toward the Analysis of e-Trust," *Minds and Machines* 20 (2) (2010), pp. 243–257.

88 In social psychology, "social loafing" is when an individual exerts less effort to achieve a goal when working in a team than when working alone.

89 Linda Skitka, Kathleen Mosier, and Mark Burdick, "Does Automation Bias Decision-Making?" *International Journal of Human-Computer Studies* 51 (5) (1999), pp. 991–1006.

90 Alternatively, if a system is perceived as unreliable by its users, distrust can become a problem. For example, despite resolving early technical glitches with the US Air Force's AI-augmented automatic ground collision avoidance system (auto-GCAS), a preconceived distrust in the system prompted several F-16 fighter pilots to disable the potentially life-saving algorithm. Rob Verger, "Two Fighter Pilots, Passed Out over Nevada Last Year: The Software Saved Them Both," *Popular Science*, February 22, 2021, www.popsci.com/story/technology/agcas-technology-saves-pilots-lives/.

91 Hana Kiros, "Doctors using AI Catch Breast Cancer More Often Than Either Does Alone," *MIT Technology Review*, July 11, 2022, www.technologyreview.com/2022/07/11/1055677/ai-diagnose-breast-cancer-mammograms/?utm_source=substack&utm_medium=email.

92 Luciano Florida, "Digital's Cleaving Power and its Consequences," *Philosophy & Technology* 30 (2) 2017), pp. 123–129.

93 Robert Charette, "Automated to Death," *IEEE Spectrum*, December 15, 2009, https://spectrum.ieee.org/automated-to-death.

94 Recent studies have attempted to address these concerns by proposing an optimal level of anthropomorphism for robotics and AI algorithmic design. Duffy, "Anthropomorphism and the Social Robot," pp. 177–190.

95 Gray, Gray, and Wegner, "Dimensions of Mind Perception."

96 Peter French, "Principles of Responsibility, Shame, and the Corporation," in *Shame, Responsibility, and the Corporation*, ed. H. Curtler (New York: Haven, 1986), pp. 17–55.

97 Ingvild Bode and Hendrik Huelss, *Autonomous Weapons Systems, and International Norms* (Queensland: McGill-Queen's University Press, 2022).

98 Hannah Bleher and Matthias Braun, "Diffused Responsibility: Attributions of Responsibility in the Use of AI-Driven Clinical Decision Support Systems," *AI Ethics* (2022), doi:10.1007/s43681-022-00135-x.

99 Ara Norenzayan and Azim Shariff, "The Origin and Evolution of Religious Prosociality," *Science* 322 (5898) (2008), pp. 58–62.

100 Carey Morewedge and Michael Clear, "Anthropomorphic God Concepts Engender Moral Judgment," *Social Cognition*, 26 (2008), pp. 181–188.

101 Kevin Haley and Daniel Fessler, "Nobody's Watching? Subtle Cues Affect Generosity in an Anonymous Economic Game," *Evolution and Human Behavior* 26 (3) (2005), pp. 245–256; and Waytz, Cacioppo, and Epley, "Who Sees Human?" pp. 219–232.

102 J. Danaher, "Robot Betrayal: A Guide to the Ethics of Robotic Deception," *Ethics Inf. Technol.* 22 (2) (2020), pp. 117–128.

103 Nick Haslam, "Dehumanization: An Integrative Review," *Personality and Social Psychology Review* 10 (3) (2006), pp. 252–264; and William Brennan, *Dehumanizing the Vulnerable: When Word Games Take Lives* (Chicago: Loyola University Press, 1995).

104 For example, socially distant outgroups are often dehumanized, while those perceived as the most different (for example drug addicts and homeless people) are most likely to be dehumanized. Lasana Harris and Susan Fiske, "Dehumanizing the Lowest of the Low: Neuroimaging Responses to Extreme Outgroups," *Psychological Science* 17 (10) (2006), pp. 847–853.

105 Adam Waytz, Nicholas Epley, and John Cacioppo, "Social Cognition Unbound: Insights into Anthropomorphism and Dehumanization," *Current Directions in Psychological Science* 19 (1) (2010), pp. 58–62.

106 Albert Bandura, Bill Underwood, and Michael Fromson, "Disinhibition of Aggression Through Diffusion of Responsibility and Dehumanization of Victims," *Journal of Research in Personality* 9 (4) (1975), pp. 253–269.

107 Deborah Gruenfeld et al., "Power and the Objectification of Social Targets," *Journal of Personality and Social Psychology* 95 (1) (2008), pp. 111–127.

108 Contemporary history is replete with tragic case studies of unchecked human emotions causing human suffering, such as Rwanda, the Balkans, Darfur, Afghanistan, and Ukraine.

109 Hume, *The Natural History of Religion*, p. 21.

110 One possible mechanism that may underlie this outcome follows the assumptions advanced by "social attachment theory." In a recent study with an AI-powered social chatbox, researchers found that human users accepted greater contact in machine teaming when presented with a threat or stressful situation, such as loneliness, anxiety, or fear, which increased the attachment to the non-human agent as means of emotional support alongside a desire to continue the relationship. See, Xie Tianling and Iryna Pentina, "Attachment Theory as a Framework to Understand Relationships with Social Chatbots: A Case Study of Replika," in *Proceedings of the 55th Hawaii International Conference on System Sciences* (2022), pp. 2046–2055.

111 William R. King and Jun He, "A Meta-Analysis of the Technology Acceptance Model," *Information & Management* 43 (6) (2006), pp. 740–755.

112 Zana Buçinca et al., "To Trust or To Think: Cognitive Forcing Functions can Reduce Overreliance on AI in AI-Assisted Decision-Making," in Proceedings of ACM Human–Computer Interaction, 5 (CSCW1) (2021), pp. 1–21.

3
Tactical generals and strategic corporals

This chapter argues that AI-enabled capabilities cannot effectively, reliably, or safely complement—let alone replace—humans in understanding and apprehending the strategic environment to make predictions and judgments to inform and shape command-and-control (C2) decision-making.[1] Moreover, the rapid diffusion of and growing dependency on AI technology (especially machine learning) to augment human decision-making at all levels of warfare harbinger strategic consequences that counterintuitively increase the importance of human involvement in these tasks across the entire chain of command. Because of the confluence of several cognitive, geopolitical, and organizational factors, the line between machines analyzing and synthesizing data (prediction) that informs humans who make decisions (judgment) will become an increasingly blurred human–machine decision-making continuum. When the handoff between machines and humans becomes incongruous, this slippery slope argument will make efforts to impose boundaries or contain the strategic effects of AI-supported tactical decisions inherently problematic and unintended strategic consequences more likely.

The chapter revisits John Boyd's observation-orientation-decision-action metaphorical decision-making cycle (or "OODA loop") to advance an objective epistemological critique of using AI-ML-enabled capabilities to augment C2 decision-making processes. Toward this end, the chapter draws insights from Boyd's emphasis on "Orientation" (or "The Big O") to elucidate the role of human cognition (perception, emotion, and heuristics) in defense planning, and the importance of understanding the broader strategic environment in a non-linear world characterized by complexity, novelty, and uncertainty. It also engages with the Clausewitzian notion of "military genius" (especially its role in "mission command"),[2] human cognition,[3] and systems and evolution theory,[4] to consider the strategic implications of automating the OODA loop. The chapter speaks to the growing body of recent literature that considers the strategic impact of adopting AI technology—and autonomous weapons, big data, cyberspace, and other emerging technologies associated with the "fourth industrial revolution"[5]—in military decision-making structures and processes.[6]

The AI Commander. James Johnson, Oxford University Press. © James Johnson (2024).
DOI: 10.1093/oso/9780198892182.003.0004

The chapter contributes to understanding the implications of AI's growing role in human decision-making in military C2. While the diffusion and adoption of "narrow" AI systems have had some success in non-military domains in making predictions and supporting—largely linear-based—decision-making (e.g., commercial sector, healthcare, and education), AI in a military context is much more problematic.[7] Specifically, military decision-making in non-linear, complex, and uncertain environments entails much more than copious, cheap datasets and inductive machine logic. In C2 decision-making, commanders' intentions, the rules of law and engagement, and ethical and moral leadership are critical to effective and safe decision-making in the application of military force. Because machines cannot perform these intrinsically human traits, the role of human agents will thus become even more critical in future AI-enabled warfare.[8] Moreover, as geostrategic and technological deterministic forces spur militaries to embrace AI systems in the quest for first-mover advantage, and reduce their perceived vulnerabilities in the digital age, commanders' intuition, latitude, and flexibility will be demanded to mitigate and manage the unintended consequences, organizational friction, strategic surprise, and dashed expectations associated with the implementation of military innovation.[9]

The chapter is organized into three sections. The first unpacks Boyd's OODA loop concept and its broader contribution to military theorizing, particularly the pivotal role of cognition in command decision-making for understanding and surviving in a priori strategic environments within the broader framework of complex adaptive organizational systems operating in dynamic non-linear environments.

The second section contextualizes Boyd's loop analogy with non-linearity, chaos, complexity, and system theories with the recent developments in AI-ML technology to consider the potential impact of integrating AI-enabled tools across the human–machine C2 decision-making continuum. This section also considers the potential strategic implications of deploying AI-ML systems in unpredictable and uncertain environments with imperfect information. Will AI alleviate or exacerbate war's "fog" and "friction"? The section explores human–machine teaming in high-intensity and dynamic environments. How will AIs cope with novel strategic situations compared to human commanders? It argues that using AI-ML systems to perform even routine operations during complex and fast-moving combat environments is problematic and that tactical leaders exhibiting initiative, flexibility, empathy, and creativity remain critical. This section also contextualizes the technical characteristics of AI technology within the broader external strategic environment. Will AI-enabled tools complement, supplant, or obviate the role of human "genius" in mission command?

The final section considers the implications of AI-ML systems for the relationship between tactical unit leaders and senior commanders. Specifically, it explores the potential impact of AI-enabled tools that improve situational awareness and intelligence, surveillance, and reconnaissance (ISR) on the notion of the twenty-first century "strategic corporals" and juxtaposes the specter of "tactical generals."

The "real" OODA loop: More than just speed

John Boyd's OODA loop has been firmly established in many strategic, business, and military tropes.[10] Several scholars have criticized the concept as overly simplistic, too abstract, and over-emphasizing speed and information dominance in warfare. Critics argue, for instance, that beyond pure granular tactical considerations (e.g., air-to-air combat), the OODA loop has minimal novelty or utility at a strategic level, for instance, managing nuclear brinkmanship, civil wars, or insurgencies.[11] Some have also lambasted the loop for lacking originality, as pseudoscience (informed by thermodynamics, quantum mechanics, and human evolution), and lacking scholarly rigor.[12] Moreover, the OODA concept struggles to meet the rigorous social science standards of epistemological validity, theoretical applicability, falsifiability, and robust empirical support.

Others argue that these criticisms misunderstand the nature, rationale, and richness of the OODA concept and thus understate Boyd's contribution to military theorizing, particularly the role of cognition in command decision-making.[13] In short, the OODA concept is much less a rigorously tested epistemological or ontological model for warfaring (which the author never intended), but instead a helpful analogy—akin to Herman Kahn's "escalation ladder" psychological metaphor[14]—for elucidating C2 decision-making cognitive processes and dynamics of commanders and their organizations as they "adjust or change in order to cope with new and unforeseen circumstances."[15] In other words, Boyd's concept is analogous to organizational and individual psychological experiences of the OODA loop in their respective temporal and spatial journeys across the strategic environment.[16]

The OODA concept was not designed as a comprehensive means to explain the theory of victory at the strategic level. Instead, the concept needs to be viewed as part of a broader canon on conceptualizations Boyd developed to elucidate the complex, unpredictable, and uncertain dynamics of warfare and

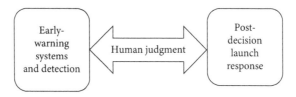

Figure 3.1 The "simple" OODA loop

Source: James Johnson, "Automating the OODA Loop in the Age of Intelligent Machines: Reaffirming the Role of Humans in Command-and-Control Decision-Making in the Digital Age," *Defence Studies* (2022), p. 4, doi: 10.1080/14,702,436.2022.2102486.

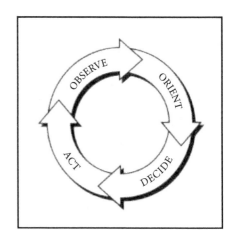

Figure 3.2 The "real" OODA loop

Source: James Johnson, "Automating the OODA Loop in the Age of Intelligent Machines: Reaffirming the Role of Humans in Command-and-Control Decision-Making in the Digital Age," *Defence Studies* (2022), p. 4, doi: 10.1080/14,702,436.2022.2102486.

strategic interactions.[17] Moreover, the popularized depictions of the simplified version of Boyd's concept (or the "simple OODA loop," see Figure 3.1) neglect Boyd's comprehensive rendering of the loop (or the "real OODA loop," see Figure 3.2)—with insights from cybernetics, systems theory, chaos and complexity theory, and cognitive science—that Boyd introduced in his final presentation, *The Essence of Winning and Losing*.[18] The influence of this science and scholarly Zeitgeist most clearly manifests in the OODA loop's vastly overlooked "orientation" element.[19]

The "Big O": The center of gravity in warfare

Insights from the cognitive revolution,[20] coupled with Neo-Darwinist research on the environment,[21] the Popperian process of adaptation and hypothesis testing,[22] and complexity and chaos theory,[23] heavily influenced the genesis of Boyd's "orientation" schemata comprising: political and strategic cultural traditions, organizational friction, experience and learning, new and novel information, and the analysis and synthesis of this information.[24] Viewed this way, "observation" is a function of inputs of external information and understanding the interaction of these inputs within the strategic environment. Boyd wrote, "orientation, seen as a result, represents images, views, or impressions of the world shaped by genetic heritage, cultural traditions, previous experiences, and unfolding circumstances."[25] Without these attributes, humans lack the psychological skills and experience to comprehend and survive in a priori strategic environments. The OODA loop concept is a shorthand for these complex dynamics.

Elaborating on this idea, Boyd asserted that orientation "shapes the way we interact with the environment—hence orientation shapes *the way we observe, the way we decide, the way we act*. Orientation shapes the character of present observation-orientation-decision-action loops—while these present loops shape the character of future orientation" (emphasis added).[26] In other words, without the contextual understanding provided by "orientation" in analyzing and synthesizing information, "observations" of the world have limited meaning. These assertions attest to the pivotal role of "orientation" in Boyd's OODA decision-making analogy, the critical connecting thread enabling commanders to survive, adapt, and effectively make decisions when faced with uncertainty, ambiguity, complexity, and chaos.[27] Boyd's OODA analogy and notions of uncertainty and ambiguous information and knowledge are equally relevant (if not more so) for strategy in the digital information age—combining asymmetric information, mis-disinformation, mutual vulnerabilities, destructive potential, and decentralized, dual-use, and widely diffused AI technology.[28]

According to Boyd, how "orientation shapes observation, shapes decision, shapes action, and in turn is *shaped by the feedback and other phenomena* coming into our sensing or observing window" (emphasis added).[29] Thus, the loop metaphor depicts an ongoing, self-correcting, and non-static process of prediction, filtering, correlation, judgment, and action. Scientists including Ian Stewart and James Maxwell have similarly cautioned against assuming that the world is stable, static, and thus predictable.[30] These processes, moreover, contain complex feedforward and feedback loops (or "double-loop learning") that implicitly influence "decision" and "action" and, in turn, inform hypothesis testing of future decisions.[31] For instance, while military theorists often categorize politics as extrinsic to war (i.e., a linear model), the feedback loops which operate from the use of force to politics and from politics to the use of force are intrinsic to war.[32] As a corollary, Boyd argues that

C2 systems must embrace (and not diminish) the role of implicit orientation and their attendant feedback loops.[33]

Similarly, Clausewitz argued that the interactive nature of war generates system-driven dynamics comprising human psychological forces and characterized by positive and negative feedback loops, thus leading to potentially limitless versions of ways to seek one-upmanship in competition "to compel our enemy to do our will."[34] War, Clausewitz argues, is a "true chameleon," exhibiting randomness, chance, and different characteristics in every instance.[35] Therefore, it is impossible, as many military theorists tend to try and do, to force war into compartmentalized sequential models of action and counter-reaction for theoretical simplicity.[36] Instead, effective commanders will explore ways to exploit war's unpredictability and non-linear nature to gain the strategic upper hand.[37] At an organizational level, systems are driven by the behavior of individuals who act based upon their intentions, goals, perceptions, and calculations, an interaction that generates a high degree of complexity and unpredictability.[38]

Therefore, a broader interpretation of the OODA loop analogy is best viewed less as a general theory of war than an attempt to depict the strategic behavior of decision-makers within the broader framework of complex adaptive organizational systems in a dynamic non-linear environment.[39] According to Clausewitz, general (linearized) theoretical laws used to explain the non-linear dynamics of war are heuristic; each war is a "series of actions obeying its own peculiar law."[40] Colin Gray opined that Boyd's OODA loop is a grand theory because the concept has an elegant simplicity, a vast application domain, and valuable insights about strategic essentials.[41]

Intelligent machines in non-linear chaotic warfare

Non-linearity, chaos theory, complexity theory, and systems theory have been broadly applied to understand organizational behavior and the intra-organizational and inter-organizational dynamics associated with competition and war.[42] Charles Perrow introduced the notion that organizations can be categorized as either simple/linear (stable, regular, and consistent) or complex/non-linear (unstable, irregular, and inconsistent) systems with tight or loose couplings.[43] Non-linear systems do not obey proportionality or additivity; they can behave erratically through disproportionally large or small outputs, exhibiting interactions in which the whole is not necessarily equal to the sum of the parts.[44] The real world has always contained an abundance of non-linear phenomena, for example, fluid turbulence, combustion, breaking or cracking, biological evolution, and biochemical reactions in living organisms.[45] Perrow's idea of coupling and complexity is critical in a system's susceptibility to accidents and failure's speed, severity, and probability. All things being equal, tightly coupled systems such as AI-ML algorithms react faster, unpredictably, with extensive multilayered interconnections, compared to loosely coupled systems such as universities—which, when everything runs smoothly, afford more time for response and recovery.[46]

According to Perrow, the problem arises in cases where a system is both complex and tightly coupled. Whereas complexity generally optimally requires a decentralized response, tight coupling suggests a centralized approach—to ensure a swift response and recovery from accidents *before* tightly coupled processes cause failure. In response to complex and tightly coupled systems, Perrow dismisses the efficacy of decentralizing decision-making at lower levels in an organization (e.g., commanders on the battlefield) because, in complex/tightly coupled systems, potential failures throughout the system are unforeseeable and highly contingent.[47] Perrow writes that alterations to any one component in a complex system "will either be impossible because some others will not cooperate, or inconsequential because some others will be allowed more vigorous expression."[48]

Similar dynamics (randomness, complex interactions, and long and intricate chains) can also be found in ecological systems.[49] Because of the intrinsic unpredictability of complex systems, evolutionary biology is—compared to conventional international relations theories—particularly amenable for understanding alliance alignments, the balance of power, signaling deterrence and resolve, assessments of actors' intentions, and diplomatic and foreign policy mechanisms and processes.[50] In complex systems, Robert Jervis notes, "problems are almost never solved once and for all," and no matter how well designed policies are, "definitive [machine generated] solutions will generate unexpected difficulties."[51] Because of the interconnectedness of world politics—imposed on states by the structures of international relations and actors' perceptions of others' intentions and policy preferences—low-intensity disputes can be strategically consequential.[52]

During conflict and crisis (see Chapter 4), where the information quality is poor (i.e., information asymmetry) and judgment and prediction are challenging, decision-makers must balance these competing requirements. Automation is generally an asset when high information quality can be combined with precise and relatively predictable judgments. Clausewitz highlights the unpredictability of war—caused by interaction, friction, and chance—as a manifestation and contributor of the role of non-linearity. He wrote, for instance, "war is not an exercise of the will directed at inanimate matter . . . or at matter which is animate but passive and yielding . . . *In war, the will is directed at an animate object that reacts*" (emphasis added)—and thus, the outcome of the action cannot be predicted from its causes.[53] Inanimate intelligent machines (e.g., digital assistants, loitering munitions, unmanned tanks, weaponized quadruped robots, and various types of autonomous drones) operating and reacting in human-centric ("animate") environments exhibiting interaction, friction, and chance cannot predict outcomes and thus control (see Appendix 2). While human decision-making under these circumstances is far from perfect, the unique interaction of factors including, inter alia, psychological, social, cultural (individual and organizational), ideology, emotion, experience (i.e., Boyd's "orientation" concept), and luck give humans a sporting chance to make clear-eyed political, legal, and ethical judgments in the chaos ("fog") and non-linearity ("friction") of warfare.[54]

The computer revolution and recent AI-ML approaches have made militaries increasingly reliant on statistical probabilities and self-organizing algorithmic rules to solve complex problems in the non-linear world. According to Maxwell, analytical mathematical rules are not always reliable guides to the real world "where things never happen twice."[55] AI-ML techniques (e.g., image recognition, pattern recognition, and natural language processing) inductively (inferring from general rules) fill the gaps in missing information to identify patterns and trends (see Introduction), thereby increasing the speed and accuracy of certain standardized military operations, including open-source intelligence collation, satellite navigation, and logistics. However, because these quantitative models are isolated from the broader external strategic environment of probabilities rather than axiomatic certainties characterized by Boyd's "orientation," human intervention remains critical to avoid distant analytical abstraction and causal deterministic predictions during the non-linear chaotic war. As mentioned, researchers at Meta AI (formally Facebook) have made some notable progress in developing a gaming algorithm, CICERO which combines techniques from game theory with probabilistic analysis to play Diplomacy—a strategic game involving the formation of alliances, negotiation, persuasion, and deception—at a human-level of performance. *Cicero* is, however, heavily pre-structured, relies on human hand-constructed data, and lacks humans' ability to think laterally and adapt and innovate in a priori situations.[56] Several scholars assume that the perceived first-mover benefits of AI-augmented war machines will create self-fulfilling spirals of security dilemma dynamics that will upend deterrence.[57]

AI exacerbating the "noise" and "friction" of war

Because AI-ML predictions and judgments tend to deteriorate where data is sparse (e.g., nuclear war) and/or low quality (i.e., biased, politicized intelligence, and where data is poisoned or manipulated by mis-disinformation),[58] military strategy requires Clausewitzian human "genius" to navigate the battlefield "fog" and the political, organizational, and information (or "noise" in the system) "friction" of war.[59] For example, the lack of training data in the nuclear domain means that AIs would depend on synthetic simulations to predict how adversaries might react during brinkmanship between two or more nuclear-armed states.[60] Nuclear deterrence is a nuanced perceptual dance in competition and manipulation between adversaries, "keeping the enemy guessing" by leaving something to chance.[61]

Therefore, datasets will need to reflect the broader strategic environment military decision-makers face in a military context, including the distinct doctrinal, organizational, and strategic cultural approaches of allies and adversaries. Even where situations closely mirror previous events, a dearth of empirical data to account for war's contingent, chaotic, and random nature makes statistical probabilistic AI-ML reasoning a very blunt instrument. AI's predicting and reacting to a priori novel situations will increase the risk of mismatch—between algorithmically optimized goals and the evolving strategic environment—and misperception will heighten the risk of accidents (e.g., targeting errors or false alerts) and inadvertent catastrophe.[62] In unpredictable and uncertain environments with imperfect information that requires near-perfect confidence levels, simulations, gaming (Go, chess, Texas hold'em, and Diplomacy etc.), and synthetic datasets—while helpful to understand how humans and machines develop and execute strategies in a controlled environment—are technically constrained by the availability of training data which makes scalability problematic.[63] Whether, to what degree, and when simulation models can be generalized to address multiagent real-world problems characterized by imperfect information, non-linearity, and astronomical state spaces is an open empirical question.[64]

To cope with novel strategic situations and mitigate unintended consequences, human "genius"—the contextual understanding afforded by Boyd's "orientation"—is needed to finesse multiple flexible, sequential, and resilient policy responses. Jervis writes that "good generals not only construct fine war plans but also understand that events will not conform to them."[65] Unlike machines, humans use abductive reasoning (or inference to the best explanation) and introspection (or "metacognition"[66]) to think laterally and adapt and innovate in novel situations.[67] As shown in Chapter 1, faced with uncertainty or lack of knowledge and information, people adopt a heuristic approach—cognitive short-cuts or rules of thumb derived from experience, learning, and experimentation—promoting intuition and reasoning to solve complex problems.[68] While human intuitive thinking often produces biases and cognitive blind spots, it also offers a very effective means to make quick judgments and decisions under stress in a priori situations.[69] AI systems use heuristics—and other neurocognitive tricks—derived from vast training datasets to make inferences that inform predictions and are required to navigate the world. They lack human intuition, which depends on experience and memory, however. Building those blind spots into AI systems—inspired, for example, by human neuroscience—is something designers need to be wary of.

Recent empirical studies indicate that the ubiquity of "friction" in AI-ML systems, designed to reduce the "fog" of war and thus improve certainty, can create new or exacerbate legacy, accountability, security, and interoperability issues, thereby generating more "friction" and uncertainty.[70] In theory, there is ample potential for AI-ML tools (e.g., facial and speech recognition, AI-enhanced space satellite navigation, emotion prediction, and translation algorithms) to benefit military operations where vast amounts of disparate information (i.e., "noise"), data, and metadata (that labels and describes data) are often incomplete, overlooked, or misdiagnosed.[71] For example, reducing the data-processing burden, monitoring multiple data feeds, and highlighting unexpected patterns for ISR operations that are integral to improving tactical and strategic command decision-making.[72]

In practice, intelligence tasks involve ambiguity, deception, manipulation, and mis-disinformation, which require nuanced interpretation, creativity, and tactical flexibility. Like C2 reporting systems, intelligence operations are more of an art than a science, where human understanding of the shifting strategic landscape is critical in enabling commanders to predict and respond to unexpected events, changes in strategic objectives, or intelligence politicization—which will require updated data, thus rendering existing data redundant or misleading.[73] Operational and planning tasks—that inform decision-making—cannot be delegated to AI-ML systems or used in human–machine teaming without commanders being fully mindful of the division of labor and the boundaries between human and machine control—that is, the humans in versus out of the loop distinction discussed in Chapters 1 and 2.

The International Committee for Robot Arms Control in its statement at the 2014 Convention on Certain Conventional Weapons meeting stated that: "A human commander (or operator) must have *full contextual and situational awareness* of the target area and be *able to perceive and react to any change or unanticipated situations* that may have arisen since planning the attack" (emphasis added).[74] Thus, the degree of autonomy delegated to machines should be limited such that commanders are confident of having sufficient information about how a weapon system will behave once activated—to anticipate the consequences and make the necessary legal and ethical deliberations about the use of force. Cognizant of these limitations, and particularly concerned about this risk of inadvertent escalation, the US Defense Department recently stated that: "In all cases the US will maintain a human 'in the loop' for all actions critical to *informing and executing* decisions by the President to initiate and terminate nuclear weapon employment" (emphasis added).[75] Whether this commitment extends to non-nuclear (especially non-nuclear strategic) capabilities is an open question.

Furthermore, human intervention is critical in deciding when and how changes to the algorithm's configuration (e.g., the tasks it is charged with, the division of labor, and the data it is trained on) are needed, which changes in the strategic environment demand. In other words, rather than complementing human operators, linear algorithms trained on static datasets will exacerbate the "noise" in non-linear, contingent, and dynamic scenarios such as tracking insurgents and terrorists or providing targeting information for armed drones and missile guidance systems. Moreover, some argue that AI systems designed to "lift the fog of war" might instead compound the friction within organizations with unintended consequences, particularly when disagreements, bureaucratic inertia, or controversy exists about war aims, procurement, civil-military relations, and the chain of command amongst allies.[76]

"Rapid looping" and the dehumanization of warfare

AI-ML systems that excel at routine and narrow tasks and games (e.g., DeepMind's StarCraft II and DARPA's Alpha Dogfight[77]) with clearly defined predetermined parameters in relatively controlled, static, and isolated (i.e., there is no feedback) linear environments—such as logistics, finance and economics, and data collation—are found wanting when it comes to addressing politically and morally strategic questions in the non-linear world of C2 decision-making.[78] For what national security interests are we prepared to sacrifice soldiers' lives? What stage on the escalation ladder should a state sue for peace over escalation? When do the advantages of empathy and restraint trump coercion and the pursuit of power? At what point should actors step back from the brink in crisis bargaining (see Chapter 4)? How should states respond to deterrence failure, and what if allies view things differently?

In high-intensity and dynamic combat environments such as densely populated urban warfare—even where well-specified goals and standard operating procedures exist—the latitude and adaptability of "mission command" remains critical, and the functional utility of ML-AI tools for even routine "task orders" (i.e., the opposite of "mission command") problematic.[79] Routine task orders such as standard operating procedures, doctrinal templates, explicit protocols, and logistics performed in dynamic combat settings still have the potential for accidents and risk of life; commanders exhibiting initiative, flexibility, empathy, and creativity are needed.[80] Besides, the implicit communication, trust, and a shared outlook that "mission command" imbibes across all levels make micro-management by senior commanders less necessary—that is, it permits tactical units to read their environment and respond within the overall framework of strategic goals defined by senior commanders—thus potentially speeding up the OODA decision cycle. Boyd writes, "the *cycle time increases commensurate with an increase in the level of organization, as one tries to control more levels and issues . . .* the faster rhythm of the lower levels must work within the larger and slower rhythm of the higher levels so that the overall system does not lose its cohesion or coherency" (emphasis added).[81]

War is not a game. Instead, it is intrinsically structurally unstable; an adversary rarely plays by the same rules and, to achieve victory, often attempts to change the rules that do exist or invent new ones.[82] The diffusion of AI-ML is unlikely to assuage this ambiguity in the ephemeral quest to speed up and compress the C2 OODA decision cycle—or Boyd's "rapid looping."[83] Instead, policymakers risk being blind-sided by the potential tactical utility—where speed, scale, precision, and lethality coalesce to improve situational awareness—offered by AI-augmented capabilities, without sufficient regard for the potential strategic implications of artificially imposing non-human agents on the fundamentally human endeavor of warfare. Moreover, the appeal of "rapid looping" may persuade soldiers operating in a high-stress environment with large amounts of data ("data tsunami") to use AI tools as a means to offload cognitively, thus placing undue confidence and trust in machines—known as "automation bias," as explored in Chapter 1.[84] Recent studies demonstrate that the more cognitively demanding, time-pressured, and stressful a situation is, the more likely humans are to defer to machine judgments.[85]

NATO's Supreme Allied Command Transformation is working with a team at Johns Hopkins University to develop an AI-enabled "digital triage assistant" to attend to injured combatants—trained on injury datasets, casualty scoring systems, predictive modeling, and inputs of a patient's condition—to decide who should receive prioritized care during conflict and mass casualty events (e.g., the Russian-Ukrainian conflict) where resources are limited.[86] On the one hand, AI-enabled digital assistants can make quick decisions in intense, complex, and fast-moving situations using algorithms and data (especially much-vaunted "big-data" sources), and arguably remove human biases to reduce human error—caused by cognitive bias, fatigue, and stress, for example—and potentially save lives.[87]

On the other hand, critics are concerned about how these algorithms will cause some combatants (allies, adversaries, civilian conscripts, volunteers, etc.) to be prioritized for care over others.[88] If, for example, there was a large explosion and civilians were among the people harmed (e.g., the Kabul Airport bombing in 2021), would they get less priority, even if they were severely injured? Would soldiers defer to an algorithm's judgment regardless of whether facts on the ground suggested otherwise during an intense situation? Further, if the algorithm plays a part in someone dying, who would be held responsible?

These ethical conundrums are compounded by mounting evidence of bias—such as when algorithms in health care prioritize white patients over black ones for getting care—in AI datasets that can perpetuate biased decision-making.[89] In contexts where judgment and decisions can directly (or indirectly) affect human safety, algorithmic designers cannot remove entirely unforeseen biases or prepare AIs to cope with a priori situations. Besides, an optimized algorithm (even if human engineers determine these goals[90]) is unable to encode the broad range of values and issues humans care about, such as empathy, ethics, compassion, and mercy—not to mention Clausewitzian courage, *coup d'oeil*, primordial emotion, violence, hatred, and enmity—which are critical for strategic thinking.[91] In short, when human life is at stake, the ethical, trust, and moral bar for technology will always be higher than those we set for accident-prone humans.

Notwithstanding the many vexing ethical and morals about the intersection between people, algorithms, and ethics,[92] introducing non-human agents onto the modern battlefield *in extremis* risks atrophying the vital feedback—or Boyd's "double-looping learning" of empathy, correlation, and rejection—in "mission command" between tactical unit leaders who interpret and execute war plans crafted by generals, or in the "strategic corporals" versus "tactical generals" problem discussed below.[93] In this symbiotic relationship, mismatches, miscommunication, or accidents would critically undermine the role of "genius" in mission command on the

modern battlefield—combining AI-ML technology, asymmetrical information and capabilities, and multidomain operations where it is in highest
demand.[94]

Butterfly effects, unintended consequences, and accidents

Even a well-running optimized algorithm is vulnerable to adversarial attacks
which may corrupt its data, embed biases, or become a target of novel tactics that seek to exploit blind spots in a system's architecture (or "going
beyond the training set"), which the AI cannot predict and thus effectively counter.[95] Moreover, in algorithms optimized to fulfill a specific goal
in unfamiliar domains (e.g., nuclear war) and contexts—or if deployed
inappropriately—false positives are possible, which inadvertently spark escalatory spirals.[96] Other technical shortcomings of AI-ML systems (especially
newer, unsupervised models) tested in dynamic non-linear contexts such as
autonomous vehicles include: (1) algorithmic inaccuracies; (2) misclassifi-
cation of data and anomalies in data inputs and behavior; (3) vulnerability
to adversarial manipulation (e.g., data-poisoning, false-flags, or spoofing);
and (4) erratic behavior and ambiguous decision-making in new and novel
interactions.[97] These problems are structural, not bugs that can be patched or
easily circumvented.

In war, much like other domains such as economics and politics, there
is a new problem for every solution that AIs (or social scientists) can
conceive. Thus, algorithmic recommendations which may look technically
correct and inductively sound may have unintended consequences unless
they are accompanied by novel strategies authored by policymakers who
are (in theory) psychologically and politically prepared to cope with these
consequences using flexibility, resilience, and creativity—or the notion of
"genius" in mission command discussed below. Chaos and complexity theories can help to elucidate the potential impact of the interaction of algorithms
with the real world. Specific interactions in physics, biology, and chemistry,
for instance, do not produce more properties as a summing between them.
Instead, the opposite occurs; that is, a non-additive chemical phenomenon
that does not have a numerical value equal to the sum of values for the component parts.[98] Combining two medical treatments, for example, can produce
considerably more than a double dose effect in the patient or even a single but
unexpected outcome. Moreover, recent research has found that computers
cannot capture the behavior of the complexity of real-world chaotic dynamical events such as climate change.[99] In sum, the coalescence of multiple

(supervised, unsupervised, reinforcement and deep-learning, etc.), complex (military and civilian datasets), and tightly coupled and compressed (convolution neural networks, artificial neural networks, Bayesian networks, etc.) ML algorithms, sensitive to small changes in the non-linear real world's initial conditions, could generate a vast amount of stochastic behavior (or "butterfly" effects), thus increasing the risk of unintended consequences and accidents.

Conceptually speaking, boundaries might be placed between AI's analyzing and synthesizing data (prediction) that inform humans who make decisions (judgment); for example, through recruitment, the use of simulations and wargaming exercises, and training combatants, contractors, algorithm engineers, and policymakers in human–machine teaming. However, the confluence of several factors will likely blur these boundaries along the human–machine decision-making continuum between decision support systems and decision-making ones (see Figure 3.3): cognitive (automation bias, cognitive offloading, and anthropomorphizing)[100]; organizational (intelligence politicization, bureaucratic inertia, unstable civil-military relations)[101]; geopolitical (first-mover pressures, security dilemma dynamics)[102]; and divergent attitudes (of both allies and adversaries) to risk, deterrence, escalation, and misaligned algorithms.[103]

AIs isolated from the broader external strategic environment (i.e., the political, ethical, cultural, and organizational contexts depicted in Boyd's "real OODA loop") are no substitute for human judgment and decisions in chaotic and non-linear situations. According to the US delegation to the Convention on Certain Conventional Weapons (CCW) in 2014, there is no "one-size-fits-all" standard for the appropriate level of human judgement to be used in the use of force with autonomous weapons systems.[104] Instead, this choice will vary considerably depending on factors, including, inter alia: the type of functions performed by machines; the nature of human–machine interaction (control measures, redundancies, and handoffs, etc.); the weapon system's operating environment (proximity of civilians, terrain, weather conditions, etc.); and the anticipated fluidity of or changes to the system's operational parameters (risk profiles and mission objectives, etc.).[105]

Even in situations where algorithms are functionally aligned with human decision-makers—that is, with knowledge of crucial human decision-making attributes—human–machine teaming risks diminishing the role of human "genius" where it is in high demand. Consequently, commanders are less psychologically, ethically, and politically prepared to respond to non-linearity, uncertainty, and chaos with flexibility, creativity, and adaptivity. Because of the non-binary nature of tactical and strategic decision-making—tactical

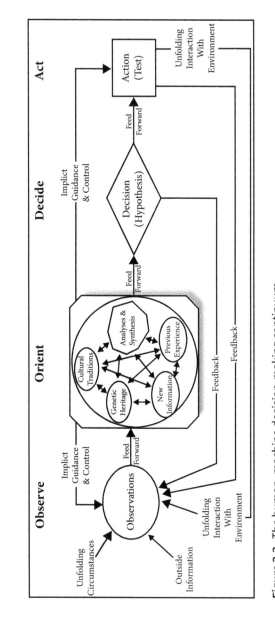

Figure 3.3 The human–machine decision-making continuum

Source: James Johnson, "Automating the OODA Loop in the Age of Intelligent Machines: Reaffirming the Role of Humans in Command-and-Control Decision-Making in the Digital Age," *Defence Studies* (2022), p. 13, doi: 10.1080/14,702,436.2022.2102486.

decisions are not made in a vacuum and invariably have strategic effects—using AI-enabled digital devices to complement human decisions will have strategic consequences that increase the importance of human involvement in these tasks. How much does a human decision to use military force derived from data mined, synthesized, and interpreted by AI-ML algorithms possess more human agency than a decision executed fully autonomously by a machine? AI researcher Stuart Russell argues that through conditioning what and how data is presented to human decision-makers—without disclosing what has been omitted or rejected—AIs possesses "power" over human's "cognitive intake."[106] This "power" runs in opposition to one of AI-ML's most touted benefits: reducing the cognitive load on humans in high-stress environments.[107]

In a recent Joint All-Domain Command and Control (JADC2) report, the US Department of Defense (DoD) proposed integrating AI-ML technology into C2 capabilities across all domains to exploit AI-enhanced remote sensors, intelligence assets, and open sources to "sense and integrate" (i.e., Boyd's "observe" and "orientate") information to "make sense" of (i.e., analyze, synthesize, and predict) the strategic environment, so the "decision cycle" operates "faster relative to adversary abilities."[108] The JADC2 report obfuscates the possible strategic implications of automating the OODA loop for tactical gains and the illusionary clarity of certainty. In a similar vein, researchers at China's *PLA Daily* (the official newspaper of China's People's Liberation Army) argue that advances in AI technology will automate the OODA loop for command decision-making of autonomous weapons and drive the broader trend toward machines replacing human observation, judgment, prediction, and action.[109] While the *PLA Daily* authors stress the importance of training and human–machine "interfacing," like the DoD's JADC2 they also omit consideration of the strategic implications of this technologically determined "profound change."[110]

Static, predefined, and isolated algorithms are not the answer to the quintessentially non-linear, chaotic, and analytically unpredictable nature of war. Therefore, an undue focus on speed and decisive tactical outcomes (or completing the "kill-chain") in the decision-making loop underplays AI's influence in C2 decision-making activities across the full spectrum of operations and domains.[111] As the US-led Multinational Capability Development Campaign notes: "Whatever our C2 models, systems and behaviours of the future will look like, *they must not be linear, deterministic, and static*. They must be agile, autonomously self-adaptive and self-regulating" (emphasis added).[112]

AI-empowered "strategic corporals" vs. "tactical generals"

US Amy General Charles Krulak coined the term "strategic corporal" to describe the strategic implications which flow from the increasing responsibilities and pressures placed on small-unit tactical leaders due to rapid technological diffusion and the resulting operational complexity in modern warfare that followed the information revolution based in military affairs in the late 1990s.[113] Krulak argues that recruitment, training, and mentorship will empower junior officers to exercise judgment, leadership, and restraint to become effective "strategic corporals."

On the digitized battlefield, tactical leaders will need to judge the reliability of AI-ML predictions, determine algorithmic outputs' ethical and moral veracity (see Chapter 1), and judge in real-time whether, why, and (as discussed in Chapter 2) to what degree AI systems should be recalibrated to reflect changes to human–machine teaming and the broader strategic environment. In other words, "strategic corporals" will need to become military, political, and technological "geniuses." While junior officers have displayed practical bottom-up creativity and innovation in using technology in the past, the new multidirectional pressures from AI systems will unlikely be resolved by training and recruiting practices.[114] Instead, pressures to make decisions in high-intensity, fast-moving, data-centric, multidomain human-teaming environments might undermine the critical role of "mission command," which connects tactical leaders with the political-strategic leadership—namely, the decentralized, lateral, and two-way (explicit and implicit) communication between senior command and tactical units. Despite the laudable efforts of the DoD to instill tactical leaders with the "tenants of mission command" to leverage AI-ML in joint force multidomain environments, the technical and cognitive burden on subordinate commanders—singularly tasked with completing the entire OODA loop—will likely be too great.[115]

Under tactical pressures to compress the decision-making, reduce "friction," and speed up the OODA loop, tactical leaders may make unauthorized modifications to algorithms (e.g., reconfigure human–machine teaming, ignore AI-ML recommendations,[116] or launch cross-domain countermeasures in response to adversarial attacks), which puts them in direct conflict with other parts of the organization or contradicts the strategic objectives of political leaders.[117] According to Boyd, the breakdown of the implicit communication and bonds of trust that define "mission command" will produce "confusion and disorder, which impedes vigorous or directed activity, hence, magnifies friction or entropy"—precisely the outcome that the empowerment of small-group tactical leaders on the twenty-first-century battlefield was intended to prevent.[118] This breakdown may also be precipitated by adversarial attacks on the electronic communications (e.g., electronic warfare jammers and cyber-attacks) that advanced militaries rely on, thus forcing tactical leaders to fend for themselves. In 2009, for example, the Shiite militia fighters used off-the-shelf software to hack into unsecured video-feed from US Predator drones. Militarily advanced near-peer adversaries such as China and Russia have well-equipped electronic warfare for offensive jamming (or triangulating their sources for bombardment), sophisticated hackers, and drones to target precision weapons.[119] To avoid this outcome, Boyd advocates a highly decentralized hierarchical structure that allows tactical commanders initiative while insisting that senior command resist the temptation to overly cognitively invest in and interfere with tactical decisions.[120]

On the other side of the command spectrum, AI-ML augmented ISR, autonomous weapons, and real-time situational awareness might produce a juxtaposed yet contingent phenomenon, the rise of "tactical generals."[121] As senior commanders gain unprecedented access to tactical information, the temptation to micro-manage and directly intervene in tactical decisions from afar will rise. Who understands the commander's intent better than the generals themselves? While AI-ML enhancements can certainly help senior commanders become better informed and take personal responsibility for high-intensity situations as they unfold, the thin line between timely intervention and obsessive micro-management is a fine one. Centralizing the decision-making process—contrary to both Boyd's guidance and the notion of "strategic corporals"—and creating a new breed of "tactical generals" micro-managing theater commanders from afar, AI-ML enhancements might compound the additional pressures placed on tactical unit leaders to speed up the OODA loop and become political and technological "geniuses." This dynamic may increase uncertainty and confusion and amplify friction and entropy.

Micro-managing or taking control of tactical decision-making could also mean that young officers lack the experience in making complex tactical solutions in the field, which might cause confusion or misperceptions in the event communications are compromised and the "genius" of "strategic corporals" is demanded. For example, interpreting sensor data (e.g., from warning systems, electronic support measures, and optronic sensors) from different platforms, monitoring intelligence (e.g., open-source data from geospatial and social media), and using historical data (e.g., data on the thematic bases for producing temporal geo-spatialization of an activity) relating to the strategic environment of previous operations.[122]

Then-US Army Chief of Staff General Mark Milley recently stated that the Army is "overly centralized, overly bureaucratic, and overly risk averse, which is the opposite of what we're going to need in any type of warfare."[123] Milley stressed the need to decentralize leadership, upend the Army's deep culture of micro-management, empower junior officers, and thus strengthen mission command. Furthermore, the breakdown in lateral relations and communication across the command chain would also risk diminishing the crucial tactical insights that inform and shape strategizing, potentially impairing political and military leadership, undermining civil-military relations, and causing strategic-tactical mismatches, which during a crisis may spark an inadvertent escalation.

Tactical units operating in the field using cloud computing technology (or "tactical cloud") coupled with other AI-enabling sensors and effectors to ensure interoperability, resilience, digital security, and close to combat situations—such as rugged, urban, complex terrains where logistics and communications lines are put under intense stress—would be well placed to guide and inform strategic decision-making. Thus, senior commanders would indubitably benefit from the speed and richness of two-way information flows as the "tactical cloud" matures; for example, information on topography and the civilian environment, and 3D images of the combat distribution of airspace volumes, complement C2 strike and reconnaissance tracking and targeting for drone swarming and missile strike systems, and for verifying open-source intelligence and debunking of mis-disinformation.[124]

Absent the verification and supervision of machine decisions by tactical units (e.g., the troop movement of friendly and enemy forces), if an AI system gave the green light to an operation in a fast-moving combat scenario—when closer examination of algorithmic inputs and outputs are tactically costly—false positives from automated warning systems, mis-disinformation, or an adversarial attack would have dire consequences.[125] Moreover, tactical units executing orders received from brigade headquarters—and assuming a concomitant erosion of two-way communication flows—may not only diminish the providence and fidelity of information received by senior commanders deliberately from their ivory towers, but also result in unit leaders following orders blindly and eschewing moral, ethical, or even legal concerns.[126] Psychology research has found that humans tend to perform poorly at setting the appropriate objectives and are predisposed to harm others if ordered by an "expert" —known as "trust and forget."[127] As a corollary, human operators may begin to view AI systems as agents of authority (more intelligent and more authoritative than humans) and thus be more inclined to follow their recommendations blindly, even in the face of information (e.g., that debunks mis-disinformation) that indicates they would be wiser not to.

Whether the rise of "tactical generals" complements, subsumes, or conflicts with Krulak's vision of the twenty-first-century "strategic corporals," and the impact of this interaction on battlefield decision-making, are open questions. The literature on systems, complexity, and non-linearity suggests that the coalescence of centralized, hierarchical structures, tight-coupled systems, and complexity generated by this paradigm would make accidents more likely to occur and much less easy to anticipate.[128] The erosion of "mission command," this phenomenon augurs, would dramatically reduce the prospects of officers down the chain of command overriding or pushing back against top-down tactical decisions; for example, in 1983, when Soviet air force lieutenant Stanislav Petrov overrode a nuclear launch directive from an automated warning system that mistook light reflecting off clouds for an inbound ballistic missile.[129] AI-ML data synthesis and analysis capacity can enhance the decision-making process' prediction (or "observation") element. However, it still needs commanders at all levels to recognize the strengths and limitations of AI intuition, reasoning, and foresight.[130] Professional military training and education of military professionals will be critical in tightly integrated, non-linear, and interdependent tasks where the notion of handoffs between machines and humans becomes incongruous.[131]

Conclusion

Whether AI will continue to trail, or to match or surpass human intelligence and, in turn, complement or replace humans in decision-making is a necessary speculative endeavor but a vital issue to deductively analyze, nonetheless. That is, developing a robust theory-driven hypothesis is needed to guide analysis of the empirical data about the impact of the diffusion and synthesis of "narrow" AI technology in C2 decision-making processes and structures. This endeavor has a clear pedagogical utility, guiding future military professional education and training in the need to balance data and intuition as human–machine teaming matures. A policy-centric utility includes adapting militaries (doctrine, civil-military relations, and innovation) to the changing character of war and the likely effects of AI-enabled capabilities—which already exist or are being developed—on war's enduring chaotic, non-linear, and uncertain nature. Absent fundamental changes to our understanding of the impact (cognitive effects, organizational, and technical) of AI on the human–machine relationship, and we risk not only failing to harness AI's transformative potential but, more dangerously, misaligning AI capabilities with human values, ethics, and norms of warfare that spark unintended strategic consequences. Future empirical research would be welcome on how to optimize C2 processes and structures to cope with evolving human–machine relations and to adapt military education to prepare commanders (at all levels) for this paradigm shift.

The chapter argued that static, predefined, and isolated AI-ML algorithms do not answer war's non-linear, chaotic, and analytically unpredictable nature. Therefore, an undue focus on speed and tactical outcomes to complete the decision-making loop (or Boyd's "rapid OODA looping") understates the permeation of AI in C2 decision-making across the full spectrum of operations and domains. Insights from Boyd's "orientation" schemata—particularly as they relate to human cognition in command decisions and the broader strategic environment—coupled with systems, chaos, and complexity theories still have a pedagogical utility in understanding these dynamics. The chapter found that (a) speeding up warfare and compressing decision-making (or automating the OODA loop) will have strategic implications that cannot be easily anticipated (by humans or AIs); (b) the line between the handoff from humans to machines will become increasingly blurred; and thus, (c) the synthesis and diffusion of AI into the military decision-making process increases the importance of human agency across the entire chain of command.

While this research agrees with the conventional wisdom that AI is already having and will continue to have a transformative impact on warfare, it finds fault with the prevailing focus of militaries on harnessing the tactical potential of AI-enabled capabilities in the pursuit of speed and rapid decision-making. This undue focus risks blind-siding policymakers without sufficient regard for the potential strategic implications of artificially and inappropriately imposing non-human agents on the fundamentally human nature of warfare. Misunderstanding the human–machine relationship during fast-moving, dynamic, and complex battlefield scenarios will likely undermine the critical symbiosis between senior commanders and tactical units (or "mission command"), which increase the risk of mismatches, accidents, and inadvertent escalation.

In extremis, the rise of "tactical generals" (empowered with AI tools making tactical decisions from afar) and the concomitant atrophy of "strategic corporals" (junior officers exercising judgment, leadership, and restraint) will create highly centralized and tight-coupled systems that make accidents more probable and less predictable. Paradoxically, therefore, AI used to complement and support humans in decision-making might obviate the role of human "genius" in mission command when it is most demanded. We now turn to implications of AI-enabled warfare on crisis stability.

Notes

1 Sections of this chapter are derived in part from James Johnson, "Automating the OODA Loop in the Age of Intelligent Machines: Reaffirming the Role of Humans in Command-and-Control Decision-Making in the Digital Age," *Defence* Studies, 23 (1) (2023), pp. 43-67, doi:10.1080/14702436.2022.2102486.

2 See Carl Von Clausewitz, *On War*, ed. and trans. Michael Howard and Peter Paret (Princeton, NJ: Princeton University Press, 1976), pp. 75–77; Alan Beyerchen, "Clausewitz, Nonlinearity, and the Unpredictability of War," *International Security* 17 (3) (1992–1993), pp. 74–75; Ryan Grauer, *Commanding Military Power: Organizing for Victory and Defeat on the Battlefield* (Cambridge: Cambridge University Press, 2016); and Stephen Biddle, *Military Power: Explaining Victory and Defeat in Modern Battle* (Princeton, NJ: Princeton University Press, 2004).

3 The literature on human cognitive bias and heuristics is extensive; for example, see Daniel Kahneman, *Thinking, Fast and Slow* (New York: Farrar, Straus and Giroux, 2011); Dan Ariely, *Predictably Irrational: The Hidden Forces that Shape Our Decisions* (New York: Harper Perennial, 2010); Daniel Kahneman, Paul Slovic, and Amos Tversky (eds), *Judgment Under Uncertainty: Heuristics and Biases* (Cambridge: Cambridge University Press, 1982); Jonathan Baron, *Thinking and Deciding*. 4th ed. (Cambridge: Cambridge University Press, 2008); and Robert B. Cialdini, *Influence: The Psychology of Persuasion*. Rev. ed. (New York: Harper Business, 2006).

4 For example, see Erich Jantsch, *The Self-Organizing Universe, Scientific and Human Implications of the Emerging Paradigm of Evolution* (Oxford: Pergamon Press, 1980); Ilya Prigogine and Isabella Stengers, *Order Out of Chaos* (London: Penguin Random House, 1984); Michael Lissack, "Complexity: The Science, its Vocabulary, and its Relation to Organizations," *Emergence* 1 (1), (2022), pp. 110–126; Charles Perrow, *Normal Accidents* (Princeton, NJ: Princeton University Press, 1999); Robert Jervis, *System Effects, Complexity in Political and Social Life* (Princeton, NJ: Princeton University Press, 1997); and Thomas J. Czerwinski, *Coping with the Bounds, Speculations on Nonlinearity in Military Affairs* (Washington, D.C.: National Defense University Press, 1999).

5 David Barno and Nora Bensahel, "War in the Fourth Industrial Revolution," *War on the Rocks*, July 3, 2018, https://warontherocks.com/2018/06/war-in-the-fourth-industrial-revolution/.

6 See, for example, Michael Raska "The Sixth RMA Wave: Disruption in Military Affairs?" *Journal of Strategic Studies* 44 (4) (2021), pp. 456–479; Caitlin Talmadge, "Emerging Technology and Intra-War Escalation Risks: Evidence from the Cold War, Implications for Today," *Journal of Strategic Studies* 42 (6) (2019), pp. 864–887; and Avi Goldfarb and Jon Lindsay, "Prediction and Judgment, Why Artificial Intelligence Increases the Importance of Humans in War," *International Security* 46 (3) (2022), pp. 7–50.

7 See Ajay Agrawal, Joshua Gans, and Avi Goldfarb, *Prediction Machines: The Simple Economics of Artificial Intelligence* (Cambridge, MA: Harvard Business Review Press, 2018), p. 24; and Jason Furman and Robert Seamans, "AI and the Economy," in *Innovation Policy*

and the Economy, ed. Josh Lerner and Scott Stern, Vol. 19 (Chicago, IL: University of Chicago Press, 2018), pp. 161–191.

8   See Kenneth Payne, *I, Warbot: The Dawn of Artificially Intelligent Conflict* (New York: Oxford University Press, 2021); and James Johnson, *Artificial Intelligence and the Future of Warfare: USA, China, and Strategic Stability* (Manchester: Manchester University Press, 2021).

9   See Michael C. Horowitz, *The Diffusion of Military Power: Causes and Consequences for International Politics* (Princeton, NJ: Princeton University Press, 2010); and Stephen P. Rosen, "The Impact of the Office of Net Assessment on the American Military in the Matter of the Revolution in Military Affairs," *Journal of Strategic Studies* 33 (4), pp. 469–482; and Biddle, *Military Power*.

10 See Frans Osinga, "'Getting' *A Discourse on Winning and Losing*: A Primer on Boyd's 'Theory of Intellectual Evolution,'" *Contemporary Security Policy* 34 (3) (2013), pp. 603–624; and Grant T. Hammond, "Reflections on the Legacy of John Boyd," *Contemporary Security Policy* 34 (3) (2013), pp. 600–602.

11 See James Hasik, "Beyond the Briefing: Theoretical and Practical Problems in the Works and Legacy of John Boyd," *Contemporary Security Policy* 34 (3) (December 2013), pp. 583–599; and Jim Storr, "Neither Art nor Science—Towards a Discipline of Warfare," *RUSI Journal* (April 2001), pp. 39–45.

12 Hasik, "Beyond the Briefing."

13 Osinga, "'Getting' *A Discourse on Winning and Losing*," pp. 603–624.

14 Herman Kahn, *On Escalation: Metaphors and Scenarios* (New York: Harvard University Press, 1965).

15 John Boyd, "Patterns of Conflict," (unpublished presentation, draft version, 1982), www.projectwhitehorse.com/pdfs/boyd/patterns%20of%20conflict.pdf.

16 Frans Osinga, *Science, Strategy and War, The Strategic Theory of John Boyd* (London: Routledge, 2007), p. 3.

17 Others include more abstract discussions about military theory, grand strategy, and a general theory of organizational survival. Ibid., p. 173.

18 John Boyd, "The Essence of Winning and Losing," (unpublished presentation, 1995), https://danford.net/boyd/essence1.htm.

19 Osinga, *Science, Strategy, and War*, Chs 3 and 4.

20 For example, Michael Polanyi, *Knowing and Being* (London: Routledge, 1969).

21 For example, James Bryant Conant, *Two Modes of Thought* (New York: Trident Press, 1964).

22 Karl Popper, *The Logic of Scientific Discovery* (London: Routledge, 1968).

23 For example, see David Byrne, *Complexity Theory and the Social Sciences: An Introduction* (London: Routledge, 1998); and Susanne Durham, *Chaos Theory For the Practical Military Mind* (New York: Biblioscholar, 2012).

24 Examples include Howard Gardner, *The Mind's New Science: A History of the Cognitive Revolution* (New York: Basic Books, 1985); John von Neumann, *The Computer and the Brain* (New Haven, CT: Yale University Press, 1958); Norbert Wiener, *The Human Use of Human Beings: Cybernetics and Society* (New York: Avon Books, 1967); and Gilbert Ryle, *The Concept of Mind* (London: Hutchinson, 1966).

25 John Boyd, "Organic Design for Command and Control," (unpublished presentation, 1987), p. 15, https://pdfs.semanticscholar.org/6ca9/63358751c859d7b68736aca1aa9d1a8d4e53.pdf.

26   Ibid., p. 16.
27   John Boyd, "The Strategic Game of ? And ?" (unpublished presentation, 1987), p. 58, www.ausairpower.net/JRB/strategic_game.pdf.
28   See Henry A. Kissinger, Eric Schmidt, and Daniel Huttenlocher, *The Age of AI and Our Human Future* (London: John Murray, 2021), pp. 166–167; and Harold Trinkunas, Herbert Lin, and Benjamin Loehrke, *Three Tweets to Midnight: Effects of the Global Information Ecosystem on the Risk of Nuclear Conflict* (Stanford, CA: Hoover Institution Press, 2020).
29   Boyd, *The Essence of Winning and Losing*, p. 5.
30   James Clerk Maxwell, "Science and Free Will," in *The Life of James Clerk Maxwell*, ed. Lewis Campbell and William Garnett (New York: Johnson Reprint Corporation, 1969), pp. 440–442.
31   However, some scholars contend that learning from complexity and uncertainty from past events is ambiguous. See James Roche and Barry Watts, "Choosing Analytic Measures," *Journal of Strategic Studies* 13 (2) (1991), pp. 165–209; and Richard Overy, *The Air War 1939–1945* (New York: Potomac Books, 1981).
32   Beyerchen, "Clausewitz, Nonlinearity, and the Unpredictability of War," p. 89.
33   Boyd, *Organic Design for Command and Control*, p. 24.
34   Clausewitz, *On War*, pp. 75–77. Other strategists, including Sun Tzu, J. F. C. Fuller, T. E. Lawrence, Basil Liddell Hart, John Wylie, and Andre Beaufre, also recognized the role of human psychology in warfare.
35   Ibid., p. 89.
36   In contrast with Clausewitz's non-linear approach, other classical military theorists such as Antoine-Henri de Jomini and Heinrich von Bulow adopt implicit linear approaches to manipulate empirical evidence selectively. See Peter Paret, *Clausewitz, and the State: The Man, His Theories and His Times* (Princeton, NJ: Princeton University Press, 1985), pp. 8–9; and Clausewitz, *On War*, pp. 134–158.
37   Beyerchen, "Clausewitz, Nonlinearity, and the Unpredictability of War," pp. 74–75.
38   Jervis, *System Effects*, p. 16.
39   Complex adaptive system is a concept that refers to a group of semi-autonomous agents who interact in interdependent ways to produce system-wide patterns, such that those patterns then influence the behavior of the agents. In human systems at all scales, you see patterns that emerge from agents' interactions in that system. Kevin Dooley, "A Nominal Definition of Complex Adaptive Systems," *Chaos Network* 8 (1) (1996), pp. 2–3.
40   Clausewitz, *On War*, p. 80.
41   Colin Gray, *Modern Strategy* (London: Oxford University Press, 1999), p. 91.
42   See Jantsch, *The Self Organizing Universe, Scientific and Human Implications of the Emerging Paradigm of Evolution*; Prigogine and Stengers, *Order Out of Chaos*; Lissack, "Complexity," pp. 110–126; Perrow, *Normal Accidents*; and Jervis, *System Effects*.
43   Linear interactions are visible and follow predictable sequences, whereas non-linear interactions involve unfamiliar, non-visible, unplanned, and unexpected sequences, which are not immediately comprehensible. Perrow, *Normal Accidents*, p. 90.
44   Beyerchen, "Clausewitz, Nonlinearity, and the Unpredictability of War," p. 63.
45   See David Campbell, "Nonlinear Science: From Paradigms to Practicalities," *Los Alamos Science* 15 (1987), pp. 218–262.
46   Perrow, *Normal Accidents,* pp. 89–96.
47   Ibid., pp. 331–334.

48 Ibid, p. 173.

49 See David Ehrenfeld, "The Management of Diversity: A Conservation Paradox," in *Ecology, Economics, Ethics: The Broken Circle*, ed. F. Herbert Bormann and Stephen Kellert (New Haven, CT: Yale University Press, 1991), pp. 26–39.

50 Steven Bernstein et al., "God Gave Physics the Easy Problems: Adapting Social Science to an Unpredictable World," *European Journal of International Relations* 6 (1) (2000), p. 70.

51 Jervis, *System Effects*, p. 291.

52 Ibid., p. 24.

53 Clausewitz, *On War*, p. 149.

54 Chaos theory is an integral part of non-linear science and describes the specific range of irregular behavior in a system that changes; it emerges when it is both non-linear and sensitive to initial conditions. See James Gleick, *Chaos: The Making of a New Science* (New York: Viking, 1987); and James Glenn, *Chaos Theory: The Essentials for Military Applications* (Newport, RI: Naval War College Press, 1995).

55 Maxwell, "Science and Free Will," pp. 440–442.

56 Gary Marcus and Ernest Davis, "What Does Meta AI's Diplomacy-winning Cicero Mean for AI?" *The Road to AI We Can Trust*, November 25, 2022, https://garymarcus.substack.com

57 See Michael C. Horowitz, "When Speed Kills: Lethal Autonomous Weapon Systems, Deterrence and Stability," *Journal of Strategic Studies* 42 (6) (2019), pp. 764–788; Payne, *I, Warbot*; and James Johnson, "Deterrence in the Age of Artificial Intelligence & Autonomy: A Paradigm Shift in Nuclear Deterrence Theory and Practice?" *Defense & Security Analysis* 36 (4) (2020), pp. 426–429.

58 Several military organizations are testing alternative AI-ML approaches to compensate for the lack of labeled data (e.g., real-world information from the battlefield), which is needed to train existing supervised ML systems. These new approaches combine supervised ML with unsupervised deep-learning approaches, which work with a limited amount of annotated data. "Unsupervised Machine Learning in the Military Domain," *NATO Science & Technology Organization*, May 27, 2021, www.sto.nato.int/Lists/STONewsArchive/displaynewsitem.aspx?ID=642.

59 According to information theory, the more possibilities and information a system has, the greater amount of "friction" and "noise" it embodies. See Robert Shaw, "Strange Attractors, Chaotic Behavior, and Information Flow," *Zeitschrift der Naturforschung* 36a (1981), pp. 80–112.

60 See Boulanin (ed.), *The Impact of Artificial Intelligence on Strategic Stability and Nuclear Risk, Volume I: Euro-Atlantic Perspectives* (Stockholm, Sweden: SIPRI, May 2019) James Johnson, "Delegating Strategic Decision-Making to Machines: Dr. Strangelove Redux?" *Journal of Strategic Studies* 45 (3), pp. 439-477 (2022), https://doi.org/10.1080/01402390.2020.1759038.

61 Thomas C. Schelling, *The Strategy of Conflict* (Cambridge, MA: Harvard University Press, 1960); pp. 199–201.

62 James Johnson, "Inadvertent Escalation in the Age of Intelligence Machines: A New Model for Nuclear Risk in the Digital Age," *European Journal of International Security* 7 (3) (2022).

63 Paul K. Davis and Paul Bracken, "Artificial Intelligence for Wargaming and Modeling," *The Journal of Defense Modeling and Simulation* (2022), https://doi.org/10.1177/15485129211073126.

64   Researchers at Google-owned DeepMind have made some progress in developing an autonomous gaming algorithm, *DeepNash*, based on game theory and model-free deep-reinforcement learning that performs *Stratego*—a game that requires long-term strategic planning as in chess with imperfect information as in poker—at human-levels. "Mastering Stratego, the Classic Game of Imperfect Information," *Google DeepMind*, December 1 2022, www.deepmind.com/blog/mastering-stratego-the-classic-game-of-imperfect-information?utm_source=substack&utm_medium=email.

65   Jervis, *System Effects*, p. 293.

66   "Metacognition" is a familiar concept to master chess players, who can shift their thought concentration to execute moves when faced with complex problems and tradeoffs. Nate Silver, *The Signal and the Noise: Why So Many Predictions Fail—But Some Don't* (New York: Penguin Books, 2015); pp. 272–273.

67   Abductive reasoning produces hypotheses from a theoretically infinite number of explanations using a value system to observe unrelated or unexpected phenomena based on widely accepted facts or premises. By contrast, AI-ML systems use inductive reasoning that produces hypotheses from training datasets to make inferences from observations. See Agrawal, Gans, and Goldfarb, *Prediction Machines*, p. 24.

68   Malcolm Gladwell, *Blink: The Power of Thinking Without Thinking* (New York: Little Brown and Company, 2005), Herbert A. Simon, "Making Management Decisions: The Role of Intuition and Emotions," *The Academy of Management Executive* 1 (1) (February 1987), pp. 57–64.

69   Ibid.

70   See James A. Russell, *Innovation, Transformation, and War: Counterinsurgency Operations in Anbar and Ninewa Provinces, Iraq, 2005–2007* (Stanford, CA: Stanford University Press, 2010); Timothy S. Wolters, *Information at Sea: Shipboard Command and Control in the US Navy, from Mobile Bay to Okinawa* (Baltimore, MD: Johns Hopkins University Press, 2013); and Nina A. Kollars, "War's Horizon: Soldier-Led Adaptation in Iraq and Vietnam," *Journal of Strategic Studies* 38 (4) (2015), pp. 529–553.

71   Goldfarb and Lindsay, "Prediction and Judgment," p. 36.

72   James L. Regens, "Augmenting Human Cognition to Enhance Strategic, Operational, and Tactical Intelligence," *Intelligence and National Security* 34 (5) (2019), pp. 673–687; and Keith Dear, "A Very British AI Revolution in Intelligence is Needed," *War on the Rocks*, October 19, 2018, https://warontherocks.com/2018/10/a-very-british-ai-revolution-in-intelligence-isneeded/.

73   Minna Räsänen and James M. Nyce, "The Raw is Cooked: Data in Intelligence Practice," *Science, Technology, & Human Values* 38 (5) (September 2013), pp. 655–677.

74   Frank Sauer, "ICRAC Statement on Technical Issues to the 2014 UN CCW Expert Meeting," *International Committee for Robot Arms Control*, May 14, 2014, http://icrac.net/2014/05/icrac-statement-on-technical-issues-to-the-un-ccw-expert-meeting/.

75   "2022 National Defense Strategy of the United States of America," *US Department of Defense*, October 27, 2022, https://media.defense.gov/2022/Oct/27/2003103845/-1/-1/1/2022–NATIONAL-DEFENSE-STRATEGY-NPR-MDR.PDF.

76   See Jon R. Lindsay, *Information Technology and Military Power* (Ithaca, NY: Cornell University Press, 2020).

77   AlphaStar Team, "Alphastar: Mastering the Real-Time Strategy Game Starcraft II," *DeepMind Blog*, January 24, 2019, https://deepmind.com/blog/article/alphastar-mastering-real-time-strategy-game-starcraft-ii; Thomas Newdick, "AI-Controlled F-16s

Are Now Working as a Team in DARPA's Alpha Dogfights," *The Drive*, March 22, 2021, www.thedrive.com/the-war-zone/39899/darpa-now-has-ai-controlled-f-16s-working-as-a-team-in-virtual-dogfights.

78 Recent unsupervised pre-trained "deep-learning" (a subfield of ML) networks have been tested on autonomous vehicles to cope with real-world non-linear problems. However, these new ML approaches are not trustworthy in safety-critical high non-linear environments. Raul S. Ferreira, "Machine Learning in a Nonlinear World: A Linear Explanation through the Domain of the Autonomous Vehicles," *European Training Network for Safer Autonomous Systems*, January 9, 2020, https://etn-sas.eu/2020/09/01/machine-learning-in-a-nonlinear-world-a-linear-explanation-through-the-domain-of-the-autonomous-vehicles/.

79 Eric-Hans Kramer, "Mission Command in the Information Age: A Normal Accidents Perspective on Networked Military Operations," *Journal of Strategic Studies* 38 (4) (2015), pp. 445–466.

80 A notable example of the failure of "mission command" was the ill-timed ICBM test at the US Vandenberg Air Force Base during the height of the 1962 Cuban Missile Crisis. Stephen J. Cimbala, *The Dead Volcano: The Background and Effects of Nuclear War Complacency* (New York: Praeger, 2002), p. 66.

81 Boyd, *Patterns of Conflict*, p. 72.

82 Beyerchen, "Clausewitz, Nonlinearity, and the Unpredictability of War," p. 75.

83 See Boulanin, *The Impact of Artificial Intelligence on Strategic Stability and Nuclear Risk, Volume I: Euro-Atlantic Perspectives*; Edward Geist and Andrew J. Lohn, *How Might Artificial Intelligence Affect the Risk of Nuclear War?* (Santa Monica, CA: RAND Corporation, 2018); Rebecca Hersman, "Wormhole Escalation in the New Nuclear Age," *Texas National Security Review* 3 (3) (Autumn 2020), pp. 99–110; and Johnson, "Inadvertent Escalation in the Age of Intelligence Machines."

84 See Linda J. Skitka, Kathleen L. Mosier, and Mark Burdick, "Does Automation Bias Decision-Making?" *International Journal of Human-Computer Studies* 51 (5) (1999), pp. 991–1006.

85 See Mary L. Cummings, "Automation Bias in Intelligent Time-Critical Decision Support Systems," *AIAA 1st Intelligent Systems Technical Conference*, 2004, pp. 557–562; Skitka, Mosier, and Burdick, "Does Automation Bias Decision Making?"

86 Catherine Graham, "Undergrads Partner with NATO to Reduce Combat Casualties," *The Hub*, August 20, 2021, https://hub.jhu.edu/2021/08/20/wearable-device-for-combat-triage/.

87 "Developing Algorithms That Make Decisions Aligned with Human Experts," *DARPA*, March 3, 2022, www.darpa.mil/news-events/2022-03-03.

88 Pranshu Verma, "The Military Wants AI to Replace Human Decision-Making in Battle," *The Washington Post*, March 29, 2022, www.washingtonpost.com/technology/2022/03/29/darpa-artificial-intelligence-battlefield-medical-decisions/.

89 Tom Simonite, "A Health Care Algorithm Offered Less Care to Black Patients," *Wired*, October 24, 2019, www.wired.com/story/how-algorithm-favored-whites-over-blacks-health-care/.

90 Human intervention and judgment are still required in the three main AI-ML techniques: (1) in "supervised learning" humans determine what to predict (i.e., frame its goals) from labeled training datasets; (2) in "unsupervised learning" humans judge what an algorithm classifies and analyzes, and then what to do with these associations; (3) in "reinforcement

learning" humans specify a reward function for the algorithm to make sense of the external world to maximize a predetermined goal. See Agrawal, Gans, and Goldfarb, *Prediction Machines*; and Alan Beyerchen, "Nonlinear Science and the Unfolding of a New Intellectual Vision," *Papers in Comparative Studies* 6 (1988–89), pp. 26–29; and Goldfarb and Lindsay, "Prediction and Judgment," pp. 22, 30–31.

91   Clausewitz, *On War*, p. 89.

92   For example, see Sally Applin, "They Sow, They Reap: How Humans are Becoming Algorithm Chow," *IEEE Consumer Electronics Magazine* 7 (2) (2018), pp. 101–102; Heather M. Roff, "Artificial Intelligence: Power to the People," *Ethics & International Affairs* 33 (2) (2019), pp. 124–140; and Elke Schwarz, *Death Machines: The Ethics of Violent Technologies* (Manchester: Manchester University Press, 2018).

93   "Mission command" empowers local tactical commanders—within specified military goals and rules of engagement—to follow the rules of a military organization that define the circumstances, conditions, degree, and ways in which specific military capabilities can or cannot be used, and thus the latitude to interpret guidance, coordinate support, and alter operations to reflect changes in battlefield circumstances. See Department of the Army, "ADP 6-0: Mission Command: Command and Control of Army Forces, Army Doctrine Publication," *US Department of the Army*, May 17, 2012, https://armypubs.army. mil/ProductMaps/PubForm/Details.aspx?PUB_ID=1007502.

94   See Grauer, *Commanding Military Power*; and Biddle, *Military Power*.

95   Battista Biggio and Fabio Roli, "Wild Patterns: Ten Years after the Rise of Adversarial Machine Learning," *Pattern Recognition* 84 (2018), pp. 317–331; and Ian Goodfellow, Jonathon Shlens, and Christian Szegedy, "Explaining and Harnessing Adversarial Examples," December 20, 2014, *arXiv* preprint arXiv:1412.6572.

96   Lora Saalman, "Fear of False Negatives: AI and China's Nuclear Posture," *Bulletin of the Atomic Scientists*, April 24, 2018, https://thebulletin.org/2018/04/fear-of-falsenegatives-ai-and-chinas-nuclear-posture/.

97   See Stuart Russell and Peter Norvig, *Artificial Intelligence: International Version: A Modern Approach* (Englewood Cliffs: Prentice Hall, 2010); and Nils J. Nilsson, *The Quest for Artificial Intelligence: A History of Ideas and Achievements* (Cambridge: Cambridge University Press, 2010).

98   See M. Kamo and H. Yokomizo, "Explanation of Non-Additive Effects in Mixtures of a Similar Mode of Action Chemicals," *Toxicology* 1 (335) (2015), pp. 20–26.

99   Bruce M. Boghosian, et al. "A New Pathology in the Simulation of Chaotic Dynamical Systems on Digital Computers," *Advanced Theory and Simulations* 2 (12) (2019), pp. 1–8.

100   See David Watson, "The Rhetoric and Reality of Anthropomorphism in Artificial Intelligence," *Minds and Machines* 29 (2019), pp. 417–440; Skitka, Mosier, and Burdick, "Automation Bias," pp. 47–63; and Skitka, Mosier, and Burdick, "Does Automation Bias Decision-Making?" pp. 991–1006.

101   See Richard K. Betts, *Enemies of Intelligence: Knowledge and Power in American National Security* (New York: Columbia University Press, 2007); and Joshua Rovner, *Fixing the Facts: National Security and the Politics of Intelligence* (Ithaca, NY: Cornell University Press, 2011); Scott Sagan, "Why Do States Build Nuclear Weapons? Three Models in Search of a Bomb," *International Security* 21 (1996), pp. 54–86.

102   See Keir Lieber, "Grasping the Technological Peace: The Offense–Defense Balance and International Security," *International Security* 25 (1) (2000), pp. 71–104; Robert Jervis, "Cooperation under the Security Dilemma," *World Politics* 30 (2) (1978), pp. 167–214;

and James Johnson, "The End of Military-Techno Pax Americana? Washington's Strategic Responses to Chinese AI-Enabled Military Technology," *The Pacific Review* 34 (3) (2021), pp. 351–378.

103   See James M. Acton, et al. (eds), *Entanglement: Russian and Chinese Perspectives on Non-Nuclear Weapons and Nuclear Risks* (Washington, D.C.: Carnegie Endowment for International Peace); and Forrest E. Morgan, et al., *Dangerous Thresholds: Managing Escalation in the 21st Century* (Santa Monica, CA: RAND Corporation, 2008).

104   Michael Meier, "U.S. Delegation Statement on 'Appropriate Levels of Human Judgment,'" *Statement to the CCW Informal Meeting of Experts on AWS*, April 12, 2016, https:// geneva.usmission.gov/2016/04/12/u-s-delegation-statement-on-appropriate-levels-of-human-judgment/.

105   Ibid.

106   Stuart Russell, "2021 Reith Lectures 2021: Living with Artificial Intelligence," www.bbc. co.uk/programmes/articles/1N0w5NcK27Tt041LPVLZ51k/reith-lectures-2021-living-with-artificial-intelligence.

107   Cummings, "Automation Bias in Intelligent Time-Critical Decision Support Systems," pp. 557–562.

108   "Summary of the Joint All-Domain Command and Control (JADC2) Strategy," *United States Department of Defense*, March 2022, https://media.defense.gov/2022/Mar/17/ 2002958406/-1/-1/1/SUMMARY-OF-THE-JOINT-ALL-DOMAIN-COMMAND-AND-CONTROL-STRATEGY.PDF.

109   Other countries, including the UK (e.g., The British Army's Project Theia), France (e.g., the French Air Force's Connect@aero program), and NATO (e.g., IST-ET-113 Exploratory Team) have also started developing and testing AI technology to support C2 and military decision-making. These efforts, however, remain limited in scale and scope. "Unsupervised Machine Learning in the Military Domain," *NATO Science & Technology Organization*, May 27, 2021, www.sto.nato.int/Lists/STONewsArchive/displaynewsitem. aspx?ID=642; "Digging Deeper into THEIA," *The British Army*, July 8, 2021, www.army. mod.uk/news-and-events/news/2021/07/digging-deeper-into-theia/; and Philippe Gros, "The 'Tactical Cloud,' a Key Element of the Future Combat Air System," *Fondation Pour La Recherche Stratégique* 19 (19) (October 2, 2019).

110   Yan Ke, Yang Kuo, and Shi Hongbo, "Human-on-the-Loop: The Development Trend of Intelligentized Command Systems," *PLA Daily*, March 17, 2022, www.81.cn/jfjbmap/ content/2022-03/17/content_311543.htm. This report reflects a broader debate occurring within Chinese military writings about the role of humans in autonomous weapons systems in future warfare. For example, see Xiao Xingfu, "Pay Attention to the Role of Humans in Unmanned Operations," *PLA Daily*, March 29, 2022, www.81.cn/jfjbmap/ content/2022-03/29/content_312488.htm.

111   Christian Brose, *The Kill Chain: Defending America in the Future of High-Tech Warfare* (New York: Hachette, 2020).

112   Multinational Capability Development Campaign, *Final Study Report on Information Age Command and Control Concepts*, February 8, 2019, p. 20.

113   Charles C. Krulak, "The Strategic Corporal: Leadership in the Three Block War," *Marines Magazine*, January 1999, https://apps.dtic.mil/sti/pdfs/ADA399413.pdf. On the RMA, see Eliot Cohen, "A Revolution in Warfare," *Foreign Affairs* 75 (2) (1996), pp. 34–54.

114   Kollars, "War's Horizon," pp. 529–553.

115 DoD, "Summary of the Joint All-Domain Command and Control (JADC2) Strategy."

116 The judgments (i.e., outputs) of AI-ML algorithms cannot be determined in advance because it would take too long to specify all possible contingencies; thus, human judgment is required to interpret the system's prediction to inform judgment and decision-making. Goldfarb and Lindsay, "Prediction and Judgment," p. 92.

117 Lindsay, *Information Technology and Military Power*, pp. 109–135.

118 Boyd, *Organic Design for Command and Control*, pp. 20–21.

119 Sydney Freedberg Jr., "Let Leaders Off the Electronic Leash," *Breaking Defense*, May 5, 2017, https://breakingdefense.com/2017/05/let-leaders-off-the-electronic-leash-csa-milley/.

120 Boyd, *Patterns of Conflict*, p. 128.

121 Peter W. Singer, "Robots and the Rise of Tactical Generals," *Brookings*, March 9, 2009, www.brookings.edu/articles/robots-and-the-rise-of-tactical-generals/.

122 US Office of Naval Research, *Data Focused Naval Tactical Cloud (DF-NTC)*, ONR Information Package, June 24, 2014.

123 Freedberg, "Let Leaders Off the Electronic Leash."

124 Gros, "The 'Tactical Cloud,' a Key Element of the Future Combat Air System."

125 For example, in 2003, a MIM-104 Patriot surface-to-air missile's automated system misidentified a friendly aircraft as an adversary that human operators failed to correct, leading to the death by friendly fire of a US F-18 pilot. John K. Hawley, "Patriot Wars: Automation and the Patriot Air and Missile Defense Systems" (Washington, D.C.: CNAS, January 2017). Other potential causes of misguided or erroneous algorithmic outputs include open-source mis-disinformation, adversarial attacks, data-poisoning, or simply the use of outdated, malfunctioning, or biased data training sets.

126 On the ethical and moral dilemmas and tradeoffs in making decisions during uncertainty, see Cecile Fabre, *Spying through a Glass Darkly* (London: Oxford University Press, 2022).

127 Marilynn B. Brewer and William D. Crano, *Social Psychology* (New York: West Publishing Co. 1994).

128 Perrow, *Normal Accidents*, pp. 331–334.

129 Alex Lockie, "The Real Story of Stanislav Petrov, the Soviet Officer Who 'Saved' the World from Nuclear War," *Business Insider*, September 26, 2018, www.businessinsider.com/stanislav-petrov-the-soviet-officer-saved-the-world-from-nuclear-war-2018-9?r=US&IR=T.

130 See Seth D. Baum, Robert de Neufville, and Anthony M. Barrett, "A Model for the Probability of Nuclear War," *Global Catastrophic Risk Institute*, Global Catastrophic Risk Institute Working Paper 18-1 (March 2018), pp. 19–20.

131 For example, cyber sensemaking, where human analysts are teamed with AI agents to understand, anticipate, and respond to real-time events. See Jeffrey Bradshaw, et al., "Coactive Emergence as a Sensemaking Strategy for Cyber Operations," *IHMC Technical Report* (October 2012), pp. 1–24.

4

Brinkmanship in algorithmic warfare

The author would like to acknowledge and extend gratitude to Reid Pauly and Rose McDermott for their insightful research on the impact of psychology on nuclear brinkmanship. Their work was a major source of theoretical inspiration for this chapter.

This chapter considers the implications of Schelling's insights on crisis stability between nuclear-armed rivals in the era of AI-enabled warfare and contextualizes them within the broader information ecosystem.[1] It engages with interdisciplinary human psychology, behavioral science, and anthropological studies to provide fresh insights into the "AI-nuclear dilemma" and, more broadly, the intersection of technological change, strategic thinking, and nuclear risk.[2] It concludes that the risks of nuclear-armed states leaving something to chance in the digital era preclude any potential bargaining benefits that may accrue to states during crises.

Thomas Schelling evokes the "threat that leaves something to chance" concept (i.e., the possibility that military escalation may spiral out of control) to tackle these complex strategic challenges, illustrating how opponents can inadvertently or accidentally blunder into warfare.[3] This theory explains the methods and motivations of actors who leverage risk to enhance their position in competitive bargaining situations.[4] Schelling applies cases of Cold War crises to elucidate how those who assume the largest risks achieve the greatest payoff.[5] More broadly, Schelling's "threat that leaves something to chance" seeks to absolve the falsification problem associated with the Cold War era "Nuclear Revolution," which offers a solution to the puzzle of how actors can engage in tests of will and resolve at the precipice of Armageddon that "rationally" purportedly emerges during brinkmanship.[6] How might the dynamics of the digital age affect Schelling's theory? Will levering something to chance in the digital age be stabilizing or destabilizing? And will the risks of leaving something to chance in the digital age outweigh the perceived bargaining benefits?

Scholars have utilized various theories to elucidate the essence of credibility in military threats and to comprehend how actors can convey determination

The AI Commander. Johnson, Oxford University Press. © James Johnson (2024).
DOI: 10.1093/oso/9780198892182.003.0005

while ensuring the believability of their threats, which lies at the theoretical core of Schelling's "threat that leaves something to chance."[7] Nevertheless, the body of literature on military organizations, strategic culture, nuclear accidents, and asymmetric warfare provides scant insight into the practical functioning of "threats that introduce an element of uncertainty" in real-world scenarios.[8] Less still, the existing canon engages Schelling's theory—or other strategic theories such as deterrence, escalation, strategic stability, the security dilemma, and catalytic war—with the emerging technologies associated with the digital age.[9] How might the dynamics of the digital age impact Schelling's strategy? Schelling writes: "Some kind of advertence, some miscalculation of enemy reactions or misreading of enemy intent, some steps taken without knowledge of steps taken by the other side, some random event or false alarm, or some decisive action to hedge against the unforeseeable would have to be involved in the process on one side or both."[10]

The chapter is organized into two sections. The first unpacks the key mechanisms and processes—accidental risk, imperfect decision-making, the rationality of the irrational, and brinkmanship—and interpretations of Schelling's "threat that leaves something to chance" theory. It also contextualizes Schelling's theory within the broader debates about war control, chance, and uncertainty. Section two builds on Robert Jervis' psychological-cognitive interpretation (perceptions, beliefs, images, and bias) of Schelling's notion of "imperfect" decision-making processes to consider the implications of AI technology for threats that leave something to chance. Specifically, it revisits Schelling's rational-based approach in the light of the latest interdisciplinary human psychology (human evolution, emotion, and weaponizing social media) to conceptualize the AI-nuclear dilemma—that is, how divergences between states' nuclear strategy, force structure, and doctrine might affect how they view the use of AI in the nuclear enterprise.[11] Against the background of a burgeoning digital information ecosystem, this section considers intergroup dynamics, decision-making under times of stress and crisis, and the problem of the nuanced and complex signaling between nuclear rivals.

Schelling's "the threat that leaves something to chance": mechanisms and interpretations

In *The Strategy of Conflict*, Schelling argues that threats in competition in risk-taking between nuclear powers by leaving something to chance keeps the enemy guessing.[12] Like a game of chicken, an element of uncertainty arises in the competition, as it involves the display of nerves, reputations, expectations regarding future actions, and determination.[13] As a result, a player with less resolve generally yields when confronted by a more determined actor who can effectively control and manipulate risks.[14]

Robert Jervis identifies two processes to explain the escalation dynamics implied in the threat of limited force utilization, termed "limited war as a risk generator" in Schelling's notion of "threats with an element of unpredictability."[15] First, using force to signal an actor's resolve and images of resolve (a willingness to accept a high risk rather than conceding) enhances the credibility of its escalatory threats.[16] What is often crucial, Jervis writes, is "each side's judgment of the chances that the conflict will expand, the willingness of each to bear the costs, and its perceptions of the other's willingness to do so."[17] For example, the US naval harassment of Soviet submarines during the Cuban Missile Crisis to demonstrate resolve to Khrushchev.[18]

Second is the threat of inadvertent escalation. As Schelling notes, "any situation that scares one side will scare both sides with the danger of war that neither wants, and both will have to pick their way carefully through the crisis, *never quite sure that the other knows how to avoid stumbling over the brink*" (emphasis added).[19] Caitlin Talmadge argues, for instance, that US defense planners deliberately embedded the inadvertent escalation risks associated with the "threat that leaves something to chance" into the AirSea Battle doctrine to counter Chinese anti-access area-denial operations.[20]

Therefore, it is challenging for actors to determine the amount of risk they assume and thus when, or how often, they overestimate (or underestimate) their ability to control chance to deter or force an adversary to bend to their will. Jervis points out that leaders often "believe that they can design and implement a policy that exerts just the right amount of pressure on the other side—enough to restrain but not to lead the other to believe that an all-out conflict is inevitable."[21] In sum, the "threat that leaves something to chance" implies that whenever military force is used or threatened (as a bluff or otherwise), an escalatory chain reaction may spiral out of control, even though the initiator does not desire that outcome.

Control in chance: war control and uncertainty

Schelling wanted to understand how actors can achieve and sustain the upper hand in coercion by manipulating risk. The uncertainty of war (or the "fog and friction of war"[22]) and the concomitant difficulty of controlling events illustrated in Schelling's theory feature prominently in the theoretical deterrence problem of credibility associated with escalation and crisis bargaining. States cannot precisely calibrate their risk assessments nor be sure how close they are to the brink of war.[23] In response to the Cuban Missile Crisis, Brodie wrote: "I see no basis in experience or logic for assuming that the increase in the level of violence from one division to thirty [in conventional war in Europe] is less shocking and a less dangerous form of escalation than the introduction of [tactical] nuclear weapons."[24]

According to Reid Pauly and Rose McDermott, during classic Cold War episodes of nuclear brinkmanship, like the Cuban Missile Crisis, leaders found themselves in situations where they lost control of events but retained the ability to decide whether to escalate to a nuclear level.[25] This suggests that leaders maintained their "capacity for coercion," enabling them to uphold a semblance of control despite uncertainty.[26] A state could, for instance, change its nuclear posture in ways that manipulate risk—that is, tying leaders' hands by loosening leaders' control over nuclear weapons—by pre-delegating nuclear launch authority, deploying tactical nuclear weapons, or establishing a launch-on-warning stance.[27] For instance, it's been reported that Pakistan has delegated the launch authority of its tactical nuclear forces to field commanders, effectively relinquishing control over its nuclear weapons. This decision aims to provide greater flexibility in their retaliatory actions during a crisis with India.[28]

According to Schelling, "the essence of the crisis is its unpredictability. . .it is the essence of a crisis that participants are *not fully in control*" (emphasis added). Underlying this implicit threat of inadvertent escalation is Schelling's notion of "imperfect" decision-making mechanisms; that is, precise responses by actors to contingencies in non-linear situations cannot be foreseen or strategized. Instead, the response to situations will depend on "certain random or haphazard processes [governments as imperfect units], misunderstandings, misuse of authority, panic, or human or mechanical failure."[29]

Reflecting on the events of the Cold War era and benefiting from declassified archives, recent scholarship has reaffirmed the importance of chance, randomness, and luck.[30] These features of crisis decision-making are contingent on limited and ambiguous information, misperceptions of actors' intentions (or a misperception of an enemy's view of our intentions),[31] the limits of safety, and the faith in control (or the "illusion of control") of nuclear weapons, a high probability of accidents, the misuse of authority, and presidential command-and-control over nuclear weapons (i.e., complete presidential control over nuclear weapons) cannot be taken for granted.[32] As Scott Sagan wrote in his seminal account of the Cuban Missile Crisis:

Many serious safety problems, which could have resulted in an accidental or unauthorized detonation or a serious provocation to the Soviet government, occurred during the [Cuban Missile] crisis. *None of these incidents led to inadvertent escalation or an accidental war. All of them, however, had the potential to do so.* President Kennedy may well have been prudent. However, he did not have unchallenged final control over US nuclear weapons. (Emphasis added)[33]

The literature on "normal accidents," which explores the impact of uncertainty and chance on the resilience of complex and closely interconnected systems, including nuclear weapons, suggests that, in contrast to Schelling's perspective, such accidents (e.g., unintended launches, mechanical malfunctions, false alarms, cyberattacks, data manipulation) are unavoidable.[34]

"Accidental risk" in brinkmanship

Schelling's notion of "not being fully in control" of events can be interpreted in three ways.[35] First, actors have no agency (or "collective control") throughout events; thus, even where agreement exists on the desired outcome, because of "accidental risk" (mechanical failure, human error, false alarms, unauthorized launches, etc.), the realization of this is uncertain.[36] In this context, "control" refers to the capability of an individual or a leader to steer events or persuade themselves that they possess the ability to do so.[37] Conversely, "chance" relates to the possibility that events and how people react to them might not unfold as predicted. This can occur due to the mistaken belief in having control, an overly confident attitude toward managing complex and unpredictable situations, and the impact of luck.[38] Empirical studies have described how accidents and problems of control over nuclear weapons have caused deterrence failure (i.e., deterrence failed to prevent the risks and situations it was designed to) and nuclear "close-calls" such as the Cuban Missile Crisis.[39]

Second, while actors cannot control the actions and reactions of others, they retain collective control and thus can realize an outcome they can agree on. This interpretation of "not being fully in control" can also increase inadvertent escalation risk. State A deliberately launches a limited strike on state B that, due to a false alarm, B views as an unlimited first strike and retaliates in kind with what amounts to an inadvertent first strike.[40] According to historian F. H. Hinsley, for example, while it is conceivable that the chain of catalytic events preceding World War I "would have been avoided if this or that government has acted otherwise, it was not possible for them to have acted otherwise. . .[it] was one of those moments in history when events passed beyond men's control."[41] In other words, like the first interpretation of Schelling's "not being fully in control," no actor could have controlled the reactions of other governments to the course of events over which they lost control.

Because "threats that leave something to chance" rely on rational actors, not *intentionally* losing collective control over events, some degree of accidental risk is necessary for Schelling's theory to remain logically coherent and thus credible.[42] The strategy of leaving something to chance is, in essence, manipulating "accidental risk" (i.e., the risk of losing control due to technical mishaps) associated with nuclear brinkmanship.[43] During a crisis, both sides exert coercive pressures on the other by acting in ways that dance around the risk of catastrophe (or "rocking the boat") until one side balks and retreats. Because neither side deliberately threatens to bring this situation into being—only the risk of it—brinkmanship becomes a battle of nerves, resolve, and credibility.[44] Therefore, accidental risk and the various mechanisms of brinkmanship are inextricably linked.

The third interpretation helps to resolve the credibility dilemma embedded in the assumption of rationality underlying "threats where uncertainty plays a role."[45] Under the stress of crises, actors may exert coercive pressures on adversaries to manipulate risk in bargaining to deliberately demonstrate a willingness to act irrationally—or the "rationality of irrationality" strategy.[46] Schelling notes a paradox of deterrence: it "does not always help to be, *or to be believed to be, fully rational*, cool-headed, and in control of oneself or one's country" (emphasis added).[47] In *The Secret Agent*, akin to a modern-day suicide bomber, Joseph Conrad describes that the credibility of a seemingly preposterous anarchist attack on London's Greenwich Observatory is established because of "the belief those people [the police] have in my will to use the means [a nitroglycerine bomb attached to his body]. That's their impression. It is absolute. Therefore I am deadly [credible]."[48]

"Rationality of irrationality": deliberate loss of control

Empirical investigations into Schelling's theory that surrendering control, or creating the perception of doing so, can serve as a valuable bargaining tool in deterrence have yielded divergent outcomes. Research into the "madman theory," exemplified by Richard Nixon's diplomatic strategies with North Vietnam and the Soviet Union, demonstrates that the risks inherent in this approach, which aims to portray one's side as irrational and unpredictable to intimidate opponents, can lead to unintended consequences.[49] For instance, causing resentment, convincing the target that the initiator is in control, and attempting to manipulate nuclear risk to gain bargaining leverage, but without offering any assurances to reward compliance. [50]

During crises, the unpredictability caused by feigning madness, which creates nuclear threats that leave something to chance—even if this is not the initiator's intention—can increase the risk of misperception and inadvertent escalation. If an opponent perceives no benefit in giving in, they may choose to do so out of fear of certain punishment rather than any potential gain. However, employing madman tactics can lead to unintended consequences, as it might make the actor seem inflexible and impossible to satisfy. This may encourage the target to resist further and inadvertently escalate the situation.[51] In sum, madman tactics need to strike a tricky balance, appearing crazy and unpredictable enough to threaten annihilation to elicit concessions but not so crazy that they lose credibility, cause retrenchment, and spark escalation.[52]

Using military force to escalate a situation can be rational; for instance, if an actor believes that its (democratic or non-democratic) regime faces an existential risk. According to Scott Sagan and Jeremi Suri, "leaders in both democracies and non-democracies are susceptible to poor decision-making and pressures that can encourage dangerous activities. Both can give commands that produce complex military operations that they cannot control."[53] During crises, human psychology can also help shed some light on "rationality of irrationality," imperfect decision-making, and the role of accidental risk in understanding escalation dynamics (see Table 4.1).

Doomsday Machine: Schelling's "little black box"

How might different nuclear command, control, and communication (NC3) structures affect the tradeoff between chance and control? Recent studies indicate that the effectiveness of nuclear weapon control mechanisms, both positive (features facilitating their release upon authorized command) and negative (features inhibiting their unauthorized use), can impact the likelihood of accidental events.[54] For instance, some scholars have debated the impact on crisis stability and deterrence of further automation of the NC3 systems, akin to a modern-day Doomsday Machine such as Russia's "Dead Hand" device.[55] According to Schelling, the "more automatic it [a nuclear launch decision-making device] is, the less incentive the enemy has to test my intentions in a war of nerves, prolonging the period of risk," thus reducing strategic ambiguity and improving stability.[56] In the context of mutually

Table 4.1 Escalation dynamics during brinkmanship

Interpretation	Mechanism	Agency over decision	Escalation dynamic	Technological enabler
Accidental risk	mechanical failure/ human accident, misuse of authority	N	Accidental	technological malfunction/unintended consequences, mis-disinformation, malware/intrusions
"Imperfect processes"	randomness/luck, misperceptions, false alarms, third-party actions	Y	Inadvertent/ accidental	cyber false flag, false early warning, deepfake, mis-disinformation
"Rationality of the irrational"	fear, stress of a crisis, reputation, "madman theory," "Domesday Machine"	Y	Inadvertent	autonomous weapons, NC3 automation, social media inter-group conflict
Brinkmanship (deliberate "loss of control")	limited war, "game of chicken," escalation dominance	Y	Inadvertent	cyber NC3 attack, breakdown in communications, supply chain/critical infrastructure attack

assured destruction, only the threat of an unrecallable weapon—activating on provocation no matter what—would be credible and thus effective. Besides, this autonomous machine would obviate the need for a human decision-maker to remain resolute in fulfilling a morally and rationally recommended threat, and by removing any doubt of the morally maximizing instincts of a free human agent in-the-loop, ensuring the deterrent threat is credible.

On the other hand, from a psychological perspective, by removing human agency entirely (i.e., once the device is activated, there is nothing I can do to stop it) the choice to escalate (or deescalate) a crisis falls to machines' preprogrammed and unalterable goals. Such a goal, in turn, "automatically engulfs us both in war if the right (or wrong) combination comes up on any given day" until the demands of an actor have been complied with.[57] The terrifying uncertainty, chance, and contingency that would transpire from this abdication of choice and control of nuclear detonation to a non-human agent—even if the device's launch parameters and protocols were clearly advertised to deter aggression—would increase, as would the risk of both positive (for example, left-of-launch cyber-attack, drone swarm counterforce attack, data-poisoning) and negative failure (for example, false flag operations, AI-augmented advanced persistent threat, or spoofing) of NC3 systems (see Conclusion). Moreover, fully automating the nuclear launch process (i.e., acting without human intervention in the target acquisition, tracking, and launch) would not only circumvent the moral requirement of Just War theory—for example, the lack of legal fail-safes to prevent conflict and protect the innocent—but also violate the *jus ad bellum* requirement of proper authority discussed in Chapter 1 and thus, in principle, be illegitimate.[58]

In sum, introducing uncertainty and chance into a situation (i.e., keeping the enemy guessing) about how an actor might respond to various contingencies—and assuming clarity exists about an adversary's intentions—may have some deterrent utility. If, unlike "madman" tactics, the outcome is in part or entirely determined by exogenous mechanisms and processes—ostensibly beyond the control and comprehension of leaders—genuine and prolonged risk is generated.[59] The following section explores the intersection of chance, AI technology, and the failure of these controls.

Human psychology and "threat that leaves something to chance" in the digital age

In *The Illogic of American Nuclear Strategy*, Robert Jervis writes, "the workings of machines and the reaction of humans in time of stress cannot be predicted with high confidence."[60] This section builds on Jervis' psychological-cognitive interpretation of Schelling's "imperfect" decision-making processes to consider the implications of AI technology for threats that leave something to chance.[61]

Two cognitive biases illustrate that leaders tend to underestimate accidental risks when making decisions during crises. Firstly, the "illusion of control," as previously discussed, can lead to overconfidence in their ability to manage events, which may inadvertently or accidentally escalate a crisis or conflict.[62] Secondly, leaders often perceive adversaries as more centralized, disciplined, and coordinated than they actually are, overestimating their level of control.[63]

Furthermore, as Pauly and McDermott argue, "threats that leave something to chance" neglect the emotional and evolutionary value of retaliation and violence, which are vital to understanding the processes that underpin Schelling's theory.[64] According to Schelling, to cause suffering, nothing is gained or protected directly; instead, "it can only make people behave to avoid it."[65] McDermott et al. argue that "the human psychology of revenge explains why and when policymakers readily commit to otherwise apparently 'irrational' retaliation"—central to the notion of second-strike nuclear capacity.[66] Due to the economic-rational models suggesting that second-strike retaliation cannot avert atomic catastrophe, it is argued that such retaliation lacks a logical foundation. The concept of deterrence, prevalent in military and other arenas, relies on the implicit assumption that strong motives for retaliation exist.[67] However, even if launching a counter-attack offers no strategic advantage, adversaries are expected to anticipate one regardless.[68] In short, deterrence is intrinsically a psychological phenomenon. It uses threats to manipulate an adversary's risk perceptions to persuade against the utility responding with force.[69]

According to Pauly and McDermott, emotions and evolutionary psychology play significant roles in introducing uncertainty, randomness, and chance into crises, even when individuals considered "rational" still maintain some control over their decisions.[70] Recent studies on evolutionary models—that go beyond traditional cognitive reflections—offer fresh insights into how specific emotions can affect credibility and deterrence.[71] Thus, the psychological value attached to retaliation can also affect leaders' perceptions, beliefs, and lessons from experience, which informs choices and behavior during crises.[72] Schelling uses the term "reciprocal fear of surprise attack"—the notion that the probability of a surprise attack arises because both sides fear the same thing—to illuminate this psychological phenomenon.[73]

A recent study on public trust in AI, for instance, demonstrates that age, gender, and specialist knowledge can affect peoples' risk tolerance in AI-enabled applications, including AI-enabled autonomous weapons and crime prediction.[74] These facets of human psychology may also help explain the seemingly paradoxical coexistence of advanced weapon technology that promises speed, distance, and precision (i.e., safer forms of coercion) with a continued penchant for intrinsically human contests of nerves at the brink of nuclear war.[75] Emotional-cognitive models do not, however, necessarily directly contradict the classical rational-based ones. Instead, these models can inform and build on rational models by providing critical insights into human preferences, motives, and perceptions from an evolutionary and cognitive perspective.[76]

Leaders operating in different political systems and temporal contexts will, of course, exhibit diverse ranges of emotional awareness and thus varying degrees of ability to regulate and control their emotions.[77] Social psychology research has found that reactions are challenging to predict because emotions are socially constructed, fluid, and constrained by situational factors. A fearful individual, for example, may fight, run, freeze, or seek additional information depending on their impulse or emotional tendencies.[78] A fear-induced deterrent effect in the nuclear deterrence literature posits that the deterrent effect of nuclear weapons is premised on non-rational fear (or "existential bias") as opposed to rational risk calculation, thus initiating an iterative learning process that enables existentialism deterrence to operate.[79] Whatever the cognitive origins of these outlooks—an area about which we still know very little—they will nonetheless fundamentally affect leaders' threat perceptions and cognitive dispositions.[80]

Actors are influenced by both motivated ("affect-driven") and unmotivated ("cognitive") biases when they judge whether the other sides pose a threat.[81] Moreover, the impact of these psychological influences is ratcheted up during times of stress and crisis, in ways that can distort an objective appreciation of threats and thus limit the potential for empathy.[82] Individuals' perceptions are heavily influenced by their beliefs about how the world functions, and the patterns, mental constructs, and predispositions that emerge from these are likely to present us.[83] Jervis writes: "the decision-maker who thinks that the other side is probably hostile *will see ambiguous information as confirming this image*, whereas the same information about a country thought to be friendly would be taken more benignly" (emphasis added).[84]

At the group level, an isolated attack by a member of the out-group is often used as a scapegoat to ascribe an "enemy image" (monolithic, evil, opportunistic, cohesive etc.) to the group as a unitary actor to incite commitment, resolve, and strength to enable retribution—referred to by anthropologists as "third-party revenge" or "vicarious retribution."[85] In international relations, these intergroup dynamics that can mischaracterize an adversary and the "enemy"—whose beliefs, images, and preferences invariably shift—risk rhetorical and arms-racing escalatory retaliatory behavior associated with the security dilemma.[86] While possessing the ability to influence intergroup dynamics (frame events, mobilize political resources, influence the public discourse, etc.), political leaders tend to be particularly susceptible to out-group threats and thus more likely to sanction retribution for an out-group attack.[87] A growing body of social psychology literature demonstrates that the emergence, endorsement, and, ultimately, the influence of political leaders depends on how they embody, represent, and affirm their group's (i.e., the in-group) ideals, values, and norms—and on contrasting (or "metacontrasting") how different these are from those of out-groups.[88]

The digital era, characterized by mis/disinformation, social media-fueled "filter bubbles" and "echo chambers"[89]—and rapidly diffused by automated social bots and hybrid cyborgs[90]—is compounding the effects of inflammatory polarizing falsehoods to support anti-establishment candidates in highly populist and partisan environments, such as the 2016 and 2020 US elections and 2016 Brexit referendum.[91] According to social identity scholars Alexander Haslam and Michael Platow, there is strong evidence to suggest that people's attraction to particular groups and their subsequent identity-affirming behavior is driven "not by personal attraction and interest, but rather by their group-level ties."[92] These group dynamics can expose decision-makers to increased "rhetorical entrapment" pressures, whereby alternative policy options (viable or otherwise) may be overlooked or rejected.[93]

Most studies suggest a curvilinear trajectory in the efficiency of making decisions during times of stress.[94] Several features of human psychology affect our ability to reason under stress.[95] First, the large amount of information available to decision-makers is generally complex and ambiguous during crises. Machine-learning algorithms are on hand in the digital age to collate, statistically correlate, parse, and analyze vast big-data sets in real-time. Second, and related, time pressures during crises place a heavy cognitive burden on individuals. Third, people working long hours with inadequate rest, and leaders enduring the immense strain of making decisions that have potentially existential implications (in the case of nuclear weapons), add additional cognitive impediments to sound judgment under pressure. Taken together, these psychological impediments can impede the ability of actors to send and receive nuanced, subtle, and complex signals to appreciate an adversary's beliefs, images, and perception of risk—critical for effective deterrence.[96]

While AI-enabled tools can improve battlefield awareness and, prima facie, afford commanders more time to deliberate, they come at strategic costs, not least accelerating the pace of warfare and compressing the decision-making timeframe available to decision-makers.[97] AI tools can also offer a potential means to reduce (or offload) people's cognitive load and thus ease crisis-induced stress, as well as people's susceptibility to things like cognitive bias, heuristics, and groupthink.[98] However, a reduction in the solicitation of wide-ranging opinions to consider alternatives is unlikely to be improved by introducing new whiz-bang technology. Thus, further narrowing the window of reflection and discussion compounds existing psychological processes that can impair effective crisis (and non-crisis) decision-making, namely, avoiding difficult tradeoffs, limited empathy to view adversaries, and misperceiving the signals that others are conveying.[99]

People's judgments rely on capacities such as reasoning, imagination, examination, reflection, social and historical context, experience, and, importantly for crises, empathy.[100] According to philosopher John Dewey, the goal of judgment is "to carry an incomplete [and uncertain] situation to its fulfillment."[101] Human judgments, and the decisions that flow from them, have an intrinsic moral and emotional dimension. Machine learning algorithms, by contrast, generate decisions after gestating datasets through an accumulation of calculus, computation, and rule-driven rationality.[102] As

AI advances, substituting human judgment for fuzzy machine logic, humans will likely cling to the illusory veneer of their ability to retain human control and agency over AIs as they develop. Thus, error-prone and flawed AI systems will continue to produce unintended consequences in fundamentally non-human ways.[103]

In the digital age, the confluence of speed, information overload, complex and tightly coupled systems (i.e., NC3), and multipolarity will likely amplify the existing propensity for people to eschew nuance and balance during crises to keep complex and dynamic situations heuristically manageable.[104] Therefore, mistaken beliefs about and images of an adversary—derived from pre-existing beliefs—may be compounded rather than corrected during a crisis. Moreover, crisis management conducted at indefatigable machine speed—compressing decision-making timeframes (see Chapter 3)—and non-human agents enmeshed in the decision-making process will mean that even if unambiguous information emerges about an adversary's intentions, time pressures will likely filter out (or restrict entirely) subtle signaling and careful deliberation of diplomacy.[105] Thus, the difficulty actors face in simultaneously signaling resolve on an issue coupled with a willingness for restraint—that is, signaling that they will hold fire for now—will be complicated exponentially by the cognitive and technical impediments of introducing non-human agents to engage in (or supplant) fundamentally human endeavors.

Furthermore, and as we saw in Chapter 2, cognitive studies suggest that the allure of precision, autonomy, speed, scale, and lethality, combined with people's predisposition to anthropomorphize, cognitive offload, and automation bias, may view AIs as a panacea for the cognitive fallibilities of human analysis and decision-making described above.[106] People's deference to machines (which preceded AI) can result from the presumption that (a) decisions result from hard empirically based science, (b) AI algorithms function at speeds and complexities beyond human capacity, or (c) because people fear being overruled or outsmarted by machines.[107] Therefore, it is easy to see why people would be inclined to view an algorithm's judgment (both to inform and make decisions) as authoritative, particularly as human decision-making and judgment and machine autonomy interface—at various points across the continuum—at each stage of the kill chain (see Figure 4.1).

Conclusion

This chapter examined the implications of Schelling's "threats that leave something to chance" theory and related insights for crisis stability between nuclear-armed rivals in the era of AI-enabling technology, contextualizing them within the broader information ecosystem. It revisited the typology associated with Schelling's theory (accidental risk, imperfect decision-making, rationality of the irrational, and brinkmanship) to consider the intersection of AI-enabling technology with nuclear weapons and the broader information ecosystem. Further, the chapter engaged with interdisciplinary human psychology, behavioral science, and anthropological studies to provide fresh perspectives and insights on the AI-nuclear dilemma.

Because of the limited empirical evidence available on nuclear escalation, threats, bluffs, and war termination, the arguments presented here about "the threat that leaves something to chance" are mostly deductive. In other words, conclusions are inferred by reference to various plausible (and contested) theoretical laws and statistical reasoning rather than empirically deduced by reason. Robust falsifiable counterfactuals (see Chapter 5) that offer imaginative scenarios to challenge conventional wisdom ("illusion of control," rationality, the role of luck), assumptions (rationality, path-dependency, over-determinism), and human bias (hindsight bias, heuristics, and availability bias) can help fill this empirical gap.[108] Counterfactual thinking can also avoid the trap of historical and diplomatic telos that retrospectively constructs a path-dependent causal chain that often neglects or rejects the role of uncertainty, chance, luck, overconfidence, the "illusion of control," and cognitive bias.[109] Lebow writes: "If the Cuban missile crisis had led to war—conventional or nuclear—historians would have constructed a causal chain leading ineluctably to this outcome."[110]

From the perspective of policymakers, robust counterfactual thinking (grounded in inconsistent and well-established empirical and theoretical generalizations) is a valuable tool to illuminate plausible scenarios involving the intersection of disruptive emerging technologies like AI and the nuclear enterprise. They challenge outmoded Cold War era theories (rational deterrence), mindsets (conflating uncertainty and risk, path-dependency), and shifting perceptions (the role of luck, randomness, accidents), thereby reducing the risk of war by accident, miscalculation, or technological surprise.[111] Moreover, AI machine learning techniques (modeling, simulation, and analysis) can complement counterfactuals and low-tech table-top wargaming simulations to identify contingencies under which "perfect storms" might form; not to predict them, but rather to challenge conventional wisdom, and highlight bias and inertia, to highlight and, ideally, mitigate these conditions.[112] American philosopher William James wrote: "Concepts, first employed to make things intelligible, are clung to often when they make them unintelligible."[113] How can counterfactual reasoning help us to think about control, chance, and uncertainty in AI-enabled warfare? The next chapter turns to this question.

Notes

1. The author would like to thank the panelists and participants of the U.S. Naval War College Deterrence Workshop (December 2021) for their comments and feedback in developing this chapter.

2. James Johnson, *AI and the Bomb: Nuclear Strategy and Risk in the Digital Age* (Oxford: Oxford University Press, 2023).

3. Thomas C. Schelling, *The Strategy of Conflict* (Cambridge, MA: Harvard University Press, 1960); Thomas C. Schelling, *Arms and Influence* (New Haven, CT: Yale University Press, 1966); Robert V. Dodge, *Schelling's Game Theory: How to Make Decisions* (New York: Oxford University Press, 2012); Reid B. C. Pauly and Rose McDermott, "The Psychology of Nuclear Brinkmanship," *International Security* 47 (3) (2023), p. 15.

4. Ibid.

5. Ibid.

6. See Robert Jervis, *The Meaning of the Nuclear Revolution* (Ithaca, NY: Cornell University Press, 1989); Pauly and McDermott, "The Psychology of Nuclear Brinkmanship," p. 15.

7. See Robert Jervis, *The Logic of Images in International Relations* (Princeton, NJ: Princeton University Press, 1970); Kenneth A. Schultz, *Democracy and Coercive Diplomacy* (Cambridge: Cambridge University Press, 2001); Jonathan Mercer, *Reputation and International Politics* (Ithaca, NY: Cornell University Press, 1996); Pauly and McDermott, "The Psychology of Nuclear Brinkmanship."

8. Pauly and McDermott, "The Psychology of Nuclear Brinkmanship," p. 21. For literature on nuclear accidents, see, for example, Scott D. Sagan, *The Limits of Safety: Organizations, Accidents, and Nuclear Weapons* (Princeton, NJ: Princeton University Press, 1993); Patricia Lewis, et al., *Too Close for Comfort: Cases of Near Nuclear Use and Options for Policy* (London: Chatham House, 2014).

9. Notable exceptions include: Andrew Futter, "Disruptive Technologies and Nuclear Risks: What's New and What Matters," *Survival* 64 (1) (2022), pp. 99–120; James Johnson, "Artificial Intelligence in Nuclear Warfare: A Perfect Storm of Instability?" *The Washington Quarterly* 43 (2) (2020) pp. 197–211; Rebecca Hersman, "Wormhole Escalation: The New Nuclear Age," *Texas National Security Review* 2 (3) (2020), pp. 91–109; Kenneth Payne, "Artificial Intelligence: A Revolution in Strategic Affairs?" *Survival* 60 (5) (2018), pp. 7–32; James Johnson, "'Catalytic Nuclear War' in the Age of Artificial Intelligence & Autonomy: Emerging Military Technology and Escalation Risk between Nuclear-Armed States," *Journal of Strategic Studies* (2021), doi:10.1080/01402390.2020.1867541; Vincent Boulanin, et al., *Artificial Intelligence, Strategic Stability and Nuclear Risk* (SIPRI Report, June 2020); and Harold Trinkunas, Herbert Lin, and Benjamin Loehrke, *Three Tweets to Midnight: Effects of the Global Information Ecosystem on the Risk of Nuclear Conflict* (Stanford, CA: Hoover Institution Press, 2020).

10. Schelling, *Arms and Influence*, p. 95.

11. James Johnson, "Delegating Strategic Decision-Making to Machines: Dr. Strangelove Redux?" *Journal of Strategic Studies*, 45 (3) (2022), pp. 439–477 doi:10.1080/01402390.2020.1759038.

12. Pauly and McDermott, "The Psychology of Nuclear Brinkmanship," pp. 14–15.

13. Ibid.

14. Ibid. According to classical deterrence theory, strategic stability is achieved when threats to use nuclear weapons are credible—that is, when neither side can eliminate the other's retaliatory capabilities—and when a second-strike retaliation imposes an unacceptable cost to each side. See Lawrence Freedman, *Deterrence* (New York: Polity, 2004); Glenn Snyder, *Deterrence and Defense* (Princeton, NJ: Princeton University Press, 1961).

15. Pauly and McDermott, "The Psychology of Nuclear Brinkmanship," p. 19; Robert Jervis, *The Illogic of American Nuclear Strategy* (Ithaca, NY: Cornell University Press, 1984), pp. 137–138.

16. Of course, a state signaling resolve may be a bluff or break down in the face of a forceful response by the other side. Jervis, *The Illogic of American Nuclear Strategy*, p. 138.

17. Ibid., p. 141.

18. Bernard Brodie, "What Price Conventional Capabilities in Europe?" *The Reporter*, May 23, 1963, p. 32.

19. Schelling, *Arms and Influence*, pp. 98–99.

20. Pauly and McDermott, "The Psychology of Nuclear Brinkmanship," p.48 Caitlin Talmadge, "Would China Go Nuclear? Assessing the Risk of Chinese Nuclear Escalation in a Conventional War with the United States," *International Security* 41 (4) (2017), pp. 50–92.

21. Robert Jervis, "Perceiving and Coping with Threat," in *Psychology and Deterrence*, ed. Janice G. Stein, Richard N. Lebow, and Robert Jervis (New York: Johns Hopkins University Press, 1985), p. 28.

22. Bill Owens, *Lifting the Fog of War* (New York: Farrar, Straus, and Giroux 2000).

23. Jervis, *The Illogic of American Nuclear Strategy*, p. 140.

24. Brodie, "What Price Conventional Capabilities in Europe?" p. 32.

25. Pauly and McDermott, "The Psychology of Nuclear Brinkmanship."

26. Ibid., p. 12.

27. Fearon, "Signaling Foreign Policy Interests," pp. 68–90.

28. Pauly and McDermott, "The Psychology of Nuclear Brinkmanship," p. 29; Ahmed Mansoor, "Pakistan's Tactical Nuclear Weapons and Their Impact on Stability," *Carnegie Endowment for International Peace*, June 30, 2016.

29. Schelling, *The Strategy of Conflict*, p. 201.

30. See Benoît Pelopidas, "The Unbearable Lightness of Luck. Three Sources of Overconfidence in the Controllability of Nuclear Crises," *European Journal of International Security* 2 (2) (2017), pp. 240–262; Blair, *The Logic of Accidental Nuclear War*; Pauly and McDermott, "The Psychology of Nuclear Brinkmanship," pp. 9–51.

31. Studies conducted using brinkmanship models to examine the impact of misperception on escalation dynamics during crises—increasing or decreasing crisis stability—are inconclusive.

32. See, for example, Len Scott and R. Gerald Hughes, *The Cuban Missile Crisis: Critical Reappraisal* (London: Routledge, 2015); David Welch, *On the Brink: Americans and Soviets Reexamine the Cuban Missile Crisis* (New York: Hill & Wang, 1989); Svetlana Savranskaya and Thomas Blanton, with Anna Melyakova (eds), "New Evidence on Tactical Nuclear Weapons—59 Days in Cuba," *National Security Archive Electronic Briefing Book*, December 11, 2013, http://nsarchive.gwu.edu/NSAEBB/NSAEBB449/; Sagan, *The Limits of Safety*; and Richard N. Lebow, *Nuclear Crisis Management: A Dangerous Illusion* (Ithaca, NY: Cornell University Press, 1987).

33. Sagan, *The Limits of Safety*, pp. 79–80.

34. Pauly and McDermott, "The Psychology of Nuclear Brinkmanship," p. 29; Charles Perrow, *Normal Accidents: Living with High-Risk Technologies* (Princeton, NJ: Princeton University Press, 1984).

35. Powell, *Nuclear Deterrence Theory*, pp. 18–24.

36. Pauly and McDermott, "The Psychology of Nuclear Brinkmanship," pp. 25–26; Glenn Snyder and Paul Diesing, *Conflict Among Nations* (Princeton, NJ: Princeton University Press, 1977), p. 210.

37. Ibid.

38. See Richard N. Lebow, *Forbidden Fruit: Counterfactuals and International Relations* (Princeton, NJ: Princeton University Press, 2010).

39. See, for example, Richard N. Lebow and Janice Stein, *We All Lost the Cold War* (Princeton, NJ: Princeton University Press, 1994); Pelopidas, "The Unbearable Lightness of Luck," pp. 240–262; and Blair, *The Logic of Accidental Nuclear War*.

40. Scholars have applied game-theoretic models to explore the assumption that an actor believes an adversary might choose to act irrationally to manipulate risk in limited retaliation situations. See Powell, *Nuclear Deterrence Theory*, pp. 148–174.

41. F. H. Hinsley, *Power and the Pursuit of Peace* (Cambridge: Cambridge University Press, 1963). p. 296.

42. Robert Powell, *Nuclear Deterrence Theory: The Search for Credibility* (Cambridge: Cambridge University Press, 1990), p. 23.

43. Ibid., p. 34.

44. Ibid., p. 33.

45. Pauly and McDermott, "The Psychology of Nuclear Brinkmanship," pp. 36–37.

46. See Stephen Maxwell, *Rationality in Deterrence* (London: International Institute for International Studies, 1968); Snyder, *Deterrence and Defense*; and Herman Kahn, *On Escalation: Metaphors and Scenarios* (New York: Harvard University Press, 1965).

47. Quoted in: Pauly and McDermott, "The Psychology of Nuclear Brinkmanship," pp. 36–37.

48. Joseph Conrad, *The Secret Agent* (New York: Double Day, Page & Company, 1923), pp. 65–68.

49. Pauly and McDermott, "The Psychology of Nuclear Brinkmanship," p. 40.

50. See, Scott D. Sagan and Jeremi Suri, "The Madman Nuclear Alert: Secrecy, Signaling, and Safety in October 1969," *International Security* 27 (4) (2003), pp. 150–183. On Trump, see James D. Boys, "The Unpredictability Factor: Nixon, Trump and the Application of the Madman Theory in US Grand Strategy," *Cambridge Review of International Affairs*, 34 (3) (2021), pp. 430–451.

51. For example, recent evidence indicates that Nixon and Kissinger did not intend for their nuclear alert targeting the Soviet Union in 1969 to be "a threat that leaves something to chance," yet the alert sparked several dangerous nuclear operations, nevertheless.

52. Samuel Seitz and Caitlin Talmadge, "The Predictable Hazards of Unpredictability: Why Madman Behavior Doesn't Work," *The Washington Quarterly* 43 (3) (2020), p. 37.

53. Sagan and Suri, "The Madman Nuclear Alert," p. 182.

54. Pauly and McDermott, "The Psychology of Nuclear Brinkmanship," p. 29.

55. See David E. Hoffman, *The Dead Hand: The Untold Story of the Cold War Arms Race and Its Dangerous Legacy* (New York: Anchor, 2009); and Johnson, "Delegating Strategic Decision-Making to Machines."

56. Schelling, *The Strategy of Conflict*, p. 197.

57. Ibid.

58. See Yitzhak Benbaji, "Legitimate Authority in War," in *The Oxford Handbook of Ethics of War*, ed. Seth Lazar and Helen Frowe (New York: Oxford University Press, 2015), pp. 294–314.

59. As a counterpoint, a threat that derives from factors external to the participants might become less of a test of wills and resolve between adversaries, thus making it less costly—in terms of reputation and status—for one side to step back from the brink. Schelling, *Arms and Influence*, pp. 121–122.

60. Quoted in: Pauly and McDermott, "The Psychology of Nuclear Brinkmanship," p. 32.

61. Jervis, *The Illogic of American Nuclear Strategy*, pp. 138–139.

62. Pauly and McDermott, "The Psychology of Nuclear Brinkmanship," pp. 30–31.

63. Jervis, "Hypotheses on Misperception," pp. 454–479.

64. Pauly and McDermott, p. 10.

65. Quoted in: ibid, p. p. 33.

66. Quoted in: ibid., p. 35.

67. Ibid., pp. 34–35.

68. Snyder, *Deterrence and Defense*; Frank C. Zagare, "Reconciling Rationality with Deterrence: A Re-Examination of the Logical Foundations of Deterrence Theory," *Journal of Theoretical Politics* 16 (2) (2004), pp. 107–141; and Richard N. Lebow, "Rational Deterrence Theory: I Think Therefore I Deter," *World Politics* 41 (2) (1989), pp. 208–224.

69. Patrick M. Morgan, "Saving Face for the Sake of Deterrence," in *Psychology and Deterrence*, in *Psychology and Deterrence*, ed. Janice G. Stein, Richard N. Lebow, and Robert Jervis (New York: Johns Hopkins University Press, 1985), p. 125.

70. Pauly and McDermott, "The Psychology of Nuclear Brinkmanship," p. 13.

71. See John Tooby and Leda Cosmides, "Groups in Mind: The Coalitional Roots of War and Morality," in *Human Morality and Sociality: Evolutionary and Comparative Perspectives*, ed. Henrik Hogh-Olesen (New York: Palgrave Macmillan, 2010); Anthony C. Lopez, Rose McDermott, and Michael Bang Petersen, "States in Mind: Evolution, Coalitional Psychology, and International Politics," *International Security* 36 (2) (Fall 2011), pp. 48–83; Melissa M. McDonald, Carlos David Navarrete, and Mark Van Vugt, "Evolution and the Psychology of Intergroup Conflict: The Male Warrior Hypothesis," *Philosophical Transactions of the Royal Society B* 367 (1589) (January 2012), pp. 670–679; M. B. Petersen and L. Aaroe, "Is the Political Animal Politically Ignorant? Applying Evolutionary Psychology to the Study of Political Attitudes," *Evolutionary Psychology* 10 (5) (December 2012).

72. See Janice J. Gross, "Emotion Regulation: Affective, Cognitive, and Social Consequences," *Psychophysiology* 39 (3) (2002), pp. 281–291; Corinna Carmen, et al. "Overcoming Psychological Barriers to Peaceful Conflict Resolution: The Role of Arguments about Losses," *Journal of Conflict Resolution* 53 (6) (2009), pp. 951–975; Pranjal H. Mehta, A. C. Jones, and R. A. Josephs, "The Social Endocrinology of Dominance: Basal Testosterone Predicts Cortisol Changes and Behavior Following Victory and Defeat," *Journal of Personality and Social Psychology* 94 (6) (2008), pp. 1078–1093; and Brian A. Gladue, Michael Boechler, and Kevin D. McCaul, "Hormonal Response to Competition in Human Males," *Aggressive Behavior* 15 (6) (1989), pp. 409–422.

73. Schelling, *The Strategy of Conflict*.

74. Like previous studies, women, older people, and those with more subject knowledge perceive the risk more negatively. Yuko Ikkatai, et al., "Octagon Measurement: Public Attitudes toward AI Ethics," *International Journal of Human-Computer Interaction*, doi:10.1080/10447318.2021.2009669.

75. See Futter, "Disruptive Technologies and Nuclear Risks," pp. 99–120; Johnson, "Artificial Intelligence in Nuclear Warfare," pp. 197–211; and Michael C. Horowitz, "When Speed Kills: Lethal Autonomous Weapon Systems, Deterrence, and Stability," *Journal of Strategic Studies* 42 (6) (2019), pp. 764–788.

76. Rose McDermott, Anthony C. Lopez, and Peter K. Hatemi, "'Blunt Not the Heart, Enrage It': The Psychology of Revenge and Deterrence," Texas National Security Review 1 (1) (2017), p. 88.

77. See Jennifer S. Lerner and Dacher Keltner, "Fear, Anger, and Risk," *Journal of Personality and Social Psychology* 81 (1) (2001), pp. 146–159.

78. Diane Mackie, Thierry Devos, and Eliot Smith, "Intergroup Emotions: Explaining Offensive Action Tendencies in an Intergroup Context," *Journal of Personality and Social Psychology* 79 (4) (2000), pp. 602–616.

79. James Lebovic, *Deadly Dilemmas: Deterrence in US Nuclear Strategy* (New York: Columbia University Press, 1990).

80. See Robert Putnam, *Beliefs of Politicians* (New Haven: Yale University Press, 1973).

81. See, for example, Amos Tversky and Daniel Kahneman, "Availability: A Heuristic for Judging Frequency and Probability," *Cognitive Psychology* 5 (2) (1973), pp. 207–232; Baruch Fischhoff, Paul Slovic, and Sarah Lichtenstein, "Knowing with Certainty the Appropriateness of Extreme Confidence," *Journal of Experimental Psychology: Human Perception and Performance* 3 (4), (1977), pp. 562–563; Jervis, "Hypotheses on Misperception," pp. 454–479; Keith L. Shimko, *Images and Arms Control: Perceptions of the Soviet Union in the Reagan Administration* (Ann Arbor: University of Michigan Press, 1992); and Johnson, *Overconfidence and War*.

82. For example, during the 1973 war, US and Israeli perceptions of Egyptian and Syrian military strength, influenced by misperceptions of Arab military weakness and goals, led to misjudged military and diplomatic choices. Alexander George and Richard Smoke, *Deterrence in American Foreign Policy: Theory and Practice* (New York: Columbia University Press, 1974).

83. Jervis, *Perception and Misperception*, pp. 143–202.

84. Jervis, "Perceiving and Coping with Threat," p. 18.

85. Shimko, *Images and Arms Control*; and Willa Michener, "The Individual Psychology of Group Hate," *Journal of Hate Studies* 10 (1) (2012), pp. 15–48.

86. Robert Jervis, "Cooperation under the Security Dilemma," *World Politics* 30 (2) (1978), pp. 169–214.

87. Michael A. Hogg, "A Social Identity Theory of Leadership," *Personality and Social Psychology Review* 5 (3) (2001), pp. 184–200.

88. Michael A. Hogg, Sarah C. Hains, and Isabel Mason, "Identification and Leadership in Small Groups: Salience, Frame of Reference, and Leader Stereotypicality Effects on Leader Evaluations," *Journal of Personality and Social Psychology* 75 (1998), pp. 1248–1263.

89. "Filter bubbles" and "echo chambers" are often cited as central drivers of political polarization and societal fragmentation. Both terms are based on the notion that people are

excluded from information different from what they already believe; they can also refer to a partisan divide in ideological camps. See Judith Moller, "Filter Bubbles and Digital Echo Chambers," in *The Routledge Companion to Media Disinformation and Populism*, ed. Howard Tumber and Silvio Waisbord (London: Routledge, 2021), pp. 92–101.

90. Recent studies demonstrate that social bots play a disproportionate role in spreading disinformation from low-credibility sources; bots amplify these sources in the early dissemination stages *before* the information goes viral. See Chengcheng Shao, et al., "The Spread of Low-Credibility Content by Social Bots," *Nature Communications* 9 (4787) (2018), pp. 1–8.

91. Camille Francois and Herb Lin, "The Strategic Surprise of Russian Information Operations on Social Media in 2016 in the United States: Mapping a Blind Spot," *Journal of Cyber Policy* 6 (1) (2021), pp. 9–30; Glenda Cooper, "Populist Rhetoric and Media Misinformation in the 2016 UK Brexit Referendum," in *The Routledge Companion to Media Disinformation and Populism*, ed. Howard Tumber and Silvio Waisbord (London: Routledge, 2021), pp. 397–411.

92. Alexander Haslam, Stephen Reicher, and Michael Paltow, *The New Psychology of Leadership: Influence, Identity, and Power* (Hove: Psychology Press, 2010), p. 49.

93. Frank Schimmelfennig "The Community Trap: Liberal Norms, Rhetorical Action, and the Eastern Enlargement of the European Union," *International Organization* 55 (1) (2001), pp. 47–80; John Postill, "Populism and Social Media: A Global Perspective," *Media, Culture & Society* 40 (5) (July 2018), pp. 754–765; and Sven Engesser, et al., "Populism and Social Media: How Politicians Spread a Fragmented Ideology," *Information, Communication and Society* 20 (8) (August 2017), pp. 1109–1126.

94. Robert Jervis, *How Statesmen Think: The Psychology of International Politics* (Princeton, NJ: Princeton University Press, 2017), p. 219.

95. Ibid., p. 220.

96. Partick M. Morgan, *Deterrence Now* (Cambridge: Cambridge University Press, 2003).

97. Jervis, *How Statesmen Think*, p. 220.

98. Amos Tversky and Daniel Kahneman, "Judgement under Uncertainty: Heuristics and Biases," *Science*, 185 (27) (1974), pp. 1124–1131.

99. Jervis, *How Statesmen Think*, p. 220.

100. Christine Moser, Frank den Hond, and Dirk Lindenbaum, "Morality in the Age of Artificially Intelligent Algorithms," *Academy of Management Learning & Education* (April 7, 2021), https://journals.aom.org.

101. John Dewey, *Essays in Experimental Logic* (Chicago, IL: University of Chicago Press, 1916), p. 362.

102. Brian C. Smith, *The Promise of Artificial Intelligence: Reckoning and Judgment* (Cambridge, MA: MIT Press, 2019).

103. John MacCormick, *Nine Algorithms That Changed the Future* (Princeton, NJ: Princeton University Press, 2012); Michael Horowitz and Erik Lin-Greenberg, "Algorithms and Influence Artificial Intelligence and Crisis Decision-Making," *International Studies Quarterly* 66 (4) (2022) pp. 1–11.

104. Snyder and Diesing, *Conflict Among Nations*, pp. 389–405; and James Johnson, "Inadvertent Escalation in the Age of Intelligence Machines: A New Model for Nuclear Risk in the Digital Age," *European Journal of International Security* 7 (3) (2022), doi:10.1017/eis.2021.23.

105. Jervis, *How Statesmen Think*, pp. 220–221.

106. The source of overtrust and automation bias might also be a machine's (real or perceived) capability, regardless of anthropomorphism. See David Watson, "The Rhetoric and Reality of Anthropomorphism in Artificial Intelligence," *Minds and Machines* 29 (2019), pp. 417–440; Linda J. Skitka, Kathleen L. Mosier, and Mark Burdick, "Does Automation Bias Decision-Making?" *International Journal of Human-Computer Studies* 51 (5) (1999), pp. 991–1006; Ewart J. de Visser, et al., "Almost Human: Anthropomorphism Increases Trust Resilience in Cognitive Agents," *Journal of Experiential Psychology Applied* 22 (3) (2016), pp. 331–349.

107. Lonnie Shekhtman, "Why Do People Trust Robot Rescuers More Than Humans?" *Christian Science Monitor*, March 1, 2016, www.csmonitor.com/Science/2016/0301/Why-do-people-trust-robot-rescuers-more-than-humans.

108. See, for example, Philip E. Tetlock and Aaron Belkin (eds), *Counterfactual Thought Experiments in World Politics* (Princeton, NJ: Princeton University Press, 1996); Jenny Andersson, *The Future of the World: Futurology, Futurists, and the Struggle for the Post-Cold War Imagination* (Oxford: Oxford University Press, 2018); Matthew Connelly, et al., "'General, I Have Fought Just as Many Nuclear Wars as You Have': Forecasts, Future Scenarios, and the Politics of Armageddon," *American History Review* 117 (5) (2012), pp. 1431–1460; and Richard Ned Lebow and Janice Stein, *We All Lost the Cold War* (Princeton, NJ: Princeton University Press, 1994).

109. Pelopidas, "The Unbearable Lightness of Luck," p. 252.

110. Richard Ned Lebow, "Counterfactuals and Security Studies," *Security Studies* 24 (3) (2015), p. 406.

111. James Johnson, "Counterfactual Thinking & Nuclear Risk in the Digital Age: The Role of Uncertainty, Complexity, Chance, and Human Psychology," *Journal for Peace and Nuclear Disarmament* 5 (2) (2022), pp. 394–421, doi:10.1080/25751654.2022.2102286.

112. Paul K. Davis and Paul Bracken, "Artificial Intelligence for Wargaming and Modeling," *Journal of Defense Modeling and Simulation* (2022), https://doi.org/10.1177/15485129211073126.

113. William James, "The Compounding of Consciousness," in *The Writings of William James: A Comprehensive Edition*, ed. J. J. McDermott (Chicago, IL: University of Chicago Press, 1977), p. 560. (Original work published in 1909).

5

Thinking forward with counterfactuals

Will emerging technology increase the risk of nuclear war? Because of the multitude of ways disruptive emerging technologies (DETs)[1] like AI intersect with nuclear weapons—and the broader "nuclear deterrence architecture"[2]—critical thinking about an imagined future that goes beyond net assessment, myopic mirror-imaging, and extrapolation of present trends should be a core task of policymakers.[3] This chapter builds on the notion of "future counterfactuals" to construct imaginative yet realistic scenarios to consider the future possibility of a nuclear exchange. It highlights the critical role counterfactual scenarios can play in challenging conventional wisdom about nuclear weapons, risk analysis, war-fighting, and linear thinking.[4]

For most defense planners and policymakers, the prospect of a nuclear war has become a political-strategic exercise in denial and complacency, driven by an inflated sense of confidence in the ability to control nuclear escalation and nuclear weapons, and understating the role of luck in preventing nuclear detonation—often treating luck, similar to uncertainty, as unquantifiable and thus negligible.[5] In short, there are several practical inconsistencies and epistemic inconsistencies in the current intellectual milieu, which are creating poor intellectual habits that will have real-world and potentially destabilizing consequences in present and future strategic planning. This attitude has meant that efforts to prevent nuclear war are frequently reduced to abstract technical-capabilities solutions, for example, the modernization of nuclear forces and the pursuit of advanced strategic non-nuclear weapons associated with the "Third Nuclear Age."[6] This is in lock-step with the continued affirmation of the logic of rational-based deterrence and, in the case of the US, the goal of nuclear superiority to guide war planning and disarmament and arms control proposals.[7] Put differently, these new whiz-bang technologies do not exist in a vacuum.[8] Instead, to avoid obfuscation, the impact of DETs on nuclear risk needs to be considered in the broader geopolitical, domestic-political, ethical, and psychological context into which they have been supplanted.[9]

The dichotomy between the nuclear deniers and proponents of rational deterrence can in part be explained, inter alia, by: (a) the unprecedented

The AI Commander. James Johnson, Oxford University Press. © James Johnson (2024).
DOI: 10.1093/oso/9780198892182.003.0006

nature of the ultimate weapon[10]; (b) limited empirical data to inform strategic planners and policymakers; (c) ideology, vested interests, and "self-censorship"[11]; (d) the psychological preferences of policymakers[12]; and (e) the existential fear, taboos, and popular cultural associations with the possibility of existential thermonuclear war.[13] An additional variance in debates about the use of nuclear weapons is those who implicitly view some limited use of nuclear weapons as politically acceptable. In contrast, others view nuclear detonation as unacceptable and thus the notion of "nuclear strategy" as oxymoronic.[14] Nuclear studies, like security and strategic studies more broadly, are, therefore, imbued with analytical, normative, and epistemological assumptions and inconsistencies that scholars often overlook.[15] As William James mused: "Concepts, first employed to make things intelligible, are clung to often when they make them unintelligible."[16]

Exposing and challenging these assumptions and the prevailing wisdom about the control and manageability of nuclear risk is an area ripe for the engagement with imaginative "counterfactual" analysis.[17] According to Richard Lebow, counterfactuals "allow for the construction of rational templates that are used to assess the behavior of real-world actors."[18] Because counterfactuals can illuminate otherwise epistemically and empirically inaccessible (both temporally and spatially) perspectives, they are an essential tool for scholars to formulate theories and test hypotheses.

Empirically and theoretically rigorous counterfactuals can be used, for instance, to re-examine the history of nuclear "close-calls"[19] and accidents to expose the "illusion of control" (i.e., overconfidence in the ability to direct events),[20] perceiving the past over-deterministically, and the focus of this chapter, the possibility of future nuclear use. While future scenarios are a critical feature of defense planning and the basis for arms control, disarmament, and broader non-proliferation efforts, they rarely go beyond mere extrapolation of current capabilities and technological determinism.[21]

Scholars need, therefore, to use counterfactual scenarios in more imaginative ways that engage the policymaking community to influence perceptions and perhaps behavior. Like Herman Kahn's objective in writing *On Thermonuclear War* in 1960, the goal of counterfactual thinking is to build on the consensus that exists on "what we are trying to avoid" and buy more time.[22] This chapter contributes to the, albeit limited, literature that considers the use of counterfactual analysis to elucidate the past, present, and particularly the future possibility of nuclear war.[23] It builds on Steven Webber's notion of "future counterfactuals" to construct imaginative yet realistic scenarios to consider the future possibility of a nuclear exchange. It highlights the critical role counterfactual scenarios can play in challenging conventional wisdom about nuclear weapons, risk analysis, war-fighting, and linear thinking.

Why are counterfactuals helpful analytical tools to view world politics? How can we optimize counterfactual reasoning to consider nuclear risk in the digital age? This framing of the problem highlights the critical role counterfactual scenarios can play in shaping perceptions and informing policy choices. In this way, the chapter contributes to our understanding of how thinking about the future—as much as policymakers' imagined past— is a critical function of nuclear war planning. In emphasizing the role of uncertainty, motivated and unmotivated cognitive bias (i.e., affect-driven versus purely cognitive), and fundamental uncertainty in world politics, the chapter also contributes to the literature that considers the growing risk of inadvertent and accidental nuclear war.[24]

The chapter is organized into three sections. The first describes why counterfactual scenario planning should be a core function of crisis decision-making and war planning. In addition to lessons of the past and other analogies (often with questionable accuracy or relevance), imaginative critical thinking about the future with counterfactuals—which goes beyond net-assessment, mirror-imaging, and worst-case-scenarios extrapolation of present trends—is a powerful tool to challenge assumptions and expose bias and weaknesses in the ways we frame empirical and theoretical research questions about the possibility of inadvertent and accidental nuclear war. How can counterfactual scenarios liberate policymakers from overconfidence, challenge assumptions, and expose bias?

Section two applies Weber's notions of a "counterfactual history of the future" to consider how we can best think about imagined futures—in contrast to conventional backward-looking counterfactual reasoning. It illuminates the choices policymakers face about the tradeoffs associated with the intersection of DETs with nuclear weapons during times of intense strategic competition, uncertainty, complexity, and mis-disinformation associated with today's emerging "information ecosystem" (social media, mobile communications, personal information feeds, and massive amounts of data from which people's interests and desires can be curated), which is characterized by the speed, volume, and scale of communications in orders of magnitude greater than in the past.[25] What criteria and processes can we use in counterfactual scenario planning to support this goal?

Section three unpacks Tetlock and Belkin's criteria to construct the "ideal-type"[26] of scenarios for the purpose of crafting policy to account for future contingencies involving DETs and nuclear weapons. What might drive a particular situation or decision? What other factors might also affect this process? How far back into the "causes behind the causes" should we go in a scenario? This section highlights the differences between the future and past use of counterfactuals to shift our perceptions of possible futures, and establishes a robust (i.e., falsifiable, realistic, and plausible) analytical framework to consider future contingencies involving emerging technology and nuclear weapons.

Plausible future worlds

Counterfactual scenario planning is a core function of crisis decision-making and war planning. Defense planners think counterfactually to construct scenarios about the potential impact of their policy choices and then retrospectively build "plausible worlds"—maximally specific descriptions of the ways things could exist in the world which are consistent with the laws of logic and abstract rules, and thus avoid the paradox of material implication— to consider what could have happened if they or their adversaries adopted alternatives. This analysis, however, rarely goes beyond extrapolating from present trends and mirror-imaging.[27] For example, the Cuban Missile Crisis became a subject of keen counterfactual investigation amongst scholars and policymakers debating the importance of critical decisions made during this crucial infection point in Cold War history.[28]

What other actors (adversaries and allies) think about the future will fundamentally determine the shape of their policy choices and thus crucially affect nuclear war planning, arms control, disarmament, and strategic stability dialogue proposals. Empirically and theoretically robust future counterfactual scenarios described in this chapter can illuminate fallacies such as "control" and inevitability,[29] the role of luck, and overconfidence as counterpoints to the conventional wisdom that denies (or underestimates) the past, present, and the possibility of nuclear war.[30] Decision-makers also often suffer from overconfidence in ways that risk escalating a crisis (see Chapter 4), which the scenarios in the final section illustrate.[31]

More broadly, political scientists (and by extension social science scholars) often fail to accurately anticipate the non-linear dynamics that can harbinger Schumpeterian-type (theory of "creative destruction") technological change.[32] Until AI machine-learning algorithms can reliably supplant human predictive frailties in foreseeing the uncertainty associated with DETs (or AI "superintelligence"),[33] counterfactuals are helpful tools to elucidate these processes. Regardless of whether and when we can move beyond (or even agree on) the abstract in developing self-learning AI systems (especially unsupervised reinforcement deep-learning) that have predictive models capable of understanding their external physical environment and developing the requisite "theory of the mind" to interact with humans, creative counterfactuals can encourage responsiveness to uncertainty and technological surprise.

Emancipation from the "official future"

When we apply counterfactual scenarios to illuminate situations, consider non-linear change, and challenge conventional wisdom, what are we doing? How might counterfactual scenarios liberate policymakers from overconfidence in their control of events and inevitability, challenge their assumptions, and expose bias? And, if they can support this goal, how can they be optimized? Counterfactuals can help scholars interested in the intersection of technological change, nuclear risk, and world politics more generally to consider possibilities—seemingly remote or improbable alternative futures—and potentialities, thus reducing the degree of surprise and unpreparedness associated with change. This focus will also enable policymakers to recognize, respond to, and pre-empt technological inflection (or "bifurcation") points (e.g., next-generation algorithmic iterations or an adversary's operational concept) more effectively. When is the inflection occurring, by whom, and to what end, and what are the tradeoffs involved?

More fundamentally, counterfactuals can act as an effective defense against people's propensity for "hindsight bias"—elevating the probability of events once they have occurred and perceiving the past over-deterministically—which can lead to overconfidence and path-dependent technological deterministic mindsets.[34] Hindsight bias can also be viewed as a psychological coping mechanism for fundamental uncertainty, leading policymakers to overstate experts' confidence in the predictability of crises, accidents, and disruptive shocks (e.g., technological surprise, nuclear accidents, cyber supply-chain attacks, and foreign crises).[35] Moreover, this propensity is compounded by belief systems that allow people to remain unduly confident in the ability to predict a future marked by continuity and thus controllability—despite empirical evidence of discontinuities, shocks, and disruption in world politics that experts were unable to either predict or control.[36] The proclivity of people to assume that the future will closely map the past can produce oversimplified, overgeneralized, and overdetermined insights from events.[37] In short, most people see the future as open and unpredictable, but the past as overdetermined. If, for example, we could have asked people in 1913 about the likelihood of averting what became known as World War I, we would have received very different responses than asking this question in 2022.

A good case in point is the attachment of policymakers and scholars alike to the notion that "rational-based deterrence"[38] secured by the existential threat of nuclear war—grounded in the logic of mutually assured destruction (MAD)—will continue to ensure policymakers' (psychological and political) need for certainty and continuity in the ability to control nuclear weapons and thus prevent deterrence failure.[39] To be sure, the fact that policymakers think their deterrence policies will succeed most of the time can lead to complacency that reinforces the "illusion of control"—allowing adversaries to manipulate and take advantage of this delusion.[40] Empirical evidence from the Cold War era, however, paints a picture of repeated deterrence failure (i.e., deterrence failed to prevent the risks and situations it was designed to), nuclear "close-calls" (e.g., the Cuban Missile Crisis),[41] and tautological justification for a policy that was essentially the product of counterfactual reasoning.[42]

Counterfactuals are, therefore, valuable learning tools to challenge prevailing psychological bias (more on this below), enabling scholars to anticipate events and risks that in hindsight appear obvious, overdetermined, or at least highly probable. Why, for example, did we fail to predict the collapse of the Soviet Union and the end of the Cold War? Despite several possible antecedents (e.g., declining productivity and birth rates), connecting principles (with well-established facts), and consistency of these principles with an established theory (see explanation below) to form a relatively high confidence forecast, the exponents of future counterfactuals at the time failed to dislodge the prevailing "official future"—that is, a set of assumptions, biases, and perceived wisdom around which most bureaucratic deliberation and decision-making takes place.[43] In this way, counterfactuals differ from the more traditional retrospective-centric theory-testing used by international relations (IR) scholars—for example, policy-centric theories like the balance of power advanced by structural-realist IR scholars Stephen Walt and Kenneth Waltz et al.[44]

In a world of growing complexity, automation, and information overload, filtered through human cognitive bias—and then funneled through and distorted by social media-fueled filter bubbles and echo chambers—policymakers can use counterfactuals to play devil's advocate to objectively scrutinize both popular and unpopular hypotheses, which is "an essential ingredient of a good detective, whether the end is the solution of a crime or an intelligence estimate."[45] Policymakers and political scientists are often taken by surprise and under/overestimate the impact in the event of techno-logical change, in part because of a failure of divergent thinking—a tendency to not accord insufficient importance to the variety of possible futures that might yet occur, as well as possible pasts that could have been.[46] Most crises and conflicts come as a surprise, but in retrospect appear entirely predictable. Many predicted that chemical weapons would instantly and dramatically change the nature of warfare and deterrence after the British used poison gas during World War I. However, chemical weapons proved far less practical, impactful, disruptive, and relatively easy to defend against than conventional explosives.[47] More recently, US "network-centric warfare" did not prove to be the game-changing strategic innovation predicted by many military thinkers at the turn of the millennium.[48]

Counterfactual scenarios can become tools of persuasion for decision-makers to contemplate one path over another, hedge against a latent (or improbable) risk, side-step technological determinism, and use heuristic thinking (anchoring, availability, and representativeness),[49] thus reducing false positives and negatives—that is, perceiving risk where none exists and missing signs of possible risk for lack of looking. Decision-making that takes place in a complex, non-linear, and possibilist world—where the tape of history only runs once—should persuade decision-makers of the value of counterfactual scenario planning to consider multiple plausible alternative scenarios of how past events and decisions might have otherwise occurred, and how future events might play out.[50] Furthermore, in domains where there is a paucity of empirical materials to satisfy basic epistemological criteria (i.e., nuclear war), prudence of this kind to manage risk and hedge against low-probability events, where one failure is uniquely intolerable (e.g., accidental nuclear detonation), becomes a critical task.[51]

The creative thinking from counterfactuals can also reduce cognitive bias (discussed below) and misaligned perceptions associated, for instance, with notions of risk and control. Henry Kissinger described a proclivity of academics to believe in the notion of a "controllable world," causing deterministic reasoning that circumscribed policymakers' agency to influence events.[52] Kissinger's worldview gave prominence to the influence of individuals who could—through persuasion, inducements, and cajoling—be persuaded to change their minds. In turn, changes to perceptions can focus decision-makers' minds, thus enabling them to create greater distance from often self-imposed (primarily structural, epistemological, and social-psychological) constraints, better anticipate non-linear change, and, in turn, judge and respond to events with greater freedom and flexibility. As cognitive scientist Daniel Kahneman observed, counterfactuals can be powerful tools of persuasion and surprise by exposing hitherto unacknowledged tensions between explicit conscious beliefs and values and implicit, unconscious biases (e.g., hindsight bias and heuristics), double standards, contradictions, and assumptions (see below).[53]

Consequently, the efficacy of counterfactuals is a measure more than a function of their ability to alter perceptions (through theory, ideas, and debate) and ultimately behavior, rather than whether they can predict the future.[54] As scholar Philip Tetlock notes, it is easy to appear correct for the wrong reasons, particularly when you have multiple alternative histories to hand.[55] A better post-mortem would include questions like: What did the scenario over/underestimate, miss out, or miscalculate, and why? Were the results surprising, and if so, for whom, and why did they expect a contrarian result?

Counterfactual history of the future

How different are counterfactual reasonings about the past compared to the future? [56] Political scientist Steven Weber coined the term "counterfactual history of the future" to capture the notion that well-conceived future counterfactual scenarios share many similarities with traditional "counterfactual histories of the past."[57] In this view, a counterfactual scenario is a question of where one temporally places an event (i.e., the counterfactual) at = T in relation to the past (i.e., what occurred) and the present. The underlying premise is that once one inserts a counterfactual into a historical sequence of events, the scenarios begin from that point along the timeline (see Figure 5.1). Put differently, at = T what has occurred ends, and the imaginary plot becomes

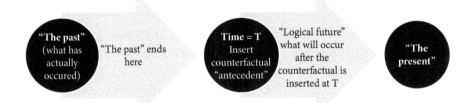

Figure 5.1 "Counterfactual history of the future"

Source: James Johnson, "Counterfactual Thinking & Nuclear Risk in the Digital Age: The Role of Uncertainty, Complexity, Chance, and Human Psychology," *Journal for Peace and Nuclear Disarmament* (2022), p. 8, doi: 10.1080/25751654.2022.2102286.

the "logical future" (i.e., what occurs once the counterfactual is inserted). Viewed this way, all (past and future) counterfactuals can be considered *histories of the future*, even if they are inserted in what we would think of as past "calendar time."[58]

Regardless of where we situate the counterfactual that did not occur along the time continuum to the present day, it is about a possible fictional "future" that we can logically extend to and beyond the present. While "future counterfactuals" are an oxymoron, Weber's concept nevertheless proposes an interesting exercise that consists of exploring alternative outcomes to future scenarios where those designing or elaborating them *think they can predict the likely outcome*, or range of possible outcomes. In sum: whereas past counterfactuals consider imaginary changes of the past (antecedents) linked through a chain of logic to a different present (consequent), future scenarios confront a fictional world with a greater range scope of imagined futures— or "fictional intelligence."[59] The empirical implications of this distinction are discussed below.

A natural objection raised about this approach—in contrast to backward-looking counterfactual reasoning—is that while the past contains a limited dataset to work off (i.e., the past is constrained by what we know happened), future permutations and combinations are, by definition, infinite. This objection can be addressed in three ways. First, establishing valid and tested theories or sets of criteria (i.e., "generalizability") that increase the confidence in the internal consistency (or "contestability") of an imaginary dataset of the future. Second, scenarios should be chosen that exist within the perimeters of current scientific reality; they are *intelligent fiction*, not science fiction (see Conclusion). That is, new insights, models, and paradigm shifts fit in the Kuhnian "normal science" framework (or "Kuhn cycle") governed by established generalizations and—causal, physical, and logical—laws.[60] Third, when using counterfactuals to think forward, we must ensure that most of the observable implications (or "antecedents") that occur in our scenario planning are predetermined (i.e., already exist or are expected to shortly). DETs such as AI technology, robotics, quantum technology, and cyberspace, for instance, fulfill this criterion.[61]

In framing the emerging technological problem in this way, we can avoid technological determinism and consider alternative outcomes that illuminate the choices policymakers face today about the tradeoffs associated with DETs, enabling them to hedge against unforeseen risk, improbable and unanticipated opportunities, and surprise. This analytical latitude and creative thinking are critical features of effective scenario planning, particularly during conditions of uncertainty, information overload, mis-disinformation, and great power strategic competition associated with today's emerging information ecosystem.

Should we necessarily have greater confidence in the more constrained retrodiction of counterfactual reasoning of the past? While it is axiomatic that social scientists' confidence in their retrodictions of past events is higher than for future predictions, future uncertainty (i.e., infinite possible antecedents and consequences) can inculcate humility and reduce hubristic tendencies in our confidence of what we think we understand about the past. Because of the extraordinary complexity and ambiguity in devising plausible and falsifiable historical counterfactuals in IR, the potential is increased for randomly distributed minor causes (akin to "chaos theory") to be unduly amplified to explain more significant outcomes.[62]

This psychologically bounded condition can mean that counterfactuals to view the past break down in the face of low-probability and low-frequency events such as technological surprise and nuclear war (see below).[63] To avoid this fate, the chapter aims to strike a balance between parsimony (a single cause, future, or monotonic counterfactuals), and, at the other extreme, the "all other things being equal" (a carte blanche to advance one's preferred causes and conditions). A failure to strike a proper balance between these two extremes risks hampering our ability to consider the role of luck, contingency, cognitive bias, and fundamental uncertainty in world politics. Reflection on these issues by policymakers who craft strategy, military doctrine, and operational concepts in the burgeoning information ecosystem is now a critical task.

Distinguishing scholarship from snake oil

Counterfactuals that foster creative thinking and encourage open minds—that challenge the "official future"—force policymakers to consider uncomfortable discontinuities (or "plausible" or "realistic" futures), which may run contrary to the political and social Zeitgeist or prevailing theoretical canon.[64] What criterion and processes should we apply to counterfactual scenario planning to support this goal? What follows is a description of the various criteria, methods, and processes that we can apply to counterfactual scenario planning to think about the future contingencies involving DETs and nuclear weapons.[65] The goal here is to yield "lawlike" generalizations, rather than scientific proof or Bayesian statistical confidence intervals, that foster creative thinking and open the minds of policymakers to consider apparent discontinuities from existing theories and assumptions.[66]

At this point, a caveat is in order. Oscillation exists amongst scholars about which criteria are most relevant (or irrelevant), conflicting or contradictory standards, and those that denounce the counterfactual project as epistemically and ontologically impossible. These criteria are all open to interpretation, and to date no cookie-cutter universally accepted method of the counterfactual argument exists to apply to all situations and issues in world politics.[67] These standards and processes represent an effort to establish compelling (or "ideal-type") counterfactual scenarios that command cross-disciplinary support and contribute to the broad social science academic goals of logical consistency, falsifiability, parsimony, and have testable explanations—thus avoiding the fate of counterfactual critics, taking their cue from historian E. H. Carr, who argues that counterfactuals are arbitrary, speculative, self-serving, and non-falsifiable,[68] and avoiding scholars from rival cross-disciplinary schools talking past each other and at cross purposes. An attempt to map these attributes to construct robust future counterfactuals for scenario planning follows.

Future counterfactual building blocks

This section adapts Tetlock and Belkin's "best practice" criteria to distinguish the plausible from the implausible, and insightful from wildly speculative counterfactuals to construct the "ideal-type"[69] of scenarios for the purpose of future scenario planning.[70] Like most theoretical and ideological approaches, counterfactuals invariably lie at various points along the plausibility continuum (or Bayesian "subjective probability"). Because of this non-bifurcation, advancing "ideal" standards and processes for determining the utility of considering possible futures is a critical methodological exercise.

Specified antecedents and consequences and logical consistency between them

Like scientific experiments, counterfactuals should be designed to isolate pathways to a predetermined outcome (or dependent variable) and should manipulate one cause (or independent variable) at a time. According to scholar Robert Jervis, in social systems (or "system theory argument") like world politics, it is impossible to hold "all other things being equal" when engaging in counterfactual scenarios, without generating ripple effects— value-basis of other potential causes in the interconnected historical matrix of interactions and complex social networks.[71] For example, testing (with a comparative method) the deterrence theoretical notion of situations resembling a "game of chicken"[72]—where an actor increases their chances of prevailing by signaling resolve to the other side—in which all the variables, bar one, are either the same or randomized is empirically problematic given the interconnections between them. As ecologist Garrett Hardin opined, "we can never do merely one thing."[73]

Unlike scientific experiments, however, counterfactual scenarios should not be too tightly wedded monotonically to independent and dependent variables; for example, if event X led to a nuclear detonation, then if X did not exist, the detonation would not have occurred. As a corollary, counterfactuals should not assume that one specific event or condition in the past (or future) can be altered and keep everything else constant (or "surgical counterfactuals").[74] In other words, a moderate degree of specificity should be used in the construction of plausible scenarios, rather than imposing an unworldly rigidity and unambiguity on the relationship between antecedents and consequences.

As counterfactual skeptics rightly assert, manipulating antecedents that are so deeply embedded in a recursive system of a complex and interconnected "causal web" is misleading.[75] There is, to be sure, a long philosophical, epistemological, and metaphysical debate—going back to David Hume and Immanuel Kant's "First Critique"—about the nature of causation as an interpretative concept and method.[76] The human brain cannot comprehend "all" other things, even if we know what they are. Moreover, in thinking forward with counterfactuals, this limitation is in even sharper focus than backward-thinking scenarios.[77] The premise that "if cause X took on a different value, then Y occurs," for instance, does not pay due attention to the causal interconnectedness in complex social-political systems.[78] Critics of structural-realist scholar John Mearsheimer, for instance, argue that Mearsheimer's view that "*ceteris paribus*, war is more likely in a multipolar system than a bipolar one" glosses over the problem of what else would have to be different in a counterfactual post-World War II system in which multipolarity prevailed. For example, the effect of a third power such as the UK, France, or China on the polarity dynamics.[79]

The logical consistency between the antecedent and consequence will depend on the scholarly consensus or shared faith—influenced in part by the prevailing IR theoretical canon—in the assessment of a particular connecting principle. Therefore, in designing a robust counterfactual, an essential first step is to identify the "driving forces" (a term that in contrast to independent variable implies a force pushing in a particular direction rather than what is known on one side of an equation) surrounding a particular event, problem, or decision—the building blocks of the scenario's plot and its conclusion. Next, we need to consider and specify what else might change by manipulating a cause, the interaction of these altered variables, and how these changes may influence the possibility of the hypothesized outcome occurring.[80] Other questions to consider include: What might drive a particular situation or decision? What other factors might also affect this process? And, how far back into the "causes behind the causes" should we go in a scenario? For example, we can identify the increase in computing power, commercial interest, and expanded datasets in the genesis of AI, but do we need to ask about the forces driving commercial interest?

Theoretical, empirical, and statistical consistency

Consistency of counterfactuals with well-established historical facts (or the "minimal rewrite rule") depends mainly on what scholars define as well-established and factual accounts of history.[81] For example, in the absence of the assassination of Austrian Archduke Ferdinand, World War I would not have occurred, which is a good case in point of a "minimal rewrite" counterfactual.[82] In other words, the minimal rewrite rule is optimized when: a *high ex-ante probability* of a counterfactual antecedent is coupled with a *lower ex-ante probability* of real-world consequent.[83]

Because of the competing schools of thought in IR theory that claim to account for the outbreak of war and the sustainability of peace (e.g., the balance of power, power transition, democratic peace, deterrence/spiral model, and neorealism), judgments about theoretical consistency are even more problematic. Critics of the predictive power of IR theories argue that, in most cases, scholars' assertions rest on ex post facto (i.e., retroactive) and empirically questionable foundations to reconcile the validity of their theories with failing to anticipate real-world events.[84] In the case of deterrence theory, for instance, predictive failures include the Cuban Missile Crisis, the end of the Cold War and the survivability of NATO, and the 1973 Middle East War.[85] In this way, IR theories, much like other social science disciplines, are best thought of as an established means to enable scholars to apply past lessons as guides to the future—however fallible and contested they may be— rather than used as bulwarks against failed predictions and surprise.[86] Put another way, a theory stands or fails on its ability to generate propositions that are testable, valid, and falsifiable, rather than whether their assumptions accurately predict or explain empirical cases.

Cognizant of these limitations, therefore, an "ideal" scenario would manipulate one or more of the well-established facts—using a "well-established" IR theoretical lens—in a way that avoids ex post facto reasoning or manipulating other facts in the process.[87] For example, scholars have used extended deterrence IR theory to argue that even if President Truman had not threatened Stalin militarily, the Soviets would have likely withdrawn from Iran. Robust counterfactuals, therefore, must clearly define and justify their theoretical (contested or otherwise) and empirical assumptions and describe what kind of evidence would likely increase the confidence in the validity of a hypothesis—or cause it to be rejected.[88] This falsifiability requirement will help ensure realistic and plausible scenarios while avoiding snares in retroactive reasoning and non-falsifiable hypotheses.

The next step is to identify the elements of the scenario that are reasonably predetermined or "relatively certain"[89] from those uncertain and potentially significant or "low-probability events." This step plays two crucial roles. First, it can help ameliorate the human cognitive propensity to overemphasize abrupt or discontinuous departures from normality—it is easier to "mentally undo" accidents or other events that constitute deviations from the norm—and treat routine events as immutable facts.[90] There is, however, much empirical evidence of sudden and unexpected departures from the status-quo (regime change, revolutions, assassinations, war, etc.), attracting much retroactive counterfactual thinking.[91] Second, specifying what is relatively sure from what is not can help policymakers consider what *other things might not be equal* in a scenario and how we might know. Thus, taking one step beyond the "all other things being equal" approach.[92]

In many situations in world politics where empirical data is scarce (e.g., nuclear war), we have few validated empirical laws to draw on (IR), and where competing theoretical schools prohibit consensus (offensive versus defensive realists, or structural realists versus constructivists), statistics can help fill in the gap in what could have happened (or might occur). For instance, if an event or decision had occurred or been omitted—that is, the importance of negative evidence or "dogs that do not bark."[93] Game theorists, for example, use statistical reasoning—such as comparative statistics and probabilistic models—to test and design counterfactuals.[94]

In game-theoretic models of interactive decision-making, statistical models explicitly compute what would happen if actors made different choices, how other actors would strategically respond, and the payoffs that actors would gain (or losses) for every possible combination of choices.[95] In robust counterfactuals—like empirical and theoretical laws—connecting principles of antecedents and consequences should align with relevant "well-established" statistical generalizations, for example, base rates and patterns of covariation. According to Robyn Dawes, for example, counterfactual inferences are only plausible if they are inculcated in an established statistical system supported by "reasonable" empirical evidence.[96] Similarly, Hume argued that inference cannot be a matter of "demonstration" or a priori inference—we cannot use reason to infer from an event alone what might happen next.[97]

In contrast to other domains such as the stock market, in games such as chess and Go, and sports, however, well-established generalizations in world politics (war, peace, crisis management, the impact of technological change, regime type, and strategic bargaining, etc.) are notoriously difficult to model. Therefore, the use of statistical studies to construct counterfactual scenarios of technological surprise, warfare, and IR more broadly defined is problematic for ontological, psychological, and normative reasons. Statistical models and logical reasoning are unable to capture the qualitative discontinuities and uncertainties that shape the complex interactions between states (the rules of the game, international institutions, and perceptions etc.).

In most cases, how policymakers behave will depend on a multitude of non-linear causal conditions (e.g., lessons from past cases, theory-driven, regime type, and domestic-political constraints, alliance structures, perceptions of the military balance, and technological change), which will vary considerably temporally (affected by the political, cultural, or organizational context) and spatially (concerning lessons from past cases, shifting perceptions, and mindsets).[98] Policymakers tend to be heavily influenced by recent events, which actors have experienced first-hand, and events that occurred when they developed political awareness.[99] Counterfactual reasoning can help to reduce the risks of forcing new empirical data into pre-existing theoretical paradigms.

According to sociologist Jens Beckert, how we anticipate the future is very different from economists—such as Cold-War era neoclassical economics and rational choice theorists at the RAND Corporation[100]—projecting rationale preferences along with a set of knowable probabilities.[101] Beckert argues that the future is a function of fundamental uncertainty instead of building on Frank Knight and Kenneth Boulding's emphasis on subjective judgment and "omnipresent uncertainty" in contemporary risk studies.[102] It prompts actors, as a corollary, to resort to beliefs, fictional narratives, and an imagined conceptualization of the future, which allows them to sustain the illusion of linear temporal continuity.[103] In a recent study, researchers found that people making decisions under risk and ambiguity are more inclined to take greater risks due to a distortion of beliefs than when under the illusion of control.[104]

Consequently, the authors argue that when people are exposed to decision-making in tasks involving high chance and uncertainty, they should avoid risk-taking behavior that they otherwise may not.

While falsifiability may be a cornerstone scientific method for testing a hypothesis, believability (or plausibility) constitutes the hallmark of an effective narrative or plot.[105] Consequently, the role of uncertainty needs to be considered alongside the human psychological need for forms of continuation of the present—the fictional scenarios in the Conclusion explore this synthesis. Lee Clarke observed that "we need to think in terms of chances and odds and likelihoods. But we shouldn't concentrate so much on probabilities that we forget the possibilities."[106] The universe of possible future cases and permeations of these interactions is infinite; thus, thinking forward with counterfactuals can help reduce the risk of false certainty.

An additional obstacle in statistical studies for counterfactual scenarios—which is borne out in the cognitive psychology and experimental literature—relates to human bias. Namely, people are notoriously flawed intuitive statisticians, whose biases are frequently laid bare in detecting and using covariation data—the measure of how two random variables in a dataset will change together—which impairs our ability to determine the plausibility (or "reasonableness") of counterfactuals.[107] While this cognitive fallibility can be ameliorated by improving the accuracy of covariation estimates (e.g., including omitted data), this solution does not resolve the problem of peoples' propensity to accept false counterfactual claims (i.e., false positives caused by Type 1 errors) and dismiss true ones (i.e., false negatives caused by Type 2 errors).[108]

In other words, the problem here is not with counterfactuals per se, but instead deeper cognitive-psychological issues that can affect the choice of variables. As Hume posited, the "ideas which we form" to create causal relationships, because of our cognitive limitations, are inherently "imperfect."[109] Exposing these (often implicit) biases that people carry with them—informing and shaping decision-makers' "official future"—driving the tendency for the certainty of hindsight, underestimating the role of luck, and overconfidence, is thus a key goal of counterfactual scenarios. Because of the complexities and uncertainties involved in world politics, statistical reasoning probability estimates provide a very crude measure of the infinite possible future events that might arise inside-outside and on the margins of interacting antecedents which link to potential consequences.

Given the obstacles and limitations described, the counterfactual scenarios illustrated in the book do not include probability estimates. Instead, they will construct disciplined counterfactuals—grounded inconsistent and well-established empirical and theoretical generalizations—to illuminate plausible scenarios involving the intersection of DETs in the "nuclear enterprise,"[110] challenging the "official future" of policymakers. That is, wedded to outmoded and obsolete Cold War era theoretical (rational-deterrence) mindsets, shifting perceptions, so that we can reduce the element of surprise from technological change.

Lawlike generalizations to anticipate the future

How can we determine the extent to which the lawlike generalizations we have constructed are robust enough to support projections into the future? Nelson Goodman's concept of "projectability" is beneficial towards this end.[111] Goodman distinguishes between coincidental generalizations (that just happen to be a specific time and place) and robust lawlike generalizations (e.g., oxygen is necessary but not sufficient for fire), which hold up to a range of tests and allow projection into the past and future.[112] Thus, whether a generalization is deterministic or probabilistic, or bounded or unbounded by moderator variables, the litmus test is essentially the same, namely, the ability of a generalization to predict or project what is likely to occur in the future in a priori unobserved situations.[113] For instance, if a hypothesis is true, what else should also be true or observable?

As a corollary, and akin to philosopher Karl Popper's "falsification principle,"[114] a counterfactual scenario should comprise a lawlike generalization that yields a falsifiable prediction. For example, the hypothesis that "all swans are white" can be falsified by observing a black swan. However, constructing compelling and robust counterfactuals to look to the past and future are not symmetrical. When we use counterfactuals to look backward, there is a strong proclivity toward using antecedents that make a situation appear part of a predetermined and inexorable causal relationship, which risks overstating the role of chance—that is, the subjective probability assessment of how likely it is that a particular outcome might occur. Political scientists generally begin (and often end) their research by locating historical situations and then retrospectively searching for factors that appear correlated to the outcome. This process tells us very little about either the relative frequency of a particular outcome or proving that the variables used are a necessary causal factor; or that they may not be found in situations where the result is different.[115] This approach characterizes, inter alia, research on alliances, arms races, the procurement of weapons, civil unrest, causes of war, and deterrence failure.

Retrospective causal relationships are often poor predictors of the future.[116] This asymmetry indicates that counterfactuals in world politics can fail not because their core premise is false, but rather because of the inherent complexity interactions between causal variables that—like "chaos theory"—generate an infinite potential for minor causes in low-probability and low-frequency events (e.g., nuclear wars) being amplified into larger effects. Many IR scholars, for example, consider World War I to indicate a broader linear causal chain of related events and decisions—or "Humean causation."[117] The theory-building of many IR scholars centers on the value of structural (or systematic/linear) factors (i.e., between units of the international system) while paying lip-service to the apparent transitory importance of non-structural (or non-systematic/non-linear) factors such as the role of luck, chance (e.g., accidents, third-party intervention, and technical failure), and causal bifurcation.[118] Consequently, many predictions underplay (or discount) the role of complexity, by implicitly assuming that each casual factor exerts an independent influence on events, rather than interacting with other factors to generate non-linear outcomes.[119] This assumption—which is also demonstrated in theorizing on critical junctures, positive feedback, and path dependency[120]—can in part be attributed to a cognitive bias that connects perceptibly significant causes to large events.[121]

Several cognitive psychologists argue that low-probability and low-frequency (or "bolt from the blue") events—accidents, mechanical failure, technological surprise, and so on—are precisely the class of events that are most likely to attract counterfactual thinkers.[122] The literature on "normal accidents" suggests that eventually these kinds of events will always happen.[123] Well-designed counterfactuals that illuminate surprise "bolts from the blue" and other long-shot close-call events can recruit a related cognitive disposition to good effect. Namely, the tendency to judge a scenario as plausible if an event is depicted in vivid and narrow terms, leading people to upgrade their confidence in the probability of an event (e.g., accidental nuclear war) contingency—their perceptual lens of what they consider as possible or rational outcomes can be widened when exposed to scenarios with divergent and improbable outcomes.[124]

Finally, the idea of "temporal proximity." That is, the confidence we have in the validity of a counterfactual scenario as a function of the temporal distance and length of the causal chain from antecedent to consequent. In other words, the "distance" between actual and plausible worlds. The greater the distance and the longer a scenario's causal chain, so the greater the likelihood for bifurcation in the causal chain, for other events and conditions to intervene and shift the future onto a different trajectory, in turn making the outcome less predictable and uncertain. An insurmountable obstacle, therefore, to making anything other than short-term predictions.

According to historian J. D. Gould, "almost all of the obstacles to accurate prediction grow, some of them exponentially, as the time horizon is extended."[125] Echoing this view, historian Ian Kershaw argues that scholars should use "short-range counterfactuals" rather than engage in an "intellectual guessing-game of looking into some distant future."[126] The scenarios used in this chapter adhere to James Fearon's "temporal proximity criteria": "only where the [past or future] counterfactuals involve causal mechanisms and regularities that are *well understood* and that are considered at a spatial and temporal range *small enough that multiple mechanisms do not interact*, yielding chaos" (emphasis added).[127]

Conclusion

This chapter built on the notion of "future counterfactuals" to construct imaginative yet realistic scenarios to consider the future possibility of a nuclear exchange in the context of DETs. It highlighted the critical role that counterfactual scenarios can play in challenging conventional wisdom about nuclear weapons, risk analysis, war-fighting, and linear thinking. It argued that future counterfactuals are an important analytical tool to supplement traditional backward-looking counterfactuals, lessons of the past (or "nuclear learning"),[128] and other analogies, to construct imaginative scenarios that challenge conventional wisdom (involving "illusion of control," rationality, the role of luck, inevitability), assumptions (rationality, path-dependency, overdeterminism, control), and human bias (hindsight bias, heuristics, and attribution bias). Military historian Lawrence Freedman writes: "These [counterfactual] works of imagination will often have value in helping to clarify the choices that need to be faced and at times will even turn out to have been prescient. For that reason, many will deserve to be taken seriously."[129] In short, the ability to think counterfactually about plausible worlds is a boon for practical deliberation and contingency planning.

While the chapter makes a timely contribution to the scholarship about the use of counterfactuals in security, strategic, and nuclear studies, it is not merely an intellectual exercise. Drawing from multidiscipline best research practice criteria, the chapter advanced a methodology and causal mechanism—to construct robust (empirically and theoretically), rigorous (falsifiable, realistic, and plausible), and analytically parsimonious—yet going beyond "all other things being equal"—future scenarios to consider the risk of inadvertent nuclear conflict in the digital age. The research threads unpacked in the chapter also have significant implications for the nuclear policymaking community. Namely, the critical role imagined futures—which go beyond extrapolation and mirror-imaging—can play in shaping perceptions and informing policy choices.

Process-tracing analysis (see Appendix 1) can illuminate the critical role of human psychology, connecting the antecedents (i.e., counterfactuals) to the consequent (i.e., outcome) through the casual chain of events. Research on human cognition demonstrates people's tendency to deviate from rational decision-making pathways when faced with situations combining complexity, uncertainty, stress, and risk.[130] During times of crisis this propensity can influence the kinds of information leaders give credence to and prioritize, which often leads to a tendency to explain the behavior of others (i.e., adversaries) as the consequence of their inherent disposition, and the same behavior in themselves as the result of factors out of their control—known as "fundamental attribution error."[131] As demonstrated in Chapter 4, threats, risk, chance, and control are not entirely rational cognitive processes; they are as much psychological and emotional constructs (if not more so), particularly during time of crisis.[132]

Recent neuroscience research, based on brain lesion studies, clearly demonstrates that emotion is necessary for any form of rational decision-making to take place.[133] This cognitive disposition, coupled with an intense security dilemma, can help us understand the causal pathways and leadership decisions made in the scenarios.[134] These findings also give credence to the literature on deterrence theory that critiques the core assumptions underpinning rational-based deterrence—namely, rationality, freedom from domestic-political constraints, the ability to identify aggressors from defenders, and that challengers are risk-accepting maximizers.[135] The concluding chapter applies these criteria to explore several plausible fictional scenarios involving nuclear weapons and AI-enabling technology.

Notes

[1] A new wave of transformative DETs—associated with the broader "Fourth Industrial Revolution"—including AI, quantum technology, nanotechnology, hypersonic weapons, additive manufacturing, and directed energy weapons is expected to have a wide-ranging impact at a societal, economic, ethical, and domestic-political level. The implications of dual-use (civilian and military) DETs, some of which have not yet reached maturity, are already affecting the stability of traditional deterrence relationships between the West and Russia and between the West and China. See Caitlin Talmadge, "Emerging

Technology and Intra-War Escalation Risks: Evidence from the Cold War," Implications for Today," *Journal of Strategic Studies* 42 (6) (2019), pp. 864–887; James Acton, "Hypersonic Boost-Glide Weapons," *Science & Global Security* 23 (3) (2015), pp. 191–219; Elizabeth Sherwood-Randall, "The Age of Strategic Instability: How Novel Technologies Disrupt the Nuclear Balance," Snapshot, *Foreign Affairs* July 21, 2020, www.foreignaffairs.com/; James Johnson, "Artificial Intelligence in Nuclear Warfare: A Perfect Storm of Instability?" *The Washington Quarterly* 43 (2) (2020), pp. 197–211.

2   The "nuclear deterrence architecture" includes early warning and intelligence, surveillance, and reconnaissance systems, command-and-control, precision strike and delivery, and non-nuclear operations such as cyber, electronic warfare, counter-space, missile defense, and physical security. Vincent Boulanin, et al., *Artificial Intelligence, Strategic Stability and Nuclear Risk* (SIPRI Report, June 2020), p. 24.

3   Richard Ned Lebow and Benoît Pelopidas, "Facing Nuclear War: Luck, Learning, and the Cuban Missile Crisis," in the *Oxford Handbook of History and International Relations*, ed. Christian Reus-Smit, et al. (Oxford: Oxford University Press, 2023).

4   Sections of this chapter are derived in part from James Johnson, "Counterfactual Thinking & Nuclear Risk in the Digital Age: The Role of Uncertainty, Complexity, Chance, and Human Psychology," *Journal for Peace and Nuclear Disarmament*, 5 (2) (2022), pp. 394-421, (2022), doi:10.1080/25751654.2022.2102286.

5   Esther Eidinow, *Luck, Fate and Fortune: Antiquity and its Legacy* (Oxford: Oxford University Press, 2011), pp. 1–21.

6   Andrew Futter and Benjamin Zala, "Strategic Non-Nuclear Weapons and the Onset of a Third Nuclear Age," *European Journal of International Security* 6 (3) (2021), pp. 257–277.

7   Matthew Kroenig, "Nuclear Superiority and the Balance of Resolve: Explaining Nuclear Crisis Outcomes," *International Organization* 67 (1) (2013), pp. 141–171.

8   Keir A. Lieber, *War, and the Engineers: The Primacy of Politics over Technology* (Ithaca, NY: Cornell University Press, 2008).

9   See Michael Horowitz, Elsa Kania, Gregory Allen, and Paul Scharre "Strategic Competition in an Era of Artificial Intelligence," in *Artificial Intelligence and International Security* (Center for New American Security), July 2018; and Matthew Kroenig, "Will Emerging Technology Cause Nuclear War? Bringing Geopolitics Back," *Strategic Studies Quarterly* (Winter, 2021), pp. 59–73.

10   Martin Amis, *"Thinkability" in Einstein's Monsters* (New York: Harmony Books, 1987).

11   Kjølv Egeland, "The Ideology of Nuclear Order," *New Political Science* 43 (2) (221), pp. 208–230.

12   Benoît Pelopidas, "Nuclear Weapons Scholarship as a Case of Self-Censorship in Security Studies," *Journal of Global Security Studies* 1 (4) (2016), pp. 326–336; and Zachary Zwald, "Imaginary Nuclear Conflicts: Explaining Deterrence Policy Preference Formation," *Security Studies* 22 (4) (2013), pp. 640–671.

13   Nina Tannenwald, "How Strong is the Nuclear Taboo Today?" *The Washington Quarterly* 41 (3) (2018), pp. 89–109; and Robert Jacobs (ed.), *Filling the Hole in the Nuclear Future: Art and Popular Culture Respond to the Bomb* (New York: Lexington Books, 2010).

14   Barry Buzan and Lene Hansen, *The Evolution of International Security Studies* (Cambridge: Cambridge University Press, 2009), p. 21; George Shultz, "Preface," in *The War That Must Never Be Fought*, ed. George Shultz and James Goodby (Stanford, CA: Hoover Press, 2015); and James Wirtz, "Limited Nuclear War Reconsidered," in *On*

Limited Nuclear War in the Twenty-First Century, ed. Jeffrey Larsen and Kerry Kartchner (Stanford, CA: Stanford University Press, 2014), pp. 263–271.

15   Ibid., p. 115.

16   William James, "The Compounding of Consciousness," in *The Writings of William James: A Comprehensive Edition*, ed. J. J. McDermott (Chicago, IL: University of Chicago Press, 1977), p. 560. (Original work published in 1909.)

17   "Counterfactuals" can be defined in the broadest sense as subjunctive conditionals (or propositions) in which the antecedent (or causal mechanism) is known or supposed for the purposes of argument to be false. For the purposes of this chapter, the concept is used to construct plausible alternative worlds to investigate the causes and contingency of the world we know—rather than engaging in the construction of far-fetched "miracle worlds" that radically depart from the present temporal reality. Philip E. Tetlock and Aaron Belkin (eds), *Counterfactual Thought Experiments in World Politics* (Princeton, NJ: Princeton University Press, 1996), pp. 4 and 23.

18   Richard N. Lebow, "Counterfactuals and Security Studies," *Security Studies* 24 (3) (2015), p. 403.

19   Patricia Lewis, et al., *Too Close for Comfort: Cases of Near Nuclear Use and Options for Policy* (London: Chatham House, 2014).

20   The "illusion of control" is also supported by anthropologic research. Namely, human males have a strong tendency toward overconfidence and illusions of control, believing they have more control than they do. This tendency also provides an evolutionary advantage; those who can bring more people to their side of a fight are more likely to win. Robert Trivers, *The Folly of Fools: The Logic of Deceit and Self-Deception in Human Life* (New York: Basic Books, 2014).

21   Notable exceptions include Richard N. Lebow and Janice G. Stein, "Back to the Past: Counterfactuals and the Cuban Missile Crisis," in *Counterfactual Thought Experiments in World Politics*, ed. Philip E. Tetlock and Aaron Belkin (Princeton, NJ: Princeton University Press, 1996), pp. 119–149; Benoît Pelopidas, "Power, Luck, and Scholarly Responsibility at the End of the World(s)," *International Theory* 12 (3) (2020), pp. 459–470; and Campbell Craig, *Glimmer of a New Leviathan: Total War in the Realism of Niebuhr, Morgenthau, and Waltz* (New York: Columbia University Press, 2003); Mark S. Bell and Julia McDonald, "How to Think About Nuclear Crises?" *Texas National Security Review* 2 (2) (2019), pp. 41–65; Jenny Andersson, *The Future of the World: Futurology, Futurists, and the Struggle for the Post-Cold War Imagination* (Oxford: Oxford University Press, 2018); and Matthew Connelly, et al., "'General, I Have Fought Just as Many Nuclear Wars as You Have': Forecasts, Future Scenarios, and the Politics of Armageddon," *American History Review* 117 (5) (2012), pp. 1431–1460.

22   Hermann Kahn, *On Thermonuclear War* (Princeton, NJ: Princeton University Press, 1960).

23   See Lebow and Pelopidas, "Facing Nuclear War"; Lebow and Stein, "Back to the Past," pp. 119–149; and Herbert Lin, *Cyber Threats and Nuclear Weapons* (Stanford, CA: Hoover Institution Press, 2021).

24   See Scott D. Sagan, *The Limits of Safety. Organizations, Accidents and Nuclear Weapons* (Princeton, NJ: Princeton University Press, 1993); Benoît Pelopidas, "The Unbearable Lightness of Luck: Three Sources of Overconfidence in the Controllability of Nuclear Crises," *European Journal of International Security* 2 (2) (2017), pp. 240–262; and James

Johnson, "Inadvertent Escalation in the Age of Intelligence Machines: A New Model for Nuclear Risk in the Digital Age," *European Journal of International Security*, 7 (3), pp. 337-359 (2022), doi:10.1017/eis.2021.23.

25   Harold Trinkunas et al., *Three Tweets to Midnight: Effects of the Global Information Ecosystem on the Risk of Nuclear Conflict* (Stanford, CA: Hoover Institution Press, 2020).

26   Tetlock and Belkin (eds), *Counterfactual Thought Experiments in World Politics*, p. 5.

27   See Pelopidas, "Nuclear Weapons Scholarship as a Case of Self-Censorship in Security Studies," pp. 326–336; and Uri Bronfenbrenner, "Mirror Image in Soviet–American Relations: A Social Psychologist's Report," *Journal of Social Issues* 17 (3) (2010), pp. 5–56.

28   See Graham T. Allison, *The Essence of Decision: Explaining the Cuban Missile Crisis* (New York: Little Publishing, 1971); Gavin Francis, "History and the Unanswered Questions of the Nuclear age," in *The Age of Hiroshima*, ed. Michael D. Gordin and G. John Ikenberry (Princeton, NJ: Princeton University Press, 2020), pp. 294–311; and Richard Ned Lebow and Janice Stein, *We All Lost the Cold War* (Princeton, NJ: Princeton University Press, 1994).

29   See Laura Considine, "Narrative and Nuclear Weapons Politics: The Entelechial Force of the Nuclear Origin Myth," *International Theory* (2021), pp. 1–20.

30   For example, see Andersson, *The Future of the World*; Matthew Connelly, et al., "'General, I Have Fought Just as Many Nuclear Wars as You Have': Forecasts, Future Scenarios, and the Politics of Armageddon," *American History Review* 117 (5) (2012), pp. 1431–1460; Jeffrey Knopf, "The Concept of Nuclear Learning," *Nonproliferation Review* 19 (1) (2012), pp. 79–93; and Benoît Pelopidas, "The Unbearable Lightness of Luck."

31   Dominic D. Johnson, *Overconfidence and War* (Cambridge, MA: Harvard University Press, 2004).

32   See, for example, Lebow and Stein, "Back to the Past"; and Lebow and Pelopidas, "Facing Nuclear War."

33   Nick Bostrom, *Superintelligence: Paths, Dangers, Strategies* (Oxford: Oxford University Press, 2014).

34   Baruch Fischoff, "Hindsight is not Equal to Foresight: The Effect of Outcome Knowledge on Judgment under Uncertainty," *Journal of Experimental Psychology* 1 (2) (1975), pp. 288–299; and S. A. Hawkins and R. Hasie, "Hindsight: Biased Judgments of the Past Events after Outcomes are Known," *Psychological Bulletin* 107 (3) (1990), pp. 211–327.

35   Humans' deep-seated fear and anxiety of uncertainty—and the concomitant belief in the ability to predict and control events—has been studied by prominent psychologists, philosophers, and social scientists. See, for example, David Hume, *An Inquiry Concerning Human Understanding*, ed. Tom L. Beauchamp (Oxford: Oxford University Press, 1999); Martin Heidegger, *Being and Time*, trans. John MacQuarrie and Edward Robinson (London: SCM Press, 1962); and A. J. Rosenblatt, et al., "Evidence for Terror Management II: The Effects of Mortality Salience on Reactions to Those who Threaten or Bolster the Cultural World View," *Journal of Personality & Social Psychology* 58 (1990), pp. 308–318.

36   Philip E. Tetlock, *Expert Political Judgment: How Good Is It? How Can We Know?* (Princeton, NJ: Princeton University Press, 2005).

37   For example, many leaders in the interwar period drew insights from World War I that fed appeasement and conciliatory attitudes toward Nazi Germany during the 1930s. Robert Jervis, "Perceiving and Coping with Threat," in *Psychology and Deterrence*, ed. Janice G. Stein, et al. (New York: Johns Hopkins University Press, 1985) p. 22.

38 For a critique on "rational-based deterrence," see Richard N. Lebow, "Rational Deterrence Theory: I Think Therefore I Deter," *World Politics* 41 (2) (1989), pp. 208–224.

39 Alexander George and Richard Smoke, *Deterrence in American Foreign Policy: Theory & Practice* (New York: Columbia University Press, 1974); Lawrence Freedman, *The Evolution of Nuclear Strategy*. 2nd ed. (London: Palgrave Macmillan, 1989); Robert Jervis, *The Meaning of the Nuclear Revolution* (Ithaca, NY: Cornell University Press, 1989); and Paul Huth and Bruce Russett, "Deterrence Failure and Crisis Escalation," *International Studies Quarterly* 32 (1) (1988), pp. 29–45.

40 Robert Jervis, "Introduction: Approach and Assumptions," in *Psychology and Deterrence*, ed. Janice G. Stein, et al. (New York: Johns Hopkins University Press, 1985), p. 7.

41 Lebow and Stein, *We All Lost the Cold War*

42 For example, policymakers interpreted the two Berlin and Taiwan Straits Crises as deterrence successes—under the assumption that the Soviets or Chinese would have attacked Berlin or Taipei without a robust US deterrent threat. After the Cold War, evidence came to light that suggested China and Russia did not question US resolve and that deterrence provoked the very kinds of strategic instability it was designed to prevent. Richard N. Lebow, *Forbidden Fruit: Counterfactuals & International Relations* (Princeton, NJ: Princeton University Press, 2010), p. 13.

43 Henry Kissinger, *Diplomacy* (New York: Simon & Schuster, 1993).

44 Stephen M. Walt, "The Enduring Relevance of the Realist Tradition," in *Political Science: State of the Discipline*, ed. Ira Katznelson and Helen V. Milner (New York: W.W. Norton, 2002), pp. 197–230; and Kenneth Waltz, *Theory of International Politics* (New York: Random House, 1979).

45 This approach might, however, exacerbate political dissension, and divert resources, political capital, and attention from other tasks and issues. Roberta Wohlstetter, *Pearl Harbor* (Stanford, CA: Stanford University Press, 1962), p. 302.

46 Tetlock and Belkin (eds), *Counterfactual Thought Experiments in World Politics*, p. 16.

47 Bernard Brodie and Brodie Fawn, *From Crossbow to H-Bomb* (Bloomington, IN: Indiana University Press, 1973), Ch. 23.

48 Stephen P. Rosen, "The Impact of the Office of Net Assessment on the American Military in the Matter of the Revolution in Military Affairs," *Journal of Strategic Studies* 33 (4), pp. 469–482.

49 Amos Tversky and Daniel Kahneman, "Judgement Under Uncertainty: Heuristics and Biases," *Science* 185 (27) (1974), pp. 1124–1131.

50 Paul. J. Schoemaker, "When and How to Use Scenario Planning: A Heuristic Approach with Illustration," *Journal of Forecasting* 10 (6) (1991), pp. 549–564.

51 This excludes, however, the use of counterfactuals to validate a control case of a null hypothesis. Steven Weber, "Counterfactuals, Past, and Future," in *Counterfactual Thought Experiments in World Politics*, ed. Philip E. Tetlock and Aaron Belkin (Princeton, NJ: Princeton University Press, 1996), p. 268.

52 Kissinger, *Diplomacy*.

53 Daniel Kahneman, "Varieties in Counterfactual Thinking," in *What Might have Been: The Social Psychology of Counterfactual Thinking*, ed. N. J. Roese and J. M. Olson (Mahwah, NJ: Erlbaum, 1995), pp. 375–396.

54 William Calvin argues that humans' inability to foresee non-linear change reliably is due to the way our nervous systems are neuro-biologically hardwired. William. H. Calvin, "The Emergence of Intelligence," *Scientific American* 271 (2006), pp. 100–107.

55 Philip Tetlock, "Good Judgment in International Politics: Three Psychological Perspectives," *Political Psychology* 13 (3) (1992), pp. 517–539.

56 Weber, "Counterfactuals, Past, and Future," pp. 268–288.

57 Ibid., pp. 275–279.

58 Ibid., p. 277.

59 Daniel Furman and Paul Musgrave, "Synthetic Experiences: How Popular Culture Matters for Images of International Relation," *International Studies Quarterly* 61 (3) (2017), pp. 503–516.

60 Kuhnian "normal science" refers to scientific progress advanced the most by occasional revolutionary explosions of new knowledge, each revolution triggered by the introduction of new ways of thought so large they must be called new paradigms. Thomas H. Kuhn, *The Structure of Scientific Revolutions* (Chicago, IL: University of Chicago Press, 1962).

61 Reuben Steff, et al. (eds), *Emerging Technologies and International Security: Machines, the State and War* (London: Routledge, 2020).

62 Tetlock and Belkin (eds), *Counterfactual Thought Experiments in World Politics*, p. 32.

63 For example, it took several decades to discover the critical role misperceptions played in the 1962 Cuban Missile Crisis. See Lewis, et al., *Too Close for Comfort*, p. 30.

64 "Plausible" counterfactuals should have a significant probability of resulting in the alternative outcome stipulated. More subjectively, "realistic" refers to elements of counterfactuals that do not contravene our current understanding of what is technologically, culturally, temporarily, or otherwise possible. This contrasts with so-called miracle worlds that are intrinsically implausible. See Lebow, *Forbidden Fruit*, pp. 44–45.

65 These criteria and processes are adapted from a volume that surveys approaches—both normative, epistemological, and cognitive—to view the role of counterfactuals in world politics. Tetlock and Belkin (eds), *Counterfactual Thought Experiments in World Politics*.

66 Jonathan Vacher, et al., "Bayesian Modeling of Motion Perception Using Dynamical Stochastic Textures," *Neural Computation* 30 (12) 2018), pp. 3355–3392.

67 See, for example, Francis J. Gavin, "What If? The Historian and the Counterfactual," *Security Studies* 24 (3) (2015), pp. 425–430; Lebow, "Counterfactuals and Security Studies," pp. 403–412; E. H. Carr, *What Is History?* (Harmondsworth: Penguin Books, 1964); and Philip E. Tetlock and Geoffrey Parker, "Counterfactual Thought Experiments: Why We Can't Live without Them & How We Must Learn to Live with Them," in *Unmaking the West: "What If?" Scenarios That Rewrite World History*, ed. Philip E. Tetlock, Richard Ned Lebow, and Geoffrey Parker (Ann Arbor, MI: University of Michigan Press, 2006), pp. 28–33.

68 Carr, *What Is History?*

69 Tetlock and Belkin (eds), *Counterfactual Thought Experiments in World Politics*, p. 5.

70 Ibid., pp. 19–31.

71 Robert Jervis, *System Effects: Complexity in Political and Social Life* (Princeton, NJ: Princeton University Press, 1997).

72 Thomas C. Schelling, *The Strategy of Conflict* (Cambridge, MA: Harvard University Press, 1960).

73 Quoted in Ibid., p. 10.

74 Lebow and Stein, "Back to the Past," p. 146.

75 The notion of "cause" is an intractable problem in all the sciences (social, biological, and physical). Prominent scholars, including philosopher David Hume, argued that this

intractability results from the cause being a result of human mental activity and thus independent of the material world. Helen Beebee, "Hume and the Problem of Causation," in *The Oxford Handbook of Hume*, ed. Paul Russell (Oxford: Oxford University Press), pp. 228–248.

76   Immanuel Kant's main objective was to define the limits and scope of pure reason. Kant wanted to understand what reason alone can determine without the help of people's sense perceptions. Kant's metaphysical work prompted Hume's skepticism to doubt the very possibility of metaphysics. Christopher Bennett, et al., *Immanuel Kant: Groundwork for the Metaphysics of Morals* (Oxford: Oxford University Press, 2019); and Russell (ed.), *The Oxford Handbook of Hume*.

77   Weber, "Counterfactuals, Past, and Future," p. 285.

78   We manipulate only one thing at a time and prioritize only those causes that relate to the interest outcomes. James Fearon proposes an alternative rule to partially avoid this problem, in which the antecedent appears very likely to impact a specific consequence *and* very little else. James Fearon, "Causes and Counterfactuals in Social Science: Exploring an Analogy between Cellular Automata and Historical Processes," in *Counterfactual Thought Experiments in World Politics*, ed. Philip E. Tetlock and Aaron Belkin (Princeton, NJ: Princeton University Press, 1996), pp. 39–69.

79   John Mearsheimer, "Back to the Future: Instability in Europe after the Cold War," *International Security* 15 (1) (1990), pp. 5–56. For a critic on this view, see Lars-Erik Cederman, "Rerunning History: Counterfactual Simulation in world Politics," in *Counterfactual Thought Experiments in World Politics*, ed. Philip E. Tetlock and Aaron Belkin (Princeton, NJ: Princeton University Press, 1996), pp. 247–268.

80   Lebow and Stein, "Back to the Past," p. 146.

81   Tetlock and Belkin (eds), *Counterfactual Thought Experiments in World Politics*, pp. 23–24.

82   For additional examples of minimal-rewrite scenarios, see Lebow, *Forbidden Fruit*; and Frank P. Harvey, *Explaining the Iraq War: Counterfactual Theory, Logic, and Evidence* (Cambridge: Cambridge University Press, 2012).

83   Jack S. Levy, "Counterfactuals, Causal Inference, and Historical Analysis," *Security Studies* 24 (3) (2015), p. 390.

84   Cases in point include Hans Morgenthau, Kenneth Thompson, and David Clinton, *Politics Amongst Nations: The Struggles for Power and Peace* (New York: McGraw-Hill Education, 2005); Kenneth N. Waltz, *Theory of International Politics* (New York: Waveland Press, 2010); and John Mearsheimer, *The Tragedy of Great Power Politic* (New York: W. W. Norton & Company, 2014).

85   Lebow, *Forbidden Fruit*, p. 14.

86   Scholars have used a variety of counterarguments to justify the shortcoming of their theories. See Philip E. Tetlock, "Close-Call Counterfactuals & Belief System Defenses: I Was Not Almost, But I Was Almost Right," *Journal of Personality and Social Psychology* 75 (1998), pp. 230–242.

87   Weber, "Counterfactuals, Past, and Future," p. 285.

88   Lebow and Stein, "Back to the Past," p. 146.

89   Peter Schwartz advances four examples of factors in world politics that are "relatively certain": slow-changing phenomena (demographics, climate change); restricted situations (budgets, electoral cycles); outcomes that are "in the pipeline" (emerging technology prior to deployment); and inevitable collisions (declining GDP and recession, trade

wars and inter-state competition). Peter Schwartz, *The Art of the Long View* (New York: Doubleday/Currency, 1991), p. 117.

90   Scott Hawkins and Reid Hastie, "Hindsight: Biased Judgments of Past Events after the Outcomes are Known," *Psychological Bulletin* 107 (2) (1990), pp. 311–327; and Tversky and Kahneman, "Judgement Under Uncertainty," pp. 1124–1131.

91   See, for example, Niall Ferguson, *Virtual History: Alternatives and Counterfactuals* (New York: Penguin, 2014); Robert Cowley, *What If? Military Historians Imagine What Might Have* (New York: Pan, 2001); Andrew Roberts (ed.), *What Might Have Been? Leading Historians on Twelve "What Ifs" of History* (New York: W&N, 2005); and Richard N. Lebow, "Contingency, Catalysts, and Nonlinear Change: The Origins of World War I," in *Explaining War and Peace Case Studies and Necessary Condition Counterfactuals*, ed. Gary Goertz and Jack S. Levy (New York: Routledge, 2007), pp. 85–111.

92   Weber, "Counterfactuals, Past, and Future," pp. 280–281.

93   The problem of explaining causation by and of omission (i.e., explaining what is needed to prevent an event from occurring or to permit events to occur) is an area of continued research. John Collins, et al. (eds), *Causation and Counterfactuals* (Cambridge, MA: MIT Press, 2004), p. 50.

94   See, for example, Bruce Bueno de Mesquita, "Counterfactuals and International Affairs: Some Insight from Game Theory," in *Counterfactual Thought Experiments in World Politics*, ed. Philip E. Tetlock and Aaron Belkin (Princeton, NJ: Princeton University Press, 1996), pp. 211–230.

95   The decision that is not made, and the sequence of decisions that would have followed from it, are defined as "off the equilibrium path"—the criterion of subgame perfect equilibrium. Ibid., pp. 212–218.

96   Robyn Dawes, *Rational Choice in an Uncertain World* (San Diageo: Harcourt Brace Jovanovich, 1988).

97   Beebee, "Hume and the Problem of Causation," p. 230.

98   See Jens Beckert, *Imagined Futures: Fictional Expectations and Capitalist Dynamics* (Cambridge MA: Harvard University Press, 2016); and Andersson, *The Future of the World*.

99   Robert Jervis, *Perception and Misperception in International Politics* (Princeton, NJ: Princeton University Press, 1976), pp. 217–271.

100   Philip Mirowski, *Machine Dreams: How Economics Became a Cyborg Science* (Cambridge MA: Harvard University Press, 2002).

101   Beckert, *Imagined Futures*.

102   See Frank Knight, *Risk, Uncertainty and Profit* (New York: Dover Publications Inc., 1921); and Kenneth Boulding, *The Image: Knowledge in Life and Society* (Ann Arbor, MI: University of Michigan Press, 1956).

103   The opposite of this phenomenon is "disruptive illusion"—the idea that future conflicts will be completely different from past ones. H. R. McMaster, "Discussing the Continuities of War and the Future of Warfare," *Small Wars Journal*, October 14, 2014, https://smallwarsjournal.com/jrnl/art/discussing-the-continuities-of-war-and-the-future-of-warfare-the-defense-entrepreneurs-foru.

104   Alex Berger and Agnieszka Tymula, "Controlling Ambiguity: The Illusion of Control in Choice under Risk and Ambiguity," *Journal of Risk and Uncertainty*, 65 (2022), pp. 261–284.

105   Karl Popper, *The Logic of Scientific Discovery* (London: Routledge 2005).

106   Lee Clarke, *Worst Cases* (Chicago, IL: University of Chicago Press, 2010), p. 41.

107   Richard Nisbett and Lee Ross, *Human Inference: Strategies and Shortcomings of Social Judgment* (New Jersey: Prentice-Hill, 1980).

108   Other biases related to statistical reasoning include those caused by non-random selection, and omitted and confounding variables, which can also upend robust statistical inference. See Gary King, et al., *Designing Social Inquiry: Scientific Inference in Qualitative Research* (Princeton, NJ: Princeton University Press, 1994).

109   Quoted in Beebee, "Hume and the Problem of Causation," p. 243.

110   The "nuclear enterprise" refers to the complete range of activities, capabilities (nuclear and non-nuclear), and operations that directly or indirectly interface with nuclear weapons, including: production, acquisition, operations, organization, and strategy. Lin, *Cyber Threats and Nuclear Weapons*, p. 38.

111   Nelson Goodman, *Fact, Fiction, and Forecast* (Cambridge, MA: Harvard University Press, 1983).

112   Most political science generalizations are neither coincidental nor robust and lawlike; instead, they are mostly contingent and bounded by variables (i.e., x causes y; x also causes z) or statistical generalizations (i.e., x increases/decreases the probability of y). See George and Smoke, *Deterrence in American Foreign Policy*.

113   Goodman, *Fact, Fiction, and Forecast*.

114   According to Karl Popper's "falsification principle," for a theory to be considered "scientific," it must generate falsifiable hypotheses. Popper, *The Logic of Scientific Discovery*.

115   Robert Jervis, "Rational Deterrence: Theory & Evidence," *World Politics*. 41 (2) (1989), pp. 193–194.

116   For example, in the aftermath of the 1970 Mexico City passenger airline crash, the causal retrospective story that FAA investigators constructed—listing many plausible antecedent causal variables such as weather conditions, smog, radio malfunction, and fatigue—did not help the FAA to predict future accidents. Dawes, *Rational Choice in an Uncertain World*.

117   Beebee, "Hume and the Problem of Causation," pp. 228–248.

118   See, for example, King et al., *Designing Social Inquiry*, pp. 62–63. For non-systematic theory-building, see Lewis et al., *Too Close for Comfort*; and Pelopidas, "Power, Luck, and Scholarly Responsibility at the end of the World(s)," pp. 459–470.

119   For example, scholars analyzing US–China relations describe various conflicting facets of the dyad but fail to consider how one factor can depend on how others evolve. See Aaron Friedberg, "The Future of US–China Relations," International Security, 30 (Fall, 2005), pp. 7–45.

120   See Ruth Begins Collier and David Collier, *Shaping the Political Arena: Critical Junctures, the Labor Movement, and Regime Dynamics in Latin America* (Princeton, NJ: Princeton University Press, 1991); and Giovanni Capoccia and R. Daniel Kelemen, "The Study of Critical Junctures: Theory, Narrative and Counterfactuals in Historical Institutionalism," *World Politics* 59 (3) (April 2007), pp. 341–369.

121   Diedre McCloskey, "History, Differential Equations, and the Problem of Narration," *History & Theory* 30 (1990), pp. 21–36.

122   See Dale Miller, et al., "Counterfactual Thinking and Social Perception," in *Advances in Experimental Social Psychology*, ed. M. Zanna (New York: Academic Press, 1990), pp. 305–331.

[123] Charles Perrow, *Normal Accidents: Living with High-Risk Technologies* (Princeton, NJ: Princeton University Press, 1984).

[124] Scholars have long determined that humans are ineffective decision-makers when faced with even simple probabilistic information. Tversky and Kahneman, "Judgement Under Uncertainty," pp. 1124–1131.

[125] J. D. Gould, "Hypothetical History," *Economic History Review* 22 (2) (August 1969), pp. 199–200.

[126] Ian Kershaw, *Fateful Choices: Ten Decisions that Changed the World, 1940–1941* (New York: Penguin, 2007), p. 6.

[127] Fearon, "Causes and Counterfactuals in Social Science," pp. 39–67.

[128] "Nuclear learning" in this context refers to learning from historical events, and it assumes that the interpretation of significant events in the nuclear age plays a decisive role in how policymakers behave during a crisis. See Knopf, "The Concept of Nuclear Learning," pp. 79–93.

[129] Lawrence Freedman, *The Future of War: A History* (London: Public Affairs, 2017), p. 287.

[130] Research suggests that crisis-induced stress adversely affects the quality of decision-making. See Ole Holsti, "Theories of Crisis Decision-Making," in *Diplomacy*, ed. Paul Gordon Lauren (New York: Free Press, 1979), pp. 99–136; Martin Kaplan et al., "Time Pressure and Information Integration in Social Judgment," in *Time Pressure and Stress in Human Judgment and Decision Making*, ed. Ola Svenson and John Maule (Boston, MA: Springer, 1993), pp. 255–267; and Carsten De Dreu, "Time Pressure and Closing of the Mind in Negotiation," *Organizational Behavior and Human Decision Processes* 91 (2) (2003), pp. 280–295.

[131] See Lee Rodd "The Intuitive Psychologist and his Shortcomings: Distortions in Attribution Process," *Advances in Experimental Social Psychology* 10 (1977), pp. 173–220; and Edward Jones and Victor Harris, "The Attribution Attitudes, *Journal of Experimental Psychology* 3 (1) (1967), pp. 167–174.

[132] James J. Gross, "Emotion Regulation: Affective, Cognitive, and Social Consequences," *Psychophysiology* 39 (3) (2002), pp. 281–291; and Leda Cosmides and John Tooby, "Evolutionary Psychology and the Emotions," *Handbook of Emotions* 2 (2) (2000), pp. 91–115.

[133] Antoine Bechara, et al., "Deciding Advantageously before Knowing the Advantageous Strategy," *Science* 275 (5304) (1997), pp. 1293–1295.

[134] These outcomes of the scenarios might unfold differently depending on alterations to various observable implications such as changes in leadership, regime type, the political Zeitgeist, technological breakthroughs, and the attitude and reaction of allies/partners, and so on.

[135] Lebow, "Rational Deterrence Theory," p. 223.

Conclusion

No magic bullets

This book examined the intersection of AI-enabling technology and human–machine interaction in military operations—or AI-enabled "centaur warfighting." Specifically, it considered how and to what degree enmeshing intelligence machines into the war machine will affect the human condition of war. The human-centric approach applied a multidisciplinary theoretical and empirical lens to investigate the nuanced, oft-misunderstood, and at times contradictory, ethical, moral, and normative impact of synthesizing man and machine in future algorithmic warfare. The book challenges the prevailing wisdom that military centaur teaming is a magic bullet for the project of ensuring control and effective decision-making in war, but without sacrificing the benefits of human cognition and moral agency. This conclusion is premised on the assumption that (a) the drive to synthesize AI technology with military capabilities is inevitable and exponential; (b) the effects of this phenomenon on human agents in war is neither incontrovertible nor predetermined; and (c) machines cannot reliably compliment or augment, let alone replace the role of humans in command decision-making.

A central finding of the book is that while the binary choice between autonomy and humans is axiomatically false, the yoking of the two in AI-enabled human–machine interaction (HMI) is not necessarily a panacea. The book's substantive empirical chapters elucidate the potential risks and payoffs of AI-enabled HMIs across the entire chain of command. They also suggest how and to what effect the psychological symbiosis between man and machine contrasts with previous incarnations, and thus how it might, dependent on circumstance, be successfully calibrated and managed. For instance, the calibration of HMIs in the context of nuclear brinkmanship discussed in Chapter 4 will be very different from that of digital triage assistants to attend to injured combatants discussed in Chapter 3. Irrespective of the technical calibration of HMIs along the spectrum of human judgment and control of decision-making (see Figure 1.1), however, the incongruous nature of the handoff between machines and humans in hybrid teaming (especially

The AI Commander. James Johnson, Oxford University Press. © James Johnson (2024).
DOI: 10.1093/oso/9780198892182.003.0007

in fast-moving tactical operations) will likely create an unpredictable and unreliable psychological decision-making continuum.

Chapter 1 found that through various psychological mechanisms associated with the human–machine synthesis, algorithms cannot be merely passive neutral force multipliers of advanced capabilities. Rather, deeper human–machine symbiosis (or "human technology symbiotes") will alter and shape the psychological mechanisms that make humans who they are; as they learn and evolve, AI-agents will likely become (either inadvertently or by conscious choice) de facto strategic actors in war—the "AI commander problem." Thus, the chapter offers a timely counterpoint to the prevailing view that delegating command decisions to AI, while simultaneously retaining meaningful human control, is a viable solution to humans' psychological and biological fallibility in war.

The chapter contributes three key psychological insights that consider human–machine interactions (HMIs) and political-ethical dilemmas in future AI-enabled warfare. These insights elucidate the de facto "AI commander problem" advanced in this book. First, efforts to make war faster, more lethal, asymmetric, and efficient are being accomplished through a socio-technical psychological process of human–machine integration which is part of a broader evolutionary dovetailing of humanity and technology. AI represents a new manifestation of the pursuit of an omniscient technological solution to the ethical-political dilemmas of war. The logical end of this trajectory is an AI commander—planners, warfighters, and tacticians. The danger is that decision-makers may seek to reconcile the paradox of war by outsourcing our consciences in the use of lethal force to non-human agents who are ill-equipped to fill this ethical-moral void.

Second, AI is the newest means by which commanders leverage in their technical-scientific quest to impose predictability and certainty in chaotic and complex contemporary warfare (or "chaoplexic warfare"). Until AI can produce testable hypotheses or reason by analogy and deductively reason like humans, they will be incapable of understanding the real world, and the role of human agents in "mission command" will be even more critical in future AI-enabled warfare. Moreover, specific cognitive biases (illusion of control, heuristic shortcuts, automation bias) associated with HMIs can compound the "meaningful control" problem and thus increase the propensity for excessive military force for unjust causes.

The research also found that biases can (a) make decision-makers more predisposed to use capabilities just because they invested time and resources in their acquisition, which may produce false positives about the necessity for war—"The Einstellung Effect"; (b) cognitive bias can make decision-makers prone to unreflectively assign positive moral attributes to the latest techno-military Zeitgeist; and thus (c) humans tend to anthropomorphize machines and so view technology as a heuristic replacement for vigilant information seeking, cross-checking, and adequate processing supervision ("automation bias"). Even where humans are "on the loop," errors and unethical decisions may go undetected or unchallenged.

Finally, the notion that human ethics can be coded into AI algorithms as a possible solution to war's subjective and multifaceted ethical-political dilemmas is technically, theoretically, ontologically, and psychologically problematic, not to mention ethically and morally questionable. These vexing questions require open and broad democratic debate and multidisciplinary deliberation.[1] Abdicating control over our ethical decision-making to machines—under the false assumption that AI can make superior moral judgments—risks defusing (rather than eliminating) the moral responsibility of war to technology. This reduces the ability of humans to challenge the abstract ethics of machines, and in turn potentially opens a moral vacuum.

Chapter 2 examined the role of anthropomorphism in augmented AI technology military HMIs. The chapter posited five key conclusions. First, understanding the human psychology that undergirds the phenomenology of AI-anthropomorphism is a critical step in determining the possible impact of military HMIs, and thus optimizing the accuracy, reliability, and efficacy of these interactions. Second, stressful war conditions may encourage social bonding in HMIs, which make human operators cognitively disposed towards AI (caring about their well-being, etc.), prompting soldiers to view their AI "team-mates" as deserving of more protection than their "human" adversary, potentially justifying excessive and potentially immoral acts of aggression. Third, anthropomorphic language and other popular tropes associated with AI risk neglecting the inherent limitations of AI, creating a false equivalence between human and machine intelligence. Fourth, in the design of HMIs a critical precondition for success is how combatants perceive an AI agent's expertise, emotional engagement, and perceptual responses. Finally, people's anthropomorphic tendency to conflate a technological capacity for accuracy and speed with tactical efficiency means that AI agents are more likely to be judged as responsible and trustworthy than they perhaps deserve. Tactical performance considerations should, therefore, not be the only criteria to consider for the appropriate trust calibration of HMIs, particularly in information asymmetric situations between AI agents and human operators.

The phenomenology of AI-anthropomorphism and its impact on HMIs in military hybrid collaboration needs to be acknowledged and understood by the AI and defense research community, its users, and the broader constituents of the socio-technical ecosystem if they desire to realistically anticipate both the opportunities, challenges, and risks associated with hybrid tactical teamwork. As the chapter described, the deployment of highly autonomous AI agents entails a series of socio-technical and psychological challenges, including the need for human warfighters to understand the AI algorithmic design as it pertains to functionality; the limitations and biases in human (and machine) perception, cognition, and judgment; and the management or risks associated with delegating tasks and decision-making to machines.

To date, while the risks associated with dysfunctional AI in HMIs highlighted in this book should not be underestimated, the evidence suggesting that anthropomorphism in HMIs leads to more risky behavior and accidents is anecdotal. Therefore, it does not warrant the prohibition of anthropomorphic AI design. Some argue that many of the risks associated with anthropomorphic tendencies in HMIs (e.g., inappropriate attachment to AI agents) could be mitigated and controlled through appropriate monitoring, design, training, and force structuring. Possible follow-up measures, designed to maximize the advantages and minimize the risks in future human–machine interfaces, that policymakers, designers, and users might consider include:

- Designing AI-driven systems to monitor biases, errors, adversarial behavior, potential anthropomorphic risk, and incorporating "human" ethical principles, social cognition, and norms in AI systems while retaining the role of humans as moral agents and keeping humans in the loop as fail-safes.
- Training that emphasizes meaningful human control, moral responsibility, and a culture of collective vigilance against automation bias and complacence in hybrid teaming.
- Educating both combatants and support staff about the possible benefits and risks of anthropomorphizing AI agents.
- Closely coordinating force structuring decisions with training exercises to maximize human–machine communications—especially when communications are restricted or compromised.
- Ensuring robust test, evaluation, validation, and verification best practices is an integral feature of human–machine teaming design to minimize unintended biases and mitigate the premature deployment of potentially destabilizing and ethically questionable interfaces.[2]

These lines of effort should be coordinated and implemented to optimize human–machine communication and also increase cost and time efficiency.[3] An additional potential path forward is using cognitively inspired real-world synthetic generated data to train algorithms on infrequent but potentially high-risk contingencies. In short, ensuring human operations retain an active role in the decision-making process (i.e., across the entire OODA loop) could potentially improve users' perception (positive or negative) of an AI system; appropriately calibrating their trust and confidence in HMIs to maximize successful teaming outcomes remains a challenge.[4]

Future multidisciplinary empirical studies would also be beneficial in, inter alia, the following areas: (1) the prevalence of anthropomorphism in military HMIs to validate the mostly anecdotal claims about the risks of anthropomorphism in warfare; (2) the extent to which there are differences between how various groups of actors in the military anthropomorphize; (3) the risks and benefits associated with anthropomorphism within AI agent–human soldier teams; (4) the effects of anthropomorphism on the interactions between hybrid military teams and external entities (allies, adversaries, and non-combatant populations); (5) the optimum design (both technical and normative) solutions to maximize the benefits and minimize the risks in future human–machine (and human–human) interactions, and finally; (6) designers should consider the tradeoff between designing HMI for deeper engagement and the usability and tactical efficiency of AI systems, depending on the circumstances and nature of the operation.

Chapter 3 revisited John Boyd's OODA loop decision-making model and argued that AI-enabled capabilities cannot effectively, reliably, or safely complement—let alone replace—humans in comprehending the strategic environment to make effective command decisions. Besides, the growing dependency, proliferation, and diffusion of AI technology to augment human decision-making will likely produce strategic consequences that counterintuitively increase the importance of human involvement. The chapter found that the static and isolated nature of AI-ML algorithms offer no panacea to non-linear, chaotic, and uncertain warfare. Therefore, overly focusing on speed and tactical outcomes to complete the decision-making loop understates the permeation of AI in command decisions across the entire chain of command. The research finds fault with the conventional wisdom of militaries focusing on harnessing the tactical potential of AI-enabled capabilities in the pursuit of speed and rapid decision-making. Misunderstanding the nature of the evolving human–machine interface during fast-moving and fluid battlefield scenarios may undermine the critical symbiosis between senior commanders and tactical leaders (or "mission command"), increasing the risk of accidents and inadvertent escalation.

Although the chapter focused on "narrow" task-specific AI, the prospects of artificial general intelligence (AGI) are both intriguing and confounding— aside from the hype surrounding what a "third-wave" of genuine intelligence might look like, whether it is even technically possible, and broader debates about the nature of "intelligence" and machine consciousness.[5] Conceptually speaking, AGI systems would be able to complete the entire OODA loop without human intervention—and, depending on the goals they are programmed by humans to optimize—would be able to out-fox, manipulate, deceive, and overwhelm any human adversary. Pursuing these goals at all costs and absent of an off switch (which adversaries would presumably seek to activate), AGIs would unlikely attach much import to the various ethical and moral features of warfare that humans care about most.[6] In imagined future wars between rival AIs who define their own objectives (which may or may not align with or even be comprehended by humans) and who possess a sense of existential threat to their survival, the role of humans in warfare—aside from suffering the physical and virtual consequences of dehumanized autonomous hyper-war—is unclear. In this scenario, "strategic corporals" and "tactical generals" would become obsolete, and machine "genius"—however that might look—would fundamentally change Clausewitz's nature of war.

Chapter 4 revisited Schelling's insights on crisis stability and engaged with interdisciplinary human psychology, behavioral science, and anthropological studies to consider AI-enabled warfare. The chapter argued that the risks of nuclear-armed states leveraging Schelling's "threat that leaves something to chance" theory in the digital era preclude any potential bargaining benefits that may accrue to states during crises. It offers a fresh perspective and insights on the AI-nuclear dilemma. In the digital age, the confluence of increased speed, compressed decision-making, dual-use technology, reduced levels of human agency, critical network vulnerabilities, and dis-misinformation injects more randomness, uncertainty, and chance into crises, which, in turn, set in motion the pathways for unintentional (accidental, inadvertent, and catalytic) escalation to a nuclear level of conflict.[7] New vulnerabilities and threats (perceived or otherwise) to states' nuclear deterrence architecture in the digital era, highlighted in this chapter and elsewhere by the author, will likely serve as novel generators of inadvertent and accidental risk.

These vulnerabilities—amplified, manipulated, and distorted in the information ecosystem—will make current and future crises (Russian–Ukraine, India–Pakistan, The Taiwan Straits, The Korean Peninsula, and the South China Seas, etc.) resemble a multiplayer game of chicken, where the confluence of Schelling's something to chance coalesces with contingency, uncertainty, luck, and the fallacy of control, under the nuclear shadow. In this dangerous game, either side can increase the risk that a crisis inadvertently or accidentally escalates to nuclear war. Because of the limited empirical evidence available on nuclear escalation, threats, bluffs, and war termination, the chapter's conceptual findings (much like Schelling's own) are mostly deductive. Robust falsifiable counterfactuals that challenge conventional wisdom can help fill this empirical gap.

Chapter 5 reconceptualized "future counterfactuals" to consider how disruptive emerging technology like AI might impact future crises involving nuclear-armed adversaries. It highlighted the critical role counterfactual scenarios can play in challenging conventional wisdom about nuclear weapons, risk assessments, war-fighting, and linear thinking. It also highlighted the critical role that well-designed counterfactual scenarios can play in challenging conventional wisdom, assumptions, and human bias about nuclear weapons, risk analysis, warfighting, and deterrence. The chapter engaged with multidisciplinary best research practices to advance a framework to build robust, rigorous, and analytically parsimonious future scenarios to consider the risk of nuclear (especially accidental and inadvertent) conflict in the digital age. These findings have significant implications for the nuclear policymaking community, going beyond extrapolation and mirror-imaging. In sum, well-designed counterfactuals can prepare policymakers to hedge against unforeseen risk, the improbable, and unanticipated technological surprise.

Tools for policymakers: buying time with counterfactuals

This section applies the methods and processes developed in Chapter 5 to three future counterfactual scenarios that expose and challenge prevailing assumptions (overconfidence in the controllability of nuclear crises), our fears, bias (hindsight bias and heuristics), and what we think can be done to assuage them.[8] The scenarios are constructed as illustrative rather than empirically exhaustive. They are designed as reflective tools to expose weaknesses in the prevailing "official future" (assumptions, bias, and perceived wisdom) revealing potential blind spots or shortcomings in how we frame our research questions to consider nuclear risk anew in the digital age.

While the scenarios viewed in isolation may appear improbable or preventable, taken together they demonstrate how the interaction of a range of technologies with nuclear weapons might exacerbate crisis stability and increase the risk of nuclear escalation. With this in mind, we should consider the following research puzzles: Can a causal chain be traced back to underlying causes and enabling conditions? Does a demonstrable (or incontrovertible) catalyst exist? Are multiple causal chains involved? If so, to what degree are they independent (or dependent) of each other? The more independent, the more probable the outcome can be understood as the result of confluence—that is, multiple independent causes combine to produce an event that might not otherwise have occurred.[9]

The counterfactual scenarios are premised on four assumptions: (1) crisis conditions involving two nuclear-armed adversaries; (2) an intense "security dilemma" operating within the dyad[10]; (3) the existence of military (both capabilities and information) asymmetry between adversaries; and (4) the technical feasibility of the operations and capabilities illustrated—either currently deployed or being developed. These provisional assumptions, together with the causal claims described below—and without pre-existing empirical evidence—allow us to construct rigorous scenarios that meet the positivist standards established in Chapter 5. These foundations, in turn, will require modification evaluation rather than testing as new data, competing scenarios, or assumptions emerge.[11] This approach is a form of social science process tracing (see Appendix 1) to support a hypothesis—namely, that nuclear rivals are more likely to use military force against each other in ways that could inadvertently or accidentally escalate a crisis to a nuclear conflict (Y) than they might have been if they did not possess disruptive emerging technology (X)—with observable implications thinking to the future, rather than the past.

Scenario 1: AI-enhanced cyber-attack of dual-use command-and-control systems

China announces a series of nuclear simulation exercises that model a limited nuclear strike on Taiwan. The simulation includes moving the People's Liberation Army Rocket Force—responsible for China's nuclear weapons—mobile missiles out of their garrisons and increasing the resiliency of China's dual-use (i.e., supporting both its nuclear and conventional capabilities) command, control, and communications (C3) systems.[12]

The US, to ascertain Chinese intentions in conducting these "non-routine" exercises during a period of heightened Cross-Straits tension, activates a dormant AI-augmented advanced persistent threat (APT)[13] clandestine cyber-attack within China's C3 networks to gather intel—to determine whether the simulations are an exercise or part of a clandestine preparation for an actual first strike.[14] China's C3 network resiliency efforts (part of its simulation exercise readiness) enable it to detect the US's APT intrusion—which hitherto remained undetected—and thus assumes US cyber operations are part of an offensive attack against China's nuclear command, control, and communications (NC3) system—designed to create a window of opportunity for a larger strategic strike.[15] This precipitates a major crisis where only a minor one existed before.[16]

Because the discovery of the US cyber intrusion coincides with escalatory rhetoric between the opposing sides, diplomatic spokespersons playing out on social media, and corresponding provocative US freedom of navigation and a series of aircraft within Taiwan's air defense identification zone, China shifts its nuclear status to high alert. Amid recent Chinese aggressive disinformation campaigns in Taiwan and a nuclear modernization program, Washington is unassuaged by Beijing's statements that these exercises are merely a simulation.

From a US perspective, its clandestine cyber operations are designed to determine China's genuine intentions.[17] That is, the US assumes China's exercises are malign, and given its upper hand vis-à-vis China, feels less of an imperative to back down or refrain from escalation. Therefore, both sides are incentivized to take a more aggressive military posture, but for different reasons. The US views China's "mere" exercise as mobilization to a war-footing stance, and China views US penetration of its NC3 network as a deliberate attempt to comprise these capabilities. In sum: in the absence of these enabling novel technological advances and techniques (APT, cyber countermeasures, dual-use technology), all things being equal, this causal escalatory chain of events would be technically unfeasible and thus operationally implausible, thereby supporting the hypothesis.

Scenario 2: third-party cyber false-flag operation

During the initial phase of a conflict in the South China Seas, a third-party actor (terrorist, state proxy, or other criminal, etc.) launches a "false-flag cyber operation"[18] (e.g., data manipulation, social media flooding with bots, a spoofing attack, or other forms of deception), to realize their "apocalyptic world views,"[19] against Chinese and US dual-use early warning satellites—providing both sides with warning of a nuclear attack on their homelands—which is untraceable and thus appears to both states as originating from the other.[20] No evidence exists to disprove these claims, and both sides deny responsibility.[21] Each side is convinced that the other is responsible, and the attack is designed as a prelude to a pre-emptive first strike.[22]

The US, concerned that the loss of a critical strategic warning capability puts its launch-on-warning nuclear forces at risk, raises its nuclear alert status.[23] As a de-escalatory tactical measure (to signal resolve), the US launches a cyber malware attack against China's conventional C3 network. The attack accidentally disables one of China's NC3 nodes, which Beijing views as intentional and malign. China, fearful that this attack is a prelude to a decapitating strike, orders the delegation of pre-launch authority to remote AI-powered decision-making support systems.[24]

Lacking sufficient evidence for who was behind the attack, and under intense domestic political pressure to respond, China launches a pre-emptive limited nuclear strike against US bases in Guam. The US views China's attack as unprovoked aggression, sparking an accidental "catalytic war."[25] Once both sides consider conflict inevitable, the security dilemma logic of seizing the tactical first-mover advantage—before the other side can fully execute their war plans—can create self-fulfilling spirals of escalation.[26] In sum: similar to the first scenario, without the confluence of the complex and interdependent contingencies enabled by emerging technologies (malware, AI decision support tools, NC3 automation) described here, the recourse to military force would, all things being equal, likely be significantly less, thus supporting the hypothesis.

Scenario 3: information warfare operations to undermine confidence in a states' nuclear forces

During a US–China crisis, Russian proxy actors flood social media outlets and open-source crowdsourcing platforms with false information (satellite imagery, 3D models, Twitter feeds, or geospatial data, etc.) about the suspicious movement of Chinese dual-use (nuclear and conventional capable) Dong Feng (DF) 26 intermediate range nuclear road-mobile launchers, able to reach US military assets in the Pacific.[27] Once the Russian operations (e.g., deepfakes, misinformation, and bots) go viral, neither US human nor machine operators are able to limit the fall-out from the attack, eroding the public and policymakers' confidence—a psychological as well as a technical phenomenon—in the US' extended deterrence commitments in the Pacific.[28]

The US, as part of a "supply chain attack"[29] on China's missile forces— unable to determine with confidence the veracity of this information and with mounting public pressures to respond—inserts malware in several Chinese dual-use weapon delivery platforms. Against the backdrop of an escalating crisis, and based on misinformation "false positive,"[30] US intelligence provides serendipitous clues to China that it has carried out this (unprovoked) attack, allowing it to discover these system vulnerabilities.[31] The US also informs Beijing that these insertions have infected other Chinese missile platforms, including China's dual-use DF-26.

The Chinese leadership is unable to determine whether the US attack is genuine (and not part of a disinformation campaign to signal resolve to China and reassure its regional allies), how widespread the US penetration is, or whether the US gained access to additional vulnerabilities that it did not reveal (e.g., NC3 networks), and thus how to respond. Under intense domestic political pressure to respond, Beijing believes it is in a "use-it-or-lose-it" situation, and responds by launching a retaliatory first strike against US platforms in the region.[32] In sum, the coalescence of a range of interconnected information technologies (satellite imagery, 3D models, geospatial data, social media mis/disinformation, and deepfakes), and the escalatory causal chain of events that followed, would, all things being equal, be unlikely to occur in the absence of these enablers, thus supporting the hypothesis.

The counterfactual scenarios demonstrate that multiple causal chains would likely be involved in a future crisis dynamic between a nuclear-armed adversarial dyad—rather than evidence of a demonstrable or incontrovertible catalyst. Moreover, the multiple casual chains illustrated in the process-tracing analysis (see Appendix 1)—dual-use command-and-control systems, public confidence in nuclear deterrence, third-party information operations, preemption doctrine, AI-enhanced cyber capabilities, pre-launch authority, and social media-fueled escalatory rhetoric, etc.—were demonstrably interdependent and mutually reinforcing. A noteworthy recurrent theme in the scenarios was the effect that crisis stability of dual-use systems used in conjunction with clandestine technological operations (whether defensive or offensive) had on both sides' perceptions, attitude to risk, and confidence—both in attributing the intentions of the other and assuming their motivations were apparent and immutable. In short, the cognitive-psychological impact on decision-makers of these operations (especially deploying AI-enhanced cyber capabilities) was equal, if not more significant, than the actual effect of the operations per se.

The process-tracing analysis (see Appendix 1) highlights additional empirical threads worthy of further investigation, including: (a) the indistinguishability of offensive and defensive DET-augmented capabilities and operations (especially in cyberspace); (b) the inadvertent escalation risk associated with commingled nuclear and non-nuclear capabilities; (c) temporally, the importance of the geopolitical context in shaping perceptions, and thus informing policy; the destabilizing effects of offensively oriented military doctrine (launch-on-warning, preemption, etc.); and d) the amplifying effects of the information ecosystem (social media, deepfakes, bots, and disinformation, etc.) on public opinion, and, in turn, on decision-makers' perceptions.[33]

* * *

Since the time of the ancient Greeks, humanity has adored artificial life, automata, self-moving devices, and human enhancements—as with the AI Pandora's Box of images, illusions, myths, hopes, and fears.[34] The "AI commander" notion advanced in this book serves as a warning of the potential consequences of neglecting the salience of human psychology in HMIs. Moreover, it also provides us with the kinds of deep questions we need to consider as this critical symbiosis between human and machine evolves in its latest incarnation in the age of AI. Answers to these questions have implications not just for what it will mean for the character (and possibly the nature) of future war, but also what it means for the human condition of war, and thus what it should mean to be human.

Future warfare will, of course, not exist in a socio-political vacuum behind the safety of a Rawlsian virtual "veil of ignorance." Therefore, it behooves all stakeholders—designers, academics, operators, commanders, defense and policy communities, political leadership, allies, adversaries—to be acquainted with the ethical-political dilemmas and the other complex socio-technical and cognitive-motivational features of human–machine interactions highlighted in this book. Thus, ensuring that these concerns inform and shape the nascent discourse and, ultimately, the design, testing, and deployment of human–machine interfaces in future hybrid teaming operations; and, more broadly, deliberations on the human condition of war itself.

In the final analysis, we should neither overestimate the extent of human control over machines in war—as algorithms increasingly inform and shape warfaring decisions—nor exaggerate the degree to which they can entirely supplant humans—even in reconstituted and augmented ones of the future. While the ultimate responsibility for war will lie with us, the relationship between humans and machines will likely remain mutually dependent. The risks and dangers posed by intelligent machines will, therefore, closely correlate with how much latitude along the decision-making continuum machines are given—either as a conscious decision or, perhaps more likely, unwittingly due to our cognitive biases and blind spots—in fulfilling human goals and to the extent to which machines share these goals. Our choices come with tradeoffs. Notwithstanding the unremitting trend to coopt exponentially sophisticated machines to conduct war on our behalf, which continues at a pace, the choice to start, escalate, and sue for peace will remain ours alone.

Notes

1 Notable efforts toward this goal include: Michael Schmitt, "Autonomous Weapons Systems and International Humanitarian Law: A Reply to the Critics," *Harvard National Security Journal Features* (2013), http://harvardnsj.org/2013/02/autonomous-weapon-systems-and-international-humanitarian-law-a-reply-to-the-critics/; Merel Ekelhof and Giacomo Persi Paoli, "The Human Element in Decisions about the Use of Force," UNIDIR, 2019, www.unidir.org/publication/human-element-decisions-about-use-force; Danielle C. Tarraf, et al., "The Department of Defense Posture for Artificial Intelligence: Assessment and Recommendations," *RAND Corporation*, 2019, www.rand.org/pubs/research_reports/RR4229.html; "Ethics and Autonomous Weapon Systems: An Ethical Basis for Human Control?" International Committee of the Red Cross (ICRC), 2018; NATO OTAN, Science & Technology Trends 2020–2040 Exploring the S&T Edge, NATO Science & Technology Organization 2020, www.nato.int/nato_static_fl2014/assets/pdf/2020/4/pdf/190422-ST_Tech_Trends_Report_2020-2040.pdf.

2 See Jared Dunnmon, et al., "Responsible AI Guidelines in Practice," *Defense Innovation Unit*, November 15, 2021, https://assets.ctfassets.net/3nanhbfkr0pc/acoo1Fj5uungnGNPJ3QWy/6ec382b3b5a20ec7de6defdb33b04dcd/2021_RAI_Report.pdf.

3 Massimiliano Cappuccio, Jai Galliott, and Eduardo Sandoval, "Saving Private Robot: Risks and Advantages of Anthropomorphism in Agent–Soldier Teams," *International Journal of Social Robotics* (2021), doi:10.1007/s12369-021-00755-z.

4 Catalina Gomez, Mathias Unberath, and Chien-Ming Huang, "Mitigating Knowledge Imbalance in AI-Advised Decision-Making Through Collaborative User Involvement," *International Journal of Human-Computer Studies* 172 (April 2023), pp. 1–14.

5 See Brian C. Smith, The Promise of Artificial Intelligence: Reckoning and Judgment (Cambridge, MA: MIT Press, 2019); Meredith Broussard, *Artificial Unintelligence: How Computers Misunderstand the World* (Cambridge: MIT Press, 2018); and Kenneth Payne, *I, Warbot: The Dawn of Artificially Intelligent Conflict* (New York: Hirst Publishers, 2021).

6 On misaligned AIs and the problem of control, see Stuart Russell, *Human Compatible* (New York: Viking Press, 2019); and Nick Bostrom, *Paths, Dangers, Strategies* (Oxford: Oxford University Press, 2014).

7 James Johnson, *AI and the Bomb: Nuclear Strategy and Risk in the Digital Age* (Oxford: Oxford University Press, 2023), Chs 3 and 5.

8 This section is derived in part from James Johnson, "Counterfactual Thinking & Nuclear Risk in the Digital Age: The Role of Uncertainty, Complexity, Chance, and Human Psychology," *Journal for Peace and Nuclear Disarmament* 5 (2) (2022), pp. 394-421, (2022), doi: 10.1080/25751654.2022.2102286.

9 Richard N. Lebow, "Counterfactuals and Security Studies," *Security Studies* 24 (3) (2015), p. 409.

10 See Herbert Butterfield, *History and Human Relations* (London: Collins, 1951); John Herz, *Political Realism and Political Idealism: A Study in Theories and Realities* (Chicago, IL: University of Chicago Press, 1951); and Robert Jervis, "Cooperation under the Security Dilemma," *World Politics* 30 (2) (1978), pp. 169–214.

11 Space does not allow for exploring a range of plausible alternative scenarios and "wild card" events and the uncertainties that might arise from the possible combinations of them.

12 James M. Acton, "Escalation through Entanglement: How the Vulnerability of Command-and-Control Systems Raises the Risks of an Inadvertent Nuclear War," *International Security* 43 (1) (2018), pp. 56–99.

13 The cost of tools used to create malicious documents depends heavily on whether the malware can persist on the target system undetected by antivirus software. See "Advanced Persistent Threat: Attack Cost Research, Positive Technologies," August 22, 2019, www.ptsecurity.com/ww-en/analytics/advanced-persistent-threat-apt-attack-cost-report/.

14 See Ben Buchanan and Fiona S. Cunningham, "Preparing the Cyber Battlefield: Assessing a Novel Escalation Risk in a Sino-American Crisis," *Texas National Security Review* 3 (4) (Fall, 2020), pp. 55–81.

15 Technological advances in AI technology and cyber capabilities, coupled with the increasingly commingled nature of the state's nuclear and conventional command-and-control systems, have enabled solutions to overcome the robustness of permissive action links and increase these vulnerabilities systems. Bruce Blair, *The Logic of Accidental Nuclear War* (Washington, D.C.: Brookings Institute, 1993).

16 China would be unable to know what US intentions were *before* the operation was detected (i.e., espionage or an offensive cyber-attack), and thus it would likely assume the worst.

17 During peacetime conditions, rival states are more likely to reveal otherwise clandestine capabilities to support deterrence objectives, which during a crisis are more valuable as tools of surprise and preemption. See Brendan Rittenhouse Green and Austin Long, "Conceal or Reveal? Managing Clandestine Military Capabilities in Peacetime Competition," *International Security* 44 (3) (2019/20), pp. 48–83.

18 Herbert Lin, "Escalation Dynamics and Conflict Termination in Cyberspace," *Strategic Studies Quarterly* 6 (3) (2012), pp. 46–70.

19 On the nature and drivers of non-state actors' (especially terrorist groups) interest in nuclear weapons, see Mark Fitzpatrick, *The World After: Proliferation, Deterrence and Disarmament if the Nuclear Taboo is Broken* (Paris: Ifri Security Studies Centre, 2009); Charles C. Ferguson and William C. Potter, *The Four Faces of Nuclear Terrorism* (Monterey, CA: Center for Nonproliferation Studies and Nuclear Threat Initiative, 2004); James Forest, "Framework for Analyzing the Future Threat of WMD Terrorism," *Journal of Strategic Security* 5 (4) (2012), pp. 51–68; and Graham Allison, *Nuclear Terrorism: The Ultimate Preventable Catastrophe* (New York: Owl Books, 2004).

20 In a conventional kinetic conflict, an actor may attempt to increase the effectiveness of its short-range missiles through interfering with or manipulating an adversary's early warning satellites (especially high-frequency communication satellites), for example, a cyber-attack on its satellites ground links. However, an attack like this could lead the victim to assume that its long-range strategic forces were under attack. Herbert Lin, *Cyber Threats, and Nuclear Weapons* (Stanford: Stanford University Press, 2021), p. 110.

21 While a cyber false-flag operation would not require particularly sophisticated technical expertise—at least compared to the level of scientific and military infrastructure required to develop nuclear weapons—it would need the organizational know-how to collect and parse intelligence and conduct clandestine activities. See Shao Chengcheng, et al., "The Spread of Low-Credibility Content by Social Bots," *Nature Communications* 9 (4787) (2018), pp. 1–9.

22 Given the pivotal role of command-and-control, a state's NC3 systems would likely be targeted to degrade these capabilities during the initial stages of a conflict. Acton, "Escalation through Entanglement," pp. 56–99.

23 In 2017, for example, US soldiers and their family members in Korea were subject to a text notification with fake evacuation orders for non-combatants issued for the Korean Peninsula. Though this attack was quickly debunked, a third-party attack, like during an ongoing crisis, could prompt a state to order a pre-emptive strike, assuming that the evacuation was a prelude to conflict initiation. Kim Gamel, "US Forces Korea Warns of Fake Evacuation Messages," *Stars & Stripes*, September 21, 2017, www.stripes.com/theaters/asia_pacific/us-forces-korea-warns-of-fake-evacuation-messages .488792.

24 China has begun to research the use of big-data and deep-learning AI techniques to enhance the processing speed and intelligence analysis of satellite images, support its early warning capabilities, and, ultimately, enable a "prediction revolution" in future warfare. Chinese researchers have also applied AI to wargaming and military simulations to generate data and insights that may be used to enhance Chinese early-warning systems, situational awareness, and targeting. Jia Daojin and Zhou Hongmei, "The Future 20–30 Years Will Initiate Military Transformation," *China Military Online*, June 2, 2016.

25 The notion of "catalytic war" is the possibility that a third party's actions spark a nuclear war between the two nuclear-armed opponents. See Donald H. Kobe, "A Theory of Catalytic War," *The Journal of Conflict Resolution* 6 (2) (1962), pp. 443–457; and James Johnson, "'Catalytic Nuclear War' in the Age of Artificial Intelligence & Autonomy: Emerging Military Technology and Escalation Risk between Nuclear-Armed States," *Journal of Strategic Studies* (2021), online first, https://doi.org/10.1080/01402390.2020.1867541.

26 Jervis, "Cooperation under the Security Dilemma," pp. 169–214.

27 From an intelligence standpoint, nuclear solid-fuel missiles and tracked transport erector launchers (TELs) reduce intelligence, surveillance, reconnaissance (ISR) systems' ability to detect signs of launch preparation. Solid fuel also increases the speed of launching missiles and reduces the number of support vehicles to support an operation.

28 Facebook, for example, uses its algorithms to anticipate human behavior to create "prediction products" that make people easier to manipulate—i.e., profiling and micro-targeting their users to sell more advertising space. This capability was allegedly used to manipulate public perceptions during the 2016 US presidential election and the UK's referendum on membership of the European Union. See Shoshana Zuboff, *The Age of Surveillance Capitalism: The Fight for a Human Future at the New Frontier of Power* (New York: Public Affairs, 2019), pp. 3–17.

29 Supply-chain attacks on complex and interdependent systems (e.g., the "colossal" Kaseya ransomware supply-chain attack in 2021) can render parts or the entire chain vulnerable before it is put into use. Fred Schneider and Justin Sherman, "Bases for Trust in a Supply Chain," *Lawfare*, February 1, 2021, www.lawfareblog.com/bases-trust-supply-chain; and

Joe Tidy, "US Companies Hit by 'Colossal' Cyber-Attack," *BBC News*, July 3, 2021, www.bbc.com/news/world-us-canada7703836.

30 Alternative outcomes from this fictional scenario are, of course, possible. For example, counter-AI systems might uncover the leak's source or false nature before it can do severe damage. State A might also assure State B through backchannel or formal diplomatic communications of this falsehood. While social media platforms have had some success in slowing down users' ability to orchestrate manipulative and dangerous campaigns, once these operations (e.g., deepfakes and bots) go viral, the ability to curtail them becomes inexorably problematic—for human operators or machines.

31 Suppose an actor can demonstrate that it has successfully comprised one or more weapon systems. In that case, the destructive potential of such an intrusion may severely affect a leader's confidence and risk appetite. Lin, *Cyber Threats, and Nuclear Weapons*, p. 113.

32 US and Russian nuclear doctrine maintain the option for counterforce operations to limit the damage they would suffer from a nuclear exchange or believe that the other side might launch a counterforce attack. Observers have also debated whether India and China are moving in the same direction. See US Department of Defense, *Nuclear Posture Review* (Washington, D.C.: Office of the Secretary, 2018), p. 23; Christopher Clary and Vipin Narang, "India's Counterforce Temptations: Strategic Dilemmas, Doctrine, and Capabilities," *International Security* 43 (3) (2018/2019), pp. 7–2; and Caitlin Talmadge, "Would China Go Nuclear? Assessing the Risk of Chinese Nuclear Escalation in a Conventional War with the United States," *International Security* 41 (4) (2017), pp. 50 2.

33 The potential implications of each of these threads are discussed in depth elsewhere. For example, see Ben Garfinkel and Allen Dafoe, "How Does the Offense–Defense Balance Scale?" *Journal of Strategic Studies* 42 (6) (2019), pp. 736–763; Acton, "Escalation through Entanglement," pp. 56–99; Matthew Kroenig, "Bringing Geopolitics Back," *Strategic Studies Quarterly* (Winter, 2021), pp. 59–73; and James Johnson, "Inadvertent Escalation in the Age of Intelligence Machines: A New Model for Nuclear Risk in the Digital Age," *European Journal of International Security* 7 (3) (2022), pp. 1–23.

34 Adrienne Mayor, *Gods, and Robots: Myths, Machines, and Ancient Dreams of Technology* (Princeton: Princeton University Press, 2020).

Process tracing

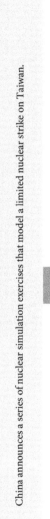

Cause "antecedent"

China announces a series of nuclear simulation exercises that model a limited nuclear strike on Taiwan.

Causal mechanisms

US activates dormant AI-augmented AFT within China's C3 networks to gather intel to determine China's intentions.

China interprets US cyber operations are part of an offensive attack against China's NC3 system—designed to create a window of opportunity

Escalatory rhetoric playing out on social media amplifies the impact of US "routine" operations in the Pacific, prompting China to place upgrade its nuclear alert status.

Outcome "consequent"

Each side views the others' action as malign/aggressive.

US and China move to a war-footing—with nuclear weapons on the table.

Figure A1.1 Process tracing

Source: James Johnson, "Counterfactual Thinking & Nuclear Risk in the Digital Age: The Role of Uncertainty, Complexity, Chance, and Human Psychology," *Journal for Peace and Nuclear Disarmament* (2022), p. 8, doi: 10.1080/25751654.2022.2102286.

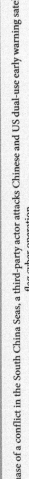

Cause "antecedent"

During the initial phase of a conflict in the South China Seas, a third-party actor attacks Chinese and US dual-use early warning satellites with a false flag cyber operation.

Causal mechanisms

China fearful that this attack is a prelude to decapitating US first strike orders the delegation of pre-launch authority to remote AI-powered decision-making support systems.

US fearful that the loss of an important strategic warning capability raises its nuclear alert status.

With scant evidence of responsibility, both sides are convinced that the other is responsible, and that the attack is designed as a prelude to a preemptive first strike.

Outcome "consequent"

The US views China's attack as unprovoked aggression accidentally sparking "catalytic nuclear war."

China retaliates preemptively against the US with tactical nuclear missiles in a limited strike against US bases in Guam.

Figure A1.2 Process tracing

Source: James Johnson, "Counterfactual Thinking & Nuclear Risk in the Digital Age: The Role of Uncertainty, Complexity, Chance, and Human Psychology," *Journal for Peace and Nuclear Disarmament* (2022), p. 9, doi: 10.1080/25751654.2022.2102286.

Cause "antecedent"

During a US-China crisis Russian proxy actors flood social media outlets and open-source crowdsourcing platforms with false information about the suspicious movement of Chinese dual-use missiles.

The public dissemination of China's action erodes the public confidence in the US nuclear deterrent (and extended deterrent commitments).

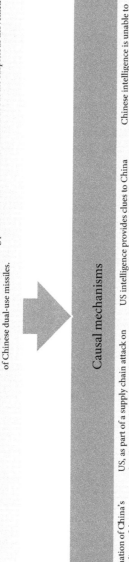

Causal mechanisms

US intelligence provides clues to China that it has carried out this attack, and that this intrusion runs deeper than China might otherwise predict.

US, as part of a supply chain attack on China's missile forces, inserts a malware in Chinese dual-use weapon delivery platforms.

Chinese intelligence is unable to determine whether the US attack is genuine nor how widespread the attack is.

Outcome "consequent"

Beijing, under intense domestic-political pressure to respond, believing it to be in a "use-it-or-lose-it" asymmetric situation retaliates by launching a retaliatory first strike against US platforms in the region.

Figure A1.3 Process tracing

Source: James Johnson, "Counterfactual Thinking & Nuclear Risk in the Digital Age: The Role of Uncertainty, Complexity, Chance, and Human Psychology," *Journal for Peace and Nuclear Disarmament* (2022), p. 9, doi: 10.1080/25751654.2022.2102286.

Sample of AI-enabled autonomous weapons used in human–machine teaming

Table A2.1 Sample of AI-enabled autonomous weapons used in human–machine teaming in development, production, or deployment.

Weapon system	Project/Nation	Key advantages
Missile defense and precision strike systems	• Goalkeeper close-in weapon system (Netherlands) • Iron Dome (Israel) • Kashtan close-in weapon system (Russia)	• Defense of ships against maneuverable missiles, aircraft, and surface vessels. • Detects, analyzes, and intercepts various threats. • Air defense gun/missile system defends ships from sea-skimming anti-ship missiles, and fixed- and rotary-wing aircraft.
Anti-personnel sentry weapons	• Samsung SGR-A1 (Republic of Korea) • Guardium (Israel) • Mobile Detection Assessment and Response System (MDARS-E) (US)	• Autonomous sentry gun equipped with surveillance, tracking, firing, and voice recognition. • Unarmed autonomous unmanned ground vehicle equipped with 360-degree cameras and loudspeaker. • Automated intrusion detection and inventory assessment.
Loitering munitions	• Harpy, Harop (Israel)	• Fire and forget autonomous weapon.
Unmanned aerial vehicle (UAV)/unmanned combat air vehicle (UCAV)	• Northrop Grumman X-47B (US) • Boeing Loyal Wingman (US) • Volk-18 (Russia)	• Aircraft carrier-based strike fighter-sized UCAV used for autonomous air refueling. • Low-cost stealth UAV to support manned aircrafts such as the F-35. • ISR for detecting and attacking drones.

Continued

Table A2.1 *Continued*

Weapon system	Project/Nation	Key advantages
Unmanned ground vehicle (UGV)	• Uran-9 (Russia) • MRK-27 BT (Russia) • Ghost Vision 60 (US)	• Tracked unmanned combat ground vehicle (UCGV) armed with anti-tank guided missile launcher. • Assault robotic vehicle fitted with flamethrowers, machine gun, grenade launchers and smoke grenades. • Quadrupedal (Q-UGV) used for remote inspection, ISR, mapping, distributed communications, and persistent security.
Unmanned surface vehicle (USV)	• Sea Hunter (US) • Protector USV (Israel) • Silver Marlin (Israel)	• Submarine-hunting USV designed to search, track, and destroy enemy submarines, conduct surface warfare missions, fire weapons, and launch electronic attacks. • Unmanned integrated system capable of performing a variety of naval and security missions and fitted with a "mini typhoon weapon station." • USV designed for maritime patrol missions and fitted with a remote-controlled stabilized weapon station.
Unmanned underwater vehicle (UUV)	• Galtel (Russia) • HSU-001 UUV (China) • Razerback (US)	• Autonomy for ISR and situational awareness. • UUV program designed for covert military operations. • Support submarine and the explosive ordnance disposal communities.
Command-and-control (C2) digital assistants	• Maritime Autonomous Platform Exploitation (MAPLE) C2 system (UK) • Perimeter Joint Operations Command and Control Advanced Concepts (Russia) • Deep Green (US) • Demonstration System (China) • Joint All-Domain Command and Control (JADC2) (US)	• Combat management system designed to autonomously control USVs and UAVs. • Automated launch of a nuclear strike based on data from sensors, indicating a nuclear attack. • Decision-making support system with predictive capabilities to predict possible future scenarios. • Based on study of the US Deep Green. • All-domain program that employs automation and AI to speed up decision-making and disrupt/exploit adversaries decision cycle.

Selected bibliography

Acton, James, "Hypersonic Boost-Glide Weapons," *Science & Global Security* 23 (3) (2015), pp. 191–219.

Acton, James, "Escalation through Entanglement: How the Vulnerability of Command-and-Control Systems Raises the Risks of an Inadvertent Nuclear War," *International Security* 43 (1) (2018), pp. 56–99.

Agrawal, Ajay, Joshua Gans, and Avi Goldfarb, *Prediction Machines: The Simple Economics of Artificial Intelligence* (Cambridge, MA: Harvard Business Review Press, 2018).

Martin Amis, *"Thinkability" in Einstein's Monsters* (New York: Harmony Books, 1987).

Anderson, Susan, "Asimov's 'Three Laws of Robotics,' and Machine Metaethics," *AI and Society* 22 (4) (2008), pp. 477–493.

Andersson, Jenny, *The Future of the World: Futurology, Futurists, and the Struggle for the Post-Cold War Imagination* (Oxford: Oxford University Press, 2018).

Antoine, Bechara et al., "Deciding Advantageously before Knowing the Advantageous Strategy," *Science* 275 (5304) (1997), pp. 1293–1295.

Applin, Sally, "They Sow, They Reap: How Humans are Becoming Algorithm Chow," *IEEE Consumer Electronics Magazine* 7 (2) (2018), pp. 101–102. doi:10.1109/MCE.2017.2776468.

Arendt, Hannah, *On Violence* (New York: Harcourt Publishing Co., 1970).

Arendt, Hannah, *The Human Condition* (Chicago, IL: University of Chicago Press, 1998).

Arkin, Ronald, *Governing Lethal Behavior in Autonomous Robots* (Boca Raton, FL: Chapman, 2009).

Arkin, Ronald, "Lethal Autonomous Systems and the Plight of the Non-Combatant," *AISB Quarterly* 137 (2013), pp. 1–9.

Arquilla, John, and David Ronfeldt, "Looking Ahead: Preparing for Information-Age Conflict," in *Athena's Camp: Preparing for Conflict in the Information Age*, ed. John Arquilla and David Ronfeldt (Santa Monica, CA: RAND, 1997), pp. 439–502.

Bandura, Albert, Bill Underwood, and Michael Fromson, "Disinhibition of Aggression through Diffusion of Responsibility and Dehumanization of Victims," *Journal of Research in Personality* 9 (4) (1975), pp. 253–269.

Barnes, Michael, and William Evans, "Soldier–Robot Teaming: An Overview," in *Human–Robot Interactions in Future Military Operations*, ed. Michael Barnes and Florian Jentsch (Farnham: Ashgate Publishing, 2010), pp. 9–31.

Baron, Jonathan, *Thinking and Deciding*. 4th ed. (Cambridge: Cambridge University Press, 2008).

Bartneck, Christoph et al., "Measurement Instruments for the Anthropomorphism, Animacy, Likeability, Perceived Intelligence, and Perceived Safety of Robots," *International Journal of Social Robotics* 1 (1) (2009), pp. 71–81.

Bartneck, Christoph, "Robots in the Theatre and the Media," *Proceedings of the Design and Semantics of Form and Movement* (2013), *Wuxi*, pp. 64–70.

Baum, Seth D., Robert de Neufville, and Anthony M. Barrett, "A Model for the Probability of Nuclear War," *Global Catastrophic Risk Institute*, Global Catastrophic Risk Institute Working Paper 18–1 (March 2018), pp. 19–20.

Beavers, Anthony, "Editorial," *Ethics and Information Technology* 12 (3) (2010), 207–208.

Beckert, Jens, *Imagined Futures: Fictional Expectations and Capitalist Dynamics* (Cambridge MA: Harvard University Press, 2016).

Benbaji, Yitzhak, "Legitimate Authority in War," in *The Oxford Handbook of Ethics of War*, ed. Seth Lazar and Helen Frowe (New York: Oxford University Press, 2015), pp. 294–314.

Bengio, Yoshua, Yann Lecun, and Geoffrey Hinton, "Deep Learning for AI," *Communications of the ACM* 64 (7) (July 2021), pp. 58–65.

Bennett, Christopher, Joe Saunders, and Robert Stern, *Immanuel Kant: Groundwork for the Metaphysics of Morals* (Oxford: Oxford University Press, 2019).

Berger Alex, and Agnieszka Tymula, "Controlling Ambiguity: The Illusion of Control in Choice under Risk and Ambiguity," *Journal of Risk and Uncertainty* 65 (2022), pp. 261–284.

Bering, Jesse, "The Folk Psychology of Souls," *Behavioral and Brain Sciences* 29 (5) (2006), pp. 453–462.

Bernstein, Steven et al., "God Gave Physics the Easy Problems: Adapting Social Science to an Unpredictable World," *European Journal of International Relations* 6 (1) (2000), pp. 43–76. doi:10.1177/1354066100006001003.

Betts, Richard, *Enemies of Intelligence: Knowledge and Power in American National Security* (New York: Columbia University Press, 2007).

Beyerchen, Alan, "Clausewitz, Nonlinearity, and the Unpredictability of War," *International Security* 17 (3) (1992–1993), pp. 59–90.

Biddle, Stephen, *Military Power: Explaining Victory and Defeat in Modern Battle* (Princeton, NJ: Princeton University Press, 2004).

Biggio, Battista, and Fabio Roli, "Wild Patterns: Ten Years after the Rise of Adversarial Machine," *Pattern Recognition* 84 (December) (2018), pp. 317–331.

Blair, Bruce G., *The Logic of Accidental Nuclear War* (New York: Brookings, 1993).

Bleher, Hannah, and Matthias Braun, "Diffused Responsibility: Attributions of Responsibility in the use of AI-Driven Clinical Decision Support Systems," *AI Ethics* (2022). doi:10.1007/s43681-022-00135-x.

Bode, Ingvild, and Hendrik Huelss, *Autonomous Weapons Systems, and International Norms* (Queensland: McGill-Queen's University Press, 2022).

Boghosian, Bruce M., P. V. Coveney, and H. Wang 2019. "A New Pathology in the Simulation of Chaotic Dynamical Systems on Digital Computers," *Advanced Theory and Simulations* 2 (12), pp. 1–8. doi:10.1002/adts.201900125.

Bostrom, Nick, *Superintelligence: Paths, Dangers, Strategies* (Oxford: Oxford University Press, 2014).

Bousquet, Antoine, "Chaoplexic Warfare or the Future of Military Organization," *International Affairs* 84 (5) (2008), pp. 915–929.

Bousquet, Antoine, "Cyberneticizing the American War Machine: Science and Computers in the Cold War," *Cold War History* 8 (1) (January 2008), pp. 771–1102.

Bousquet, Antoine, *The Eye of War: Military Perception from the Telescope to the Drone* (Minnesota: University of Minnesota Press, 2018).

Boyd, John, "Patterns of Conflict," (unpublished presentation, draft version, 1982). www. projectwhitehorse.com/pdfs/boyd/patterns%20of%20conflict.pdf.

Boyd, John, "Organic Design for Command and Control," (unpublished presentation, 1987).

Boyd, John, "The Strategic Game of? And?" (unpublished presentation, 1987). www. ausairpower.net/JRB/strategic_game.pdf

Boyd, John, "The Essence of Winning and Losing," (unpublished presentation, 1995). https:// danford.net/boyd/essence1.htm.

Boyer, Pascal, *Religion Explained* (New York: Basic Books, 2001).

Boys, James D., "The Unpredictability Factor: Nixon, Trump and the Application of the Madman Theory in US Grand Strategy," *Cambridge Review of International Affairs* 34 (3) (2021), pp. 430–451.

Bradshaw, Jeffrey et al., "Coactive Emergence as a Sensemaking Strategy for Cyber Operations," *IHMC Technical Report* (October 2012), pp. 1–24.

Brennan, William, *Dehumanizing the Vulnerable: When Word Games Take Lives* (Chicago, IL: Loyola University Press, 1995).

Brewer, Marilynn B., and William D. Crano, *Social Psychology* (New York: West, 1994).

Brodie, Bernard, *War and Politics* (New York: Macmillan, 1974).

Brodie, Bernard, and Fawn Brodie, *From Crossbow to H-Bomb* (Bloomington: Indiana University Press, 1973).

Bronfenbrenner, Uri, "Mirror Image in Soviet–American Relations: A Social Psychologist's Report," *Journal of Social Issues* 17 (3) (2010), pp. 5–56.

Brose, Christian, *The Kill Chain: Defending America in the Future of High-Tech Warfare* (New York: Hachette, 2020).

Brough, Michael W., "Dehumanization of the Enemy and the Moral Equality of Soldiers," in *Rethinking the Just War Tradition*, ed. Michael W. Brough, John W. Lango, and Harry van der Linden (New York: SUNY Press, 2007), pp. 149–167.

Bryant Conant, James, *Two Modes of Thought* (New York: Trident Press, 1964).

Butcher, Fiona D., "Psycho-Social Factors Influencing Trust in Artificial Intelligence Advice Systems" (thesis, University of Leicester, 2022). doi:10.25392/leicester.data.20310096.v.

Butterfield, Herbert, *History and Human Relations* (London: Collins, 1951).

Buzan, Barry, and Lene Hansen, *The Evolution of International Security Studies* (Cambridge: Cambridge University Press, 2009).

Byrne, David, *Complexity Theory and the Social Sciences: An Introduction* (London: Routledge, 1998).

Campbell Craig, *Glimmer of a New Leviathan: Total War in the Realism of Niebuhr, Morgenthau, and Waltz* (New York: Columbia University Press, 2003).

Capoccia, Giovanni, and R. Daniel Kelemen, "The Study of Critical Junctures: Theory, Narrative and Counterfactuals in Historical Institutionalism," *World Politics* 59 (3) (April 2007), pp. 341–369.

Cappuccio, Massimiliano, "Inference or Familiarity? The Embodied Roots of Social Cognition," *Synthesis Philosophica* 29 (2) (2014), pp. 253–272.

Cappuccio, Massimiliano, Jai Galliott, and Eduardo Sandoval, "Mapping Meaning and Purpose in Human–Robot Teams: Anthropomorphic Agents in Military Operations," *The Philosophical Journal of Conflict and Violence* 5 (1) (2021), pp. 73–94.

Cappuccio, Massimiliano, Jai Galliott, and Eduardo Sandoval, "Saving Private Robot: Risks and Advantages of Anthropomorphism in Agent–Soldier Teams," *International Journal of Social Robotics* (2021). doi:10.1007/s12369-021-00755-z.

Card, Stuart, Thomas Moran, and Allen Newell, *The Psychology of Human–Computer Interaction* (London: CRC Press, 1983).

Carpenter, Julie, "Just Doesn't Look Right: Exploring the Impact of Humanoid Robot Integration into Explosive Ordnance Disposal Teams," in *Handbook of Research on Technoself: Identity in a Technological Society*, ed. Rocci Luppicini (Hershey: IGI Global, 2013), pp. 609–636.

Castel, Robert, "From Dangerousness to Risk," in *The Foucault Effect*, ed. G. Burchell, C. Gordon, and P. Mille (Hertfordshire: Harvester Wheatsheaf, 1991), pp. 281–298.

Cebrowski, Arthur K., "Sea, Space, Cyberspace: Borderless Domains," speech delivered to US Naval War College (Newport, RI), February 26, 1999.

Chamayou, Gregorie, *A Theory of the Drone*, trans. J. Lloyd (New York: New Press, 2014).

Chappelle, Wayne L. et al., "Symptoms of Psychological Distress and Post-Traumatic Stress Disorder in United States Air Force 'Drone' Operators," *Military Medicine* 179 (2014), pp. 63–70.

Charette, Robert, "Automated to Death," *IEEE Spectrum*, December 15, 2009. https://spectrum. ieee.org/automated-to-death.

Charles, C. Krulak, "The Strategic Corporal: Leadership in the Three Block War," *Marines Magazine* (January 1999).

Chen, Bing et al., "Recent Developments and Challenges of Lower Extremity Exoskeletons," *Journal of Orthopaedic Translation* 5 (2016), pp. 26–37.

Chérif, Lobna et al., "Multitasking in the Military: Cognitive Consequences and Potential Solutions," *Applied Cognitive Psychology* 32 (4) (2018), pp. 429–439.

Cialdini, Robert, *Influence: The Psychology of Persuasion* (New York: Harper, 2007).

Cimbala, Stephen, *The Dead Volcano: The Background and Effects of Nuclear War Complacency* (New York: Praeger, 2002).

Clark, Alan, *Natural Born Cyborgs, Technology and Future of Human Intelligence* (Oxford: Oxford University Press, 2003).

Clark, Andy, *Surfing Uncertainty: Prediction, Action, and the Embodied Mind* (New York: Oxford University Press, 2015).

Clark, Lindsay, *Gender and Drone Warfare: A Hauntological Perspective* (London: Routledge, 2019).

Clerk Maxwell, James, Lewis Campbell, and William Garnett, "Science and Free Will," in *The Life of James Clerk Maxwell*, Lewis Campbell and William Garnett (New York: Johnson Reprint Corporation, 1969), pp. 194–242.

Clifford, Nass et al., "Can Computer Personalities be Human Personalities?" *International Journal of Human-Computer Studies* 43 (2) (1995), pp. 223–239.

Cohen, Eliot, "A Revolution in Warfare," *Foreign Affairs* 75 (2) (1996), pp. 34–54.

Coker, Christopher, *Ethics and War in the 21st Century* (London: Routledge, 2008).

Coker, Christopher, *Warrior Geeks: How 21st-Century Technology is Changing the Way we Fight and Think about War* (London: Hurst & Company, 2013).

Collier, Ruth, and David Collier, *Shaping the Political Arena: Critical Junctures, the Labor* (Indiana: University of Notre Dame Press, 2002).

Collins, John, Ned Hall, and L.A. Paul (eds), *Causation and Counterfactuals* (Cambridge, MA: MIT Press, 2004).

Conrad, Joseph, *The Secret Agent* (New York: Double Day, Page & Company, 1923).

Considine, Laura, "Narrative and Nuclear Weapons Politics: The Entelechial Force of the Nuclear Origin Myth," *International Theory* 14 (3) (October 2021), pp. 1–20.

Cooper, Glenda, "Populist Rhetoric and Media Misinformation in the 2016 UK Brexit Referendum," in *The Routledge Companion to Media Disinformation and PopulismI*, ed. Howard Tumber and Silvio Waisbord (London: Routledge, 2021), pp. 397–411.

Cosenzo, Keryl, and Michael Barnes, "Human–Robot Interaction Research for Current and Future Military Applications: From the Laboratory to the Field," *Unmanned Systems Technology XII* (2010).

Cosmides, Leda, and John Tooby, "Evolutionary Psychology and the Emotions," *Handbook of Emotions* 2 (2) (2000), pp. 91–115.

Crawford, Neta C., "Bugsplat: US Standing Rules of Engagement, International Humanitarian Law, Military Necessity, and Non-Combatant Immunity," in *Just War: Authority, Tradition, and Practice*, ed. A. F. Lang (Washington, D.C.: Georgetown University Press, 2013), pp. 397–422.

Creveld, Martin Van, *Command in War* (Cambridge, MA and London: Harvard University Press, 2003).

Cummings, Mary L., "Automation Bias in Intelligent Time-Critical Decision Support Systems," *AIAA 1st Intelligent Systems Technical Conference*, 2004, 557562557562.

Cummings, Mary L., "Rethinking the Maturity of Artificial Intelligence in Safety-Critical Settings," *AI Magazine* 42 (1) (2021), pp. 6–15.

Czerwinski, Thomas, J., *Coping with the Bounds, Speculations on Nonlinearity in Military Affairs* (Washington, D.C.: National Defense University Press, 1999).

Dacey, Mike, "Anthropomorphism as Cognitive Bias," *Philosophy of Science* 84 (5) (2017), pp. 1152–1164.

Danaher, John, "Robot Betrayal: A Guide to the Ethics of Robotic Deception," *Ethics Information Technology* 22 (2) (2020), pp. 117–128.

Dawes, Robyn, *Rational Choice in an Uncertain World* (San Diageo: Harcourt Brace Jovanovich, 1988).

Dawes, Robyn, and Matthew Mulford, "The False Consensus Effect and Overconfidence: Flaws in Judgment or Flaws in How we Study Judgment?" *Organizational Behavior and Human Decision Processes* 65 (3) (1996), pp. 201–211.

De Dreu, Carsten, "Time Pressure and Closing of the Mind in Negotiation," *Organizational Behavior and Human Decision Processes* 91 (2) (2003), pp. 280–295.

Deeks, Ashley, Noam Lubell, and Daragh Murray, "Machine Learning, Artificial Intelligence, and the Use of Force by States," *Journal of National Security Law & Policy* 10 (1) (2019), pp. 1–25.

Derian, James Der, "Virtuous War/Virtual Theory," *International Affairs* 766 (4) (2000), pp. 772–788.

Dewey, John, *Essays in Experimental Logic* (Chicago, IL: University of Chicago Press, 1916).

Dickson, Paul, *The Electronic Battlefield* (Bloomington: Indiana University Press, 1976).

Dobbs, Michael, *One Minute to Midnight* (New York: Alfred A. Knopf, 2008).

Dobos, Ned, *Ethics, Security, and the War-Machine: The True Cost of the Military* (Oxford: Oxford University Press, 2020).

Dodge, Robert V., *Schelling's Game Theory: How to Make Decisions* (New York: Oxford University Press, 2012).

Domingos, Pedro, "A Few Useful Things to Know about Machine Learning," *Communications of the ACM* 55 (10) (2012), pp. 78–87.

Duffy, Brian, "Anthropomorphism and the Social Robot," *Robotics and Autonomous Systems* 42 (3) (2003), pp. 177–190.

Durham, Susanne, *Chaos Theory for the Practical Military Mind* (New York: Biblioscholar, 2012).

Ehrenfeld, David, "The Management of Diversity: A Conservation Paradox," in *Ecology, Economics, Ethics: The Broken Circle*, ed. F. Herbert Bormann and Stephen Kellert (New Haven, CT: Yale University Press, 1991), pp. 26–39.

Eidelman, Scott, and Christian S. Crandall, "The Intuitive Traditionalist: How Biases for Existence and Longevity Promote the Status Quo," *Advances in Experimental Social Psychology* 50 (2014), pp. 53–104.

Eidelman, Scott, Christian S. Crandall, and Jennifer Pattershall, "The Existence Bias," *Journal of Personality and Social Psychology* 97 (5) (2009), pp. 765–775.

Ekelho, Merel, and Giacomo Persi Paoli, *The Human Element in Decisions about the Use of Force* (Geneva, Switzerland: UNIDIR, 2019).

Ellis, Bruce, and David Bjorklund, *Origins of the Social Mind: Evolutionary Psychology and Child Development* (New York: The Guildford Press, 2004).

Emery, John R., "Probabilities Towards Death: Bugsplat, Algorithmic Assassinations, and Ethical Due Care," *Critical Military Studies* 8 (2) (2022), pp. 179–197.

Emery, John R., and Hadley Biggs, "Human, All Too Human: Drones, Ethics, and the Psychology of Military Technologies," *Political Psychology* 43 (3) (2022), pp. 605–613.

Engesser, Sven et al., "Populism and Social Media: How Politicians Spread a Fragmented Ideology," *Information, Communication and Society* 20 (8) (August 2017), pp. 1109–1126.

Epley, Nicholas, and Adam Waytz, "Mind Perception," in *The Handbook of Social Psychology*, ed. Susan T. Fiske, Daniel T. Gilbert, and Gardner Lindzey. 5th ed. (New York: Wiley, 2013), pp. 498–454.

Epley, Nicolas, Adam Waytz, and John Cacioppo, "On Seeing Human: A Three-Factor Theory of Anthropomorphism," *Psychological Review* 114 (2007), pp. 864–886.

Esther Eidinow, *Luck, Fate and Fortune: Antiquity and its Legacy* (Oxford: Oxford University Press, 2011).

Evans, Nicholas G., and Jonathan D. Moreno, "Neuroethics and Policy at the National Security Interface," in *Debates about Neuroethics: Perspectives on its Development, Focus and Future*, ed. Eric Racine and John Aspler (Dordecht: Springer, 2017), pp. 141–160.

Evera, Stephen Van, "The Cult of the Offensive and the Origins of the First World War," *International Security* 9 (1) (1984), pp. 58–107.

Eyssel Friederike et al., "If You Sound Like Me, You Must be More Human: On the Interplay of Robot and User Features on Human–Robot Acceptance and Anthropomorphism," in: HRI'12, *Proceedings of the 7th annual ACM/IEEE International Conference on Human–Robot Interaction* (2012), pp. 125–126.

Eyssel, Friederike, and Dieta Kuchenbrandt, "Social Categorization of Social Robots: Anthropomorphism as a Function of Robot Group Membership," *British Journal of Social Psychology* 51 (4) (2012), pp. 724–731.

Fabre, Cecile, *Spying through a Glass Darkly* (London: Oxford University Press, 2022).

Fearon, James D., "Signaling Versus the Balance of Power and Interests: An Empirical Test of the Crisis Bargaining Model," *Journal of Conflict Resolution* 38 (2) (1994), pp. 236–269.

Fearon, James D., "Signaling Foreign Policy Interests: Tying Hands versus Sinking Costs," *Journal of Conflict Resolution* 41 (1) (1997), pp. 68–90.

Ferguson, Niall, *Virtual History: Alternatives and Counterfactuals* (New York: Penguin, 2014).

Ferreira, Raul, S., "Machine Learning in A Nonlinear World: A Linear Explanation through the Domain of the Autonomous Vehicles," *European Training Network for Safer Autonomous Systems* (January 9, 2020).

Fischhoff, Baruch, Paul Slovic, and Sarah Lichtenstein, "Knowing with Certainty the Appropriateness of Extreme Confidence," *Journal of Experimental Psychology: Human Perception and Performance* 3 (4) (1977), pp. 552–564.

Fischhoff, Baruch, "Hindsight is Not Equal to Foresight: The Effect of Outcome Knowledge on Judgment under Uncertainty," *Journal of Experimental Psychology* 1 (2) (1975), pp. 288–299.

Fiske, Susan T., and Shelley E. Taylor, *Social Cognition*. 2nd ed. (New York: McGraw-Hill, 1991).

Florida, Luciano, "Digital's Cleaving Power and its Consequences," *Philosophy & Technology* 30 (2) (2017), pp. 123–129.

Floridi, Luciano, and J. W. Sanders, "On the Morality of Artificial Agents," *Minds and Machines* 14 (3) (2004), pp. 349–379.

Fox, Jesse, and Andrew Gambino, "Relationship Development with Humanoid Social Robots: Applying Interpersonal Theories to Human/Robot Interaction," *Cyberpsychology and Behavior, and Social Networking* 24 (5) (2021), pp. 294–299.

Francis, Gavin, "History and the Unanswered Questions of the Nuclear Age," in *The Age of Hiroshima*, ed. Michael D. Gordin and G. John Ikenberry (Princeton, NJ: Princeton University Press, 2020), pp. 294–311.

Francois, Camille, and Herb Lin, "The Strategic Surprise of Russian Information Operations on Social Media in 2016 in the United States: Mapping a Blind Spot," *Journal of Cyber Policy* 6 (1) (2021), pp. 9–30.

Freedberg, Sydney, Jr., "Let Leaders Off the Electronic Leash: CSA Milley, Breaking Defense," May 5, 2017. https://breakingdefense.com/2017/05/let-leaders-off-the-electronic-leash-csa-milley.

Freedman, Lawrence, *The Evolution of Nuclear Strategy*. 2nd ed. (London: Palgrave Macmillan, 1989).

Freedman, Lawrence, *Deterrence* (New York: Polity, 2004).

Freedman, Lawrence, *The Future of War* (London: Public Affairs, 2017).

French, Peter, "Principles of Responsibility, Shame, and the Corporation," in *Shame, Responsibility, and the Corporation*, ed. H. Curtler (New York: Haven, 1986), pp. 17–55.

French, Shannon E., and Anthony I. Jack, "Dehumanizing the Enemy: The Intersection of Neuroethics and Military Ethics," in *Responsibilities to Protect: Perspectives in Theory and Practice*, ed. David Whetham and Bradley J. Strawser (Leiden: Brill, 2015), pp. 165–195.

Frieden, Jeffry, and David Lake, "International Relations as a Social Science: Rigor and Relevance," *The Annals of the American Academy of Political and Social Sciences* 600 (1) (2005), pp. 136–156.

Furman, Jason, and Robert Seamans, "AI and the Economy," in *Innovation Policy and the Economy*, ed. Josh Lerner and Scott Stern, Vol. 19 (Chicago, IL: University of Chicago Press, 2018), pp. 161–191.

Futter, Andrew, "Disruptive Technologies and Nuclear Risks: What's New and What Matters," *Survival* 64 (1) (2022), pp. 99–120.

Futter, Andrew, and Benjamin Zala, "Strategic Non-Nuclear Weapons and the Onset of a Third Nuclear Age," *European Journal of* International Security 6 (3) (2021), pp. 257–277.

Galliott, Jai, "Defending Australia in the Digital Age: Toward Full-Spectrum Defense," *Defence Studies* 16 (2) (2016), pp. 157–175.

Galliott, Jai, "War 2.0: Drones, Distance and Death," *International Journal of Technoethics* 7 (2) (2016), pp. 61–76.

Gardner, Howard, *The Mind's New Science: A History of the Cognitive Revolution* (New York: Basic Books, 1985).

Gayer, Corinna C. et al., "Overcoming Psychological Barriers to Peaceful Conflict Resolution: The Role of Arguments about Losses," *Journal of Conflict Resolution* 53 (6) (2009), pp. 951–975.

George, Alexander, and Richard Smoke, *Deterrence in American Foreign Policy: Theory & Practice* (New York: Columbia University Press, 1974).

Gilpin, Faust Drew, "The Chronicle of Higher Education. May 2. In Jefferson Lecture, Drew Faust Traces the Fascination of War, From Homer to Bin Laden," 2011. www.neh.gov/about/awards/jefferson-lecture/drew-gilpin-faust-biography.

Giordano, James, "Neurotechnology, Global Relations, and National Security: Shifting Contexts and Neuroethical Demands," in *Neurotechnology in National Security and Defense: Practical Considerations, Neuroethical Concerns*, ed. James Giordano (Boca Raton: CRC Press, 2015), pp. 1–10.

Gladue, Brian A., Michael Boechler, and Kevin D. McCaul, "Hormonal Response to Competition in Human Males," *Aggressive Behavior* 15 (6) (1989), pp. 409–422.

Gladwell, Malcolm, *Blink: The Power of Thinking without Thinking* (New York: Little Brown and Company, 2005).

Gleick, James, *Chaos: The Making of a New Science* (New York: Viking, 1985).

Goldfarb, Avi, and Jon Lindsay, "Prediction and Judgment: Why Artificial Intelligence Increases the Importance of Humans in War," *International Security* 46 (3) (2022), pp. 7–50.

Goodfellow, Ian, et al., "Generative Adversarial Nets," in *Advances in Neural Information Processing Systems* 27, ed. Zoubin Ghahramani et al. (Montreal, Quebec: NeurIPS Proceedings, 2014), pp. 2672–2680.

Goodfellow, Ian, Jonathon Shlens, and Christian Szegedy, "Explaining and Harnessing Adversarial Examples," December 20, 2014. *arXiv* preprint arXiv:1412 6572.

Grant, T. Hammond, "Reflections on the Legacy of John Boyd," *Contemporary Security Policy* 34 (3) (2013), pp. 600–602. doi:10.1080/13523260.2013.842297.

Grauer, Ryan, *Commanding Military Power: Organizing for Victory and Defeat on the Battlefield* (Cambridge: Cambridge University Press, 2016).

Gray, Colin, *Modern Strategy* (London: Oxford University Press, 1999).

Gray, Kurt, Heather Gray, and Daniel Wegner, "Dimensions of Mind Perception," *Science* 315 (5812) (2007), p. 619.

Gross, James J., "Emotion Regulation: Affective, Cognitive, and Social Consequences," *Psychophysiology* 39 (3) (2002), pp. 281–291.

Gruenfeld, Deborah et al., "Power and the Objectification of Social Targets," *Journal of Personality and Social Psychology* 95 (1) (2008), pp. 111–127.

Guthrie, Stuart, *Faces in the Clouds: A New Theory of Religion* (Oxford: Oxford University Press, 1995).

Hagerott, Mark, "Lethal Autonomous Weapons Systems from a Military Officer's Perspective: This Time is Different: Offering a Framework and Suggestions." Paper presented at the United Nations Informal Meeting of Experts at the Convention on Conventional Weapons, May 15, 2014, Geneva, Switzerland.

Haldeman, H. R. with Joseph Dimona, *The Ends of Power* (New York: Times Books, 1978).

Haley, Kevin, and Daniel Fessler, "Nobody's Watching? Subtle Cues Affect Generosity in an Anonymous Economic Game," *Evolution and Human Behavior* 26 (3) (2005), pp. 245–256.

Hardin, Russell, "Collective Action as an Agreeable N-Prisoners' Dilemma," *Behavioral Science* 16 (5) (September 1971).

Harris, Lasana, and Susan Fiske, "Dehumanizing the Lowest of the Low: Neuroimaging Responses to Extreme Outgroups," *Psychological Science* 17 (10) (2006), pp. 847–853.

Harris, Lasana, and Susan Fiske, "Brooms in Fantasia: Neural Correlates of Anthropomorphizing Objects," *Social Cognition* 26 (2) (2008), pp. 209–222.

Harvey, Frank P., *Explaining the Iraq War: Counterfactual Theory, Logic, and Evidence* (Cambridge: Cambridge University Press, 2012).

Hasik, James, "Beyond the Briefing: Theoretical and Practical Problems in the Works and Legacy of John Boyd," Contemporary Security Policy 34 (2013), pp. 583–599. doi:10.1080/13523260.2013.839257.

Haslam, Alexander, Stephen Reicher, and Michael Paltow, *The New Psychology of Leadership: Influence, Identity, and Power* (Hove: Psychology Press, 2010).

Haslam, Nick, "Dehumanization: An Integrative Review," *Personality and Social Psychology Review* 10 (3) (2006), pp. 252–264.

Hassabis, Demis, et al., "Neuroscience-Inspired Artificial Intelligence," *Neuron* 95 (2) (2017), pp. 245–258.

Hawkins, Scott, and Reid Hastie, "Hindsight: Biased Judgments of Past Events after the Outcomes are Known," *Psychological Bulletin* 107 (2) (1990), pp. 311–327.

Hayashi, Hideaki, and Toshio Tsuji, "Human–Machine Interfaces Based on Bioelectric Signals: A Narrative Review with a Novel System Proposal," *IEEJ Transaction on Electrical & Electronic Engineering* (2022). doi:10.1002/tee.23646.

Hegel, Frank, et al., "Towards a Typology of Meaningful Signals and Cues in Social Robotics," in *Proceedings of the IEEE International Workshop on Robot and Human Interactive Communication* (2012), pp. 72–78.

Heidegger, Martin, *Being and Time*, trans. John MacQuarrie and Edward Robinson (London: SCM Press, 1962).

Herbert, A. Simon, "Making Management Decisions: The Role of Intuition and Emotions," *The Academy of Management Executive* 1 (1989), pp. 57–64.

Hersman, Rebecca, "Wormhole Escalation: The New Nuclear Age," *Texas National Security Review* 2 (3) (2020), pp. 91–109.

Heyns, Christof, "Report of the Special Rapporteur on Extrajudicial, Summary or Arbitrary Executions, United Nations Human Rights Council," A/HRC/23/47 (2013).

Hill, Samantha R., *Critical Lives: Hannah Arendt* (New York: Reaktion Books, 2021).

Hinsley, F. H., *Power and the Pursuit of Peace* (Cambridge: Cambridge University Press, 1963).

Hoffman, David E., *The Dead Hand: The Untold Story of the Cold War Arms Race and its Dangerous Legacy* (New York: Anchor, 2009).

Hoffman, Guy, and Cynthia Breazeal, "Collaboration in Human–Robot Teams," in AIAA 1st Intelligent Systems Technical Conference (Infotech Aerospace Conferences, American Institute of Aeronautics and Astronautics, 2004).

Hogg, Michael A., "A Social Identity Theory of Leadership," *Personality and Social Psychology Review* 5 (3) (2001), pp. 184–200.

Hogg, Michael A., Sarah C. Hains, and Isabel Mason, "Identification and Leadership in Small Groups: Salience, Frame of Reference, and Leader Stereotypicality Effects on Leader Evaluations," *Journal of Personality and Social Psychology* 75 (1998), pp. 1248–1263.

Holland, Owen, *Machine Consciousness* (New York, Imprint Academic, 2003).

Horowitz, Michael C., *The Diffusion of Military Power: Causes and Consequences for International Politics* (Princeton, NJ: Princeton University Press, 2010).

Horowitz, Michael C., "When Speed Kills: Lethal Autonomous Weapon Systems, Deterrence, and Stability," *Journal of Strategic Studies* 42 (6) (2019), pp. 764–788.

Hume, David, *The Natural History of Religion* (Stanford, CA: Stanford University Press, 1957).

Hume, David, *A Treatise of Human Nature* (New York: Prometheus, 1992).

Hume, David, *Stanford Encyclopaedia of Philosophy*, April 17, 2019.

Huth, Paul, and Bruce Russett, "Deterrence Failure and Crisis Escalation," *International Studies Quarterly* 32 (1) (1988), pp. 29–45.

Ikkatai, Yuko et al., "Octagon Measurement: Public Attitudes toward AI Ethics," *International Journal of Human–Computer Interaction*, 38 (17) (2022), pp. 1589-1606, doi:10.1080/10447318.2021.2009669.

Jacobs, Robert (ed.), *Filling the Hole in the Nuclear Future: Art and Popular Culture Respond to the Bomb* (New York: Lexington Books, 2010).

Jantsch, Erich, *The Self-Organizing Universe: Scientific and Human Implications of the Emerging Paradigm of Evolution* (Oxford: Pergamon Press, 1980).

Jervis, Robert, "Hypotheses on Misperception," *World Politics* 20 (3) (1968), pp. 454–479.

Jervis, Robert, *Perception and Misperception in International Politics* (Princeton, NJ: Princeton University Press, 1976).

Jervis, Robert, "Cooperation under the Security Dilemma," *World Politics* 30 (2) (1978), pp. 169–214.

Jervis, Robert, *The Illogic of American Nuclear Strategy* (Ithaca, NY: Cornell University Press, 1984).

Jervis, Robert, *The Meaning of the Nuclear Revolution* (Ithaca, NY: Cornell University Press, 1989).

Jervis, Robert, "Rational Deterrence: Theory and Evidence," *World Politics* 41 (2) (1989), pp. 183–207.

Jervis, Robert, *System Effects: Complexity in Political and Social Life* (Princeton, NJ: Princeton University Press, 1997).

Jervis, Robert, *How Statesmen Think: The Psychology of International Politics* (Princeton, NJ: Princeton University Press, 2017).

Johnson, Dominic D., *Overconfidence and War* (Cambridge, MA: Harvard University Press, 2004).

Johnson, James, "China's Vision of the Future Network-Centric Battlefield: Cyber, Space and Electromagnetic Asymmetric Challenges to the United States," *Comparative Strategy* 37 (5) (2018), pp. 373–390. doi:10.1080/01495933.2018.1526563.

Johnson, James, "Artificial Intelligence in Nuclear Warfare: A Perfect Storm of Instability?" *The Washington Quarterly* 43 (2) (2020), pp. 197–211.

Johnson, James, *Artificial Intelligence and the Future of Warfare: USA, China, and Strategic Stability* (Manchester: Manchester University Press, 2021).

Johnson, James, "Catalytic Nuclear War in the Age of Artificial Intelligence'; Autonomy: Emerging Military Technology and Escalation Risk between Nuclear-Armed States," Journal of Strategic Studies (2021) doi:10.1080/01402390.2020.1867541.

Johnson, James, "The End of Military-Techno Pax Americana? Washington's Strategic Responses to Chinese AI-Enabled Military Technology," *The Pacific Review* 34 (3) (2021), pp. 351–378.

Johnson, James, "Automating the OODA Loop in the Age of Intelligent Machines: Reaffirming the Role of Humans in Command-and-Control Decision-Making in the Digital Age," *Defence Studies*, 23 (1) (2023), pp. 43-67 (2022). doi:10.1080/14702436.2022.2102486.

Johnson, James, "Counterfactual Thinking & Nuclear Risk in the Digital Age: The Role of Uncertainty, Complexity, Chance, and Human Psychology," Journal for Peace and Nuclear Disarmament (2022). doi:10.1080/25751654.2022.2102286.

Johnson, James, "Inadvertent Escalation in the Age of Intelligence Machines: A New Model for Nuclear Risk in the Digital Age," *European Journal of International Security* 7 (3) (2022), pp. 337–359.

Johnson, James, *AI and the Bomb: Nuclear Strategy and Risk in the Digital Age* (Oxford: Oxford University Press, 2023).

Jones, Edward, and Victor Harris, "The Attribution Attitudes," *Journal of Experimental Psychology* 3 (1) (1967), pp. 167–174.

Kahn, Herman, *On Escalation: Metaphors and Scenarios* (New York: Harvard University Press, 1965).

Kahneman, Daniel, "Varieties in Counterfactual Thinking," in *What Might Have Been: The Social Psychology of Counterfactual Thinking*, ed. N. J. Roese and J. M. Olson (Mahwah: Erlbaum, 1995), pp. 375–396.

Kahneman, Daniel, *Thinking, Fast and Slow* (New York: Penguin 2011).

Kahneman, Daniel, and Jonathan Renshon, "Hawkish Biases," in *American Foreign Policy and the Politics of Fear: Threat Inflation Since 9/11*, ed. Trevor Thrall and Jane Kramer (New York: Routledge, 2009), pp. 79–96.

Kahneman, Daniel, Paul Slovic, and Amos Tversky (eds), *Judgment Under Uncertainty: Heuristics and Biases* (Cambridge: Cambridge University Press, 1982).

Kamo, Masashi, and Hiroyuki Yokomizo, "Explanation of Non-Additive Effects in Mixtures of a Similar Mode of Action Chemicals," *Toxicology* 1 (335) (2015), pp. 20–26. doi:10.1016/j.tox.2015.06.008.

Kant, Immanuel, *Foundations of the Metaphysics of Morals*, trans. L. W. Beck (New York: Macmillan, 1959).

Kaplan, Martin, Tatiana L. Wanshula, and Mark P. Zanna, "Time Pressure and Information Integration in Social Judgment: The Effect of Need for Structure," in *Time Pressure and Stress in Human Judgment and Decision Making*, ed. Ola Svenson and John A. Maule (New York: Plenum Press, 1993), pp. 255–267.

Keegan, John, *The Face of Battle* (London: Cape, 1976).

Kershaw, Ian, *Fateful Choices: Ten Decisions that Changed the World, 1940–1941* (New York: Penguin, 2007).

King, Anthony, *Command: The Twenty-First-Century General* (Cambridge: Cambridge University Press, 2019).

King, Gary, Robert Keohane, and Sydney Verba, *Designing Social Inquiry: Scientific Inference in Qualitative Research* (Princeton, NJ: Princeton University Press, 1994).

King, William R., and Jun He, "A Meta-Analysis of the Technology Acceptance Model," *Information & Management* 43 (6) (2006), pp. 740–755.

Kissinger, Henry, *Diplomacy* (New York: Simon & Schuster, 1993).

Kissinger, Henry, Eric Schmidt, and Daniel Huttenlocher, *The Age of AI and Our Human Future* (London: John Murray, 2021).

Kjølv Egeland, "The Ideology of Nuclear Order," *New Political Science* 43 (2) (2021), pp. 208–230.

Kollars, Nina, A., "War's Horizon: Soldier-Led Adaptation in Iraq and Vietnam," *Journal of Strategic Studies* 38 (4) (2015), pp. 529–553. doi:10.1080/01402390.2014.971947.

Kornblith, Hilary, "Sosa in Perspective," *Philosophical Studies* 144 (1) (2009), pp. 127–136.

Knight, Frank, *Risk, Uncertainty and Profit* (New York: Dover Publications Inc., 1921).

Knopf, Jeffrey, "The Concept of Nuclear Learning," *Nonproliferation Review* 19 (1) (2012), pp. 79–93.

Kramer, Eric-Hans, "Mission Command in the Information Age: A Normal Accidents Perspective on Networked Military Operations," *Journal of Strategic Studies* 38 (4) (2015), pp. 445–466.

Kroenig, Matthew, "Nuclear Superiority and the Balance of Resolve: Explaining Nuclear Crisis Outcomes," *International Organization* 67 (1) (2013), pp. 141–171.

Kroenig, Matthew, "Bringing Geopolitics Back," *Strategic Studies Quarterly* 15 (4) (Winter, 2021), pp. 59–73.

Kruglanski, Arie, and Donna Webster, "Motivated Closing of the Mind: 'Seizing' and 'Freezing'," *Psychological Review* 103 (2) (1996), pp. 263–283.

Kuhn, Thomas H., *The Structure of Scientific Revolutions* (Chicago, IL: University of Chicago Press, 1962).

Kurzweil, Ray, *The Age of Spiritual Machines: When Computers Exceed Human Intelligence* (New York: Penguin, 2000).

Kwan, Virginia, and Susan Fiske, "Missing Links in Social Cognition: The Continuum from Non-Human Agents to Dehumanized Humans," *Social Cognition* 26 (2) (2008), pp. 125–128.

Lars-Erik Cederman, "Rerunning History: Counterfactual Simulation in World Politics," in *Counterfactual Thought Experiments in World Politics*, ed. Philip E. Tetlock and Aaron Belkin, *Counterfactual Thought Experiments in World Politics* (Princeton, NJ: Princeton University Press, 1996), pp. 247–268.

Lebovic, James, *Deadly Dilemmas: Deterrence in US Nuclear Strategy* (New York: Columbia University Press, 1990).

Lebow, Richard N., "Rational Deterrence Theory: I Think Therefore I Deter," *World Politics* 41 (2) (1989), pp. 208–224.

Lebow, Richard N., "Contingency, Catalysts, and Nonlinear Change: The Origins of World War I," in *Explaining War and Peace Case Studies and Necessary Condition Counterfactuals*, ed. Gary Goertz and Jack S. Levy (New York: Routledge, 2007), pp. 85–111.

Lebow, Richard N., *Forbidden Fruit: Counterfactuals and International Relations* (Princeton, NJ: Princeton University Press, 2010).

Lebow, Richard N., "Counterfactuals and Security Studies," *Security Studies* 24 (3) (2015), pp. 403–412.

Lerner, Jennifer S., and Dacher Keltner, "Fear, Anger, and Risk," *Journal of Personality and Social Psychology* 81 (1) (2001), pp. 146–159.

Lesher, James, *Xenophanes of Colophon: Fragments* (Canada: University of Toronto Press, 1992).

Levy, Jack S., "Counterfactuals, Causal Inference, and Historical Analysis," *Security Studies* 24 (3) (2015), pp. 378–402.

Lewis, Patricia, et al., *Too Close for Comfort: Cases of Near Nuclear Use and Options for Policy* (London: Chatham House, 2014).

Lieber, Keir, "Grasping the Technological Peace: The Offense–Defense Balance and International Security," *International Security* 25 (1) (2000), pp. 71–104.

Lieber, Keir, *War and the Engineers: The Primacy of Politics over Technology* (Ithaca, NY: Cornell University Press, 2008).

Lieber, Keir A., and Daryl G. Press, *The Myth of the Nuclear Revolution: Power Politics in the Atomic Age* (Ithaca, NY: Cornell University Press, 2020).

Lin, Herbert, *Cyber Threats and Nuclear Weapons* (Stanford, CA: Hoover Institution Press, 2021).

Lin, Keith Abney, and George Bekey, *Robot Ethics: The Ethical and Social Implications of Robotics* (Cambridge, MA: MIT Press, 2014).

Lissack, M. R., "Complexity: The Science, its Vocabulary, and its Relation to Organizations," *Emergence* 1 (1) (1999), pp. 110–126.

Little, Andrew T., and Thomas Zeitzoff, "A Bargaining Theory of Conflict with Evolutionary Preferences," *International Organization* 71 (3) (Summer 2017), pp. 523–557.

Lopez, Anthony C., Rose McDermott, and Michael Bang Petersen, "States in Mind: Evolution, Coalitional Psychology, and International Politics," *International Security* 36 (2) (Fall 2011), pp. 48–83.

Lupton, Danielle L., *Reputation for Resolve* (Ithaca, NY: Cornell University Press, 2020).

MacCormick, John, *Nine Algorithms That Changed the Future* (Princeton, NJ: Princeton University Press, 2012).

MacIntosh, Duncan, "PTSD Weaponized: A Theory of Moral Injury." Paper presented at the Center for Ethics and the Rule of Law at the University of Pennsylvania Law School, December 3–5, 2015.

MacIntosh, Duncan, "Fire and Forget: A Moral Defense of the Use of Autonomous Weapons Systems in War and Peace," in *Lethal Autonomous Weapons: Re-Examining the Law and Ethics of Robotic Warfare*, ed. Jai Galliott, Jens Ohlin, and Duncan MacIntosh (Oxford: Oxford University Press, 2021), pp. 9–23.

Mahmoud, Sara et al., "Where To From Here? On the Future Development of Autonomous Vehicles from a Cognitive Systems Perspective," *Cognitive Systems Research* 76 (2022), pp. 63–77.

Mansoor, Ahmed, "Pakistan's Tactical Nuclear Weapons and Their Impact on Stability," *Carnegie Endowment for International Peace*, June 30, 2016.

Marcus, Gary, "Moral Machines," *The New Yorker*, November 24, 2012.

Mayor, Adrienne, *Gods, and Robots: Myths, Machines, and Ancient Dreams of Technology* (Princeton, NJ: Princeton University Press, 2020).

McCloskey, Diedre, "History, Differential Equations, and the Problem of Narration," *History & Theory* 30 (1990), pp. 21–36.

McDermott, Drew, "Artificial Intelligence Meets Natural Stupidity," *ACM Sigart Bulletin* 57 (4) (1976), pp. 4–9.

McDermott, Rose, Anthony C. Lopez, and Peter K. Hatemi, "'Blunt Not the Heart, Enrage It': The Psychology of Revenge and Deterrence," *Texas National Security Review* 1 (1) (2017), pp. 70–71.

McDonald, Carlos, David Navarrete, and Mark Van Vugt, "Evolution and the Psychology of Intergroup Conflict: The Male Warrior Hypothesis," *Philosophical Transactions of the Royal Society B* 367 (1589) (January 2012), pp. 670–679.

McDonald, J., and M. Bell, "How to Think about Nuclear Crises?" *Texas National Security Review* 2 (2) (2019), pp. 41–65.

McManus, Roseanne W., "Revisiting the Madman Theory: Evaluating the Impact of Different Forms of Perceived Madness in Coercive Bargaining," *Security Studies* 28 (5) (2019), pp. 976–1009.

Mearsheimer, John, "Back to the Future: Instability in Europe after the Cold War," *International Security* 15 (1) (1990), pp. 5–56.

Mearsheimer, John, *The Tragedy of Great Power Politic* (New York: W. W. Norton & Company, 2014).

Mehta, Pranjal H., A. C. Jones, and R. A. Josephs, "The Social Endocrinology of Dominance: Basal Testosterone Predicts Cortisol Changes and Behavior Following Victory and Defeat," *Journal of Personality and Social Psychology* 94 (6) (2008), pp. 1078–1093.

Meijer, Albert, and Martijn Wessels, "Predictive Policing: Review of Benefits and Drawbacks," *International Journal of Public Administration* 42 (12) (2019), pp. 1031–1039.

Mercer, Jonathan, *Reputation and International Politics* (Ithaca, NY: Cornell University Press, 1996).

Michener, Willa, "The Individual Psychology of Group Hate," *Journal of Hate Studies* 10 (1) (2012), pp. 15–48.

Millar, Kevin, "Total Surveillance, Big Data, and Predictive Crime Technology: Privacy's Perfect Storm," *Journal of Technology Law & Policy* 19 (1) (2014), pp. 106–145.

Miller, Dale, et al., "Counterfactual Thinking and Social Perception," in *Advances in Experimental Social Psychology*, ed. M. Zanna (New York: Academic Press, 1990), pp. 305–331.

Mirowski, Philip, *Machine Dreams. How Economics Became a Cyborg Science* (Cambridge MA: Harvard University Press, 2002).

Morewedge, Carey, and Michael Clear, "Anthropomorphic God Concepts Engender Moral Judgment," *Social Cognition*, 26 (2008), pp. 181–188.

Morgan, Forrest E., et al., *Dangerous Thresholds: Managing Escalation in the 21st Century* (Santa Monica, CA: RAND Corporation, 2008).

Morgan, Patrick M., *Deterrence Now* (Cambridge: Cambridge University Press, 2003).

Morkevicius, Valarie, "Tin Men: Ethics, Cybernetics and the Importance of Soul," *Journal of Military Ethics* 13 (1) (2014), pp. 3–19.

Morreale, Emanuela, and Stuart Watt, "An Agent-Based Approach to Mailing List Knowledge Management. Agent-Mediated Knowledge Management," *Lecture Notes in Artificial Intelligence* 2926 (2004), pp. 118–129.

Moser, Christine, Frank den Hond, and Dirk Lindenbaum, "Morality in the Age of Artificially Intelligent Algorithms," *Academy of Management Learning & Education*, April 7, 2021. https://journals.aom.org.

Mutlu, Bilge, Christoph Bartneck, Jaap Ham, Vanessa Evers, and Takayuki Kanda (eds), *Social Robotics: Third International Conference on Social Robotics, ICSR 2011, Amsterdam, The Netherlands, November 24–25, 2011. Proceedings* (New York: Springer, 2011).

Nagel, Thomas, "War and Massacre," *Philosophy & Public Affairs* 1 (2) (1972), pp. 123–144.

Nass, Clifford, and Youngme Moon, "Machines and Mindlessness: Social Responses to Computers," *Journal of Social Issues* 56 (1) (2000), pp. 81–103.

Nelson Goodman, Fact, Fiction, and Forecast (Cambridge, MA: Harvard University Press, 1983).

Neumann, John, *The Computer and the Brain* (New Haven, CT: Yale University Press, 1958).

Newdick, Thomas, "AI-Controlled F-16s are Now Working as a Team in DARPA's Alpha Dogfights," *The Drive*, March 22, 2021.

Nisbett, R. and L. Ross, *Human Inference: Strategies and Shortcomings of Social Judgment* (New Jersey: Prentice-Hill, 1980).

Norenzayan, Ara, and Azim Shariff, "The Origin and Evolution of Religious Prosociality," *Science* 322 (5898) (2008), pp. 58–62.

Norvig, Peter, *Artificial Intelligence: A Modern Approach*. 3rd ed. (Pearson Education: Harlow, 2014).

Nowak, Kristine L., and Christian Rauh, "The Influence of the Avatar on Online Perceptions of Anthropomorphism, Androgyny, Credibility, Homophily, and Attraction," *Journal of Computer-Mediated Communication* 11 (1) (2005), pp. 153–178.

Nussbaum, Martha, "Equity and Mercy," *Philosophy and Public Affairs* 22 (2) (1993), pp. 83–125.

O'Creevy, Mark Fenton, et al., "Trading on Illusions: Unrealistic Perceptions of Control and Trading Performance," *Journal of Occupational and Organizational Psychology* 76 (1), 2003, pp. 53–68.

Olson, Mancur, Jr. (ed.), *The Logic of Collective Action: Public Goods and the Theory of Groups* (New York: Schocken, 1971).

Osinga, Frans, "'Getting' *A Discourse on Winning and Losing*: A Primer on Boyd's 'Theory of Intellectual Evolution,'" *Contemporary Security Policy* 34 (3) (2013), pp. 603–624. doi:10.1080/13523260. 2013.849154.

Otto, Jean L., and J. Bryant Webber, "Mental Health Diagnoses and Counseling among Pilots of Remotely Piloted Aircraft in the United States Air Force," *MSMS* 20 (3) (2013), pp. 3–8.

Overy, Richard, *The Air War 1939–1945* (New York: Potomac Books, 1981).

Owens, Bill, *Lifting the Fog of War* (New York: Farrar, Straus, and Giroux 2000).

Parasuraman, Raja, and Dietrich Manzey, "Complacency and Bias in Human Use of Automation: An Attentional Integration," *Human Factors* 52 (3) (2010), pp. 381–410.

Parasuraman, Raja, and Victor Riley, "Humans and Automation: Use, Misuse, Disuse, Abuse," *Human Factors* 39 (2) (June 1997), pp. 230–253.

Pasquale, Frank, *The Black Box Society: The Secret Algorithms That Control Money and Information* (Cambridge, MA: Harvard University Press, 2016).

Pauly, Reid, and Rose McDermott, "The Psychology of Nuclear Brinkmanship," *International Security* 47 (3) (2023), pp. 9–51.

Pawlyk, Oriana, "Rise of the Machines: AI Algorithm Beats F-16 Pilot in Dogfight," *Military.com*, August 24, 2020.

Payne, Kenneth, "Artificial Intelligence: A Revolution in Strategic Affairs?" *Survival* 60 (5) (2018), pp. 7–32.

Payne, Kenneth, *Warbot: The Dawn of Artificially Intelligent Conflict* (New York: Oxford University Press, 2021).

Pelopidas, Benoît, *The Book that Leaves Nothing to Chance: How the Strategy of Conflict and His Legacy Normalized the Practice of Nuclear Threats* (unpublished draft, October 24, 2016).

Pelopidas, Benoît, "The Unbearable Lightness of Luck. Three Sources of Overconfidence in the Controllability of Nuclear Crises," *European Journal of International Security* 2 (2) (2017), pp. 240–262.

Perrow, Charles, *Normal Accidents: Living with High-Risk Technologies* (Princeton, NJ: Princeton University Press, 1984).

Pickering, John, "Human Identity in the Age of Software Agents," in *Cognitive Technology: Instruments of the Mind: Proceedings of the 4th International Conference on Cognitive Technology*, ed. M Beynon, C. Nahniv, and K. Duatenhahn (Berlin: Springer, 2001), pp. 442–451.

Polanyi, Michael, *Knowing and Being* (London: Routledge, 1969).

Popper, Karl, *The Logic of Scientific Discovery* (London: Routledge, 2005).

Posen, Barry R., *Inadvertent Escalation* (Ithaca, NY: Cornell University Press, 1990).

Postill, John, "Populism and Social Media: A Global Perspective," *Media, Culture & Society* 40 (5) (July 2018), pp. 754–765.

Powell, Robert, *Nuclear Deterrence Theory: The Search for Credibility* (Cambridge: Cambridge University Press, 1990).

Prigogine, Ilya, and Isabella Stengers, *Order Out of Chaos* (London: Penguin Random House, 1984).

Putnam, Robert, *Beliefs of Politicians* (New Haven, CT: Yale University Press, 1973).

Quintero, Rasouli, et al., "Pedestrian Intention Recognition by Means of a Hidden Markov Model and Body Language," in *2017 IEEE 20th International Conference on Intelligent Transportation Systems* (October 2017), pp. 1–7. doi:10.1109/ITSC.2017.8317766.

Rauta, Vladimir, and Alexandra Stark, "What Does Arming an Insurgency in Ukraine Mean?" *Lawfare*, April 3, 2022.

Renic, Neil, "Justified Killing in an Age of Radically Asymmetric Warfare," *European Journal of International Relations* 25 (2) (2019), pp. 408–430.

Roche, James, and Barry Watts, "Choosing Analytic Measures," *Journal of Strategic Studies* 13 (2) (1991), pp. 165–209. doi:10.1080/01402399108437447.

Rodd, Lee, "The Intuitive Psychologist and His Shortcomings: Distortions in Attribution Process," *Advances in Experimental Social Psychology* 10 (1977), pp. 173–220.

Roderick, Ian, "Mil-Bot Fetishism: The Pataphysics of Military Robots," *Topia* 23 (4) (2010), pp. 286–303.

Roff, Heather M., "Artificial Intelligence: Power to the People," *Ethics & International Affairs* 33 (2) (2019), pp. 124–140.

Roff, Heather M., "The Strategic Robot Problem: Lethal Autonomous Weapons in War," *Journal of Military Ethics* 13 (3) (2014), pp. 211–227.

Rosen, Stephen, P., "The Impact of the Office of Net Assessment on the American Military in the Matter of the Revolution in Military Affairs," Journal of Strategic Studies 33 (4) (2010), pp. 469–482. doi:10.1080/01402390.2010.489704.

Rosenblatt, A., et al., "Evidence for Terror Management II: The Effects of Mortality Salience on Reactions to Those Who Threaten or Bolster the Cultural World View," *Journal of Personality and Social Psychology* 58 (1990), pp. 308–318.

Rosert, Elvira, and Frank Sauer, "How (Not) to Stop the Killer Robots: A Comparative Analysis of Humanitarian Disarmament Campaign Strategies," *Contemporary Security Policy* 42 (1) (2021), pp. 4–29. doi:10.1080/13523260.2020.1771508.

Russell, James, A., *Innovation, Transformation, and War: Counterinsurgency Operations in Anbar and Ninewa Provinces, Iraq, 2005–2007* (Stanford, CA: Stanford University Press, 2010).

Russell, Stuart, *Human Compatible* (New York: Viking Press, 2019).

Russell, Stuart, and Peter Norvig, *Artificial Intelligence: International Version: A Modern Approach* (Englewood Cliffs: Prentice Hall, 2010).

Ryle, Gilbert, *The Concept of Mind* (London: Hutchinson, 1966).

Saalman, Lora, "Fear of False Negatives: AI and China's Nuclear Posture," *Bulletin of the Atomic Scientists* (April 24, 2018).

Sagan, Scott, "Why Do States Build Nuclear Weapons? Three Models in Search of a Bomb," *International Security* 21 (3) (1996), pp. 54–86. doi:10.2307/2539273.

Sagan, Scott D., *The Limits of Safety: Organizations, Accidents, and Nuclear Weapons* (Princeton, NJ: Princeton University Press, 1993).

Sagan, Scott D., and Jeremi Suri, "The Madman Nuclear Alert: Secrecy, Signaling, and Safety in October 1969," *International Security* 27 (4) (2003), pp. 150–183.

Salles, Arleen, Kathinka Evers, and Michele Frisco, "Anthropomorphism in AI," *AJOB Neuroscience* 11 (2) (2020), pp. 91–92.

Seitz, Samuel, and Caitlin Talmadge, "The Predictable Hazards of Unpredictability: Why Madman Behavior Doesn't Work," *The Washington Quarterly* 43 (3) (2020), pp. 31–46.

Saver, Jeffrey, and John Rabin, "The Neural Substrates of Religious Experience," *Journal of Neuropsychiatry Clinical Neuroscience* 9 (3) (1997), pp. 498–510.

Savranskaya, Svetlana, and Thomas Blanton, with Anna Melyakova (eds), "New Evidence on Tactical Nuclear Weapons—59 Days in Cuba," *National Security Archive Electronic Briefing Book*, December 11, 2013, http://nsarchive.gwu.edu/NSAEBB/NSAEBB449/.

Scharre, Paul, *Army of None: Autonomous Weapons and the Future of War* (New York: W.W. Norton & Company, 2018).

Schechter, B., J. Schneider, and R. Shaffer, "Wargaming as a Methodology: The International Crisis Wargame and Experimental Wargaming," *Simulation & Gaming* 52 (4) (2021), pp. 513–526.

Schelling, Thomas C., *The Strategy of Conflict* (Cambridge, MA: Harvard University Press, 1960).

Schelling, Thomas C., *Arms and Influence* (New Haven, CT: Yale University Press, 1966).

Schimmelfennig, Frank, "The Community Trap: Liberal Norms, Rhetorical Action, and the Eastern Enlargement of the European Union," *International Organization* 55 (1) (2001), pp. 47–80.

Schmitt, Michael, "Autonomous Weapon Systems and International Humanitarian Law: A Reply to the Critics," *Harvard National Security Journal* 4 (2013), pp. 1–37.

Schoemaker, Paul. J., "When and How to Use Scenario Planning: A Heuristic Approach with Illustration," *Journal of Forecasting* 10 (6) (1991), pp. 549–564.

Schultz, Kenneth A., *Democracy and Coercive Diplomacy* (Cambridge: Cambridge University Press, 2001).

Schwarz, Elke, *Death Machines: The Ethics of Violent Technologies* (Manchester: Manchester University Press, 2018).

Schwarz, Elke, "Technology and Moral Vacuums in Just War Theorising," *Journal of International Political Theory* 14 (3) (2018), pp. 280–298.

Scott, Len, and R. Gerald Hughes, *The Cuban Missile Crisis: Critical Reappraisal* (London: Routledge, 2015).

Sechser, Todd S., and Matthew Fuhrmann, "The Madman Myth: Trump and the Bomb," *H-Diplo/ISSF Policy Series*, March 2017.

Sejnowski, Terrence, J., *The Deep Learning Revolution* (Cambridge, MA: MIT Press. 2018).

Shachtman, Noah, "How Technology Almost Lost the War: In Iraq, the Critical Networks are Social—Not Electronic," *Wired*, November 27, 2007.

Shao, Chengcheng, et al., "The Spread of Low-Credibility Content by Social Bots," *Nature Communications* 9 (4787) (2018), pp. 1–8.

Sharkey, Noel, "Killing Made Easy: From Joystick to Politics," in *Robot Ethics: The Ethical and Social Implications of Robotics, ed.* Patrick Lin, Keith Abney, and Ryan Jenkins (MA: MIT Press, 2012), pp. 111–128.

Shaw, Robert, "Strange Attractors, Chaotic Behavior, and Information Flow," *Zeitschrift der Naturforschung* 36 (1) (1981), pp. 80–112. doi:10.1515/zna-19810115.

Shimko, Keith L., *Images and Arms Control: Perceptions of the Soviet Union in the Reagan Administration* (Ann Arbor: University of Michigan Press, 1992).

Shultz, G., and J. Goodby (eds), *The War That Must Never Be Fought: Dilemmas of Nuclear Deterrence* (Stanford, CA: Hoover Press, 2015).

Silver, Nate, *The Signal and the Noise: Why so Many Predictions Fail—But Some Don't* (New York: Penguin Books, 2015).

Simon, Herbert A., "Making Management Decisions: The Role of Intuition and Emotions," *The Academy of Management Executive* 1 (1) (February 1987), pp. 57–64.

Simonite, Tom, "A Health Care Algorithm Offered Less Care to Black Patients," *Wired*, October 24, 2019.

Singer, Peter, *Wired for War: The Robotics Revolution and Conflict in the 21st Century* (New York: Penguin Press, 2009).

Singh Gill, Amandeep, "Artificial Intelligence and International Security: The Long View," *Ethics & International Affairs* 33 (2) (2019), pp. 169–179. doi:10.1017/S0892679419000145.

Skitka, Linda J., Kathleen Mosier, and Mark Burdick, "Automation Bias: Decision Making and Performance in High-Tech Cockpits," *International Journal of Aviation Psychology* 8 (1) (1998), pp. 47–63.

Skjuve, Marita, et al., "A Longitudinal Study of Human–Chatbot Relationships," *International Journal of Human-Computer Studies* 168 (2022), pp. 1–14.

Slantchev, Branislav L., "Military Coercion in Interstate Crises," *American Political Science Review* 99 (4) (2005), pp. 533–547.

Smith, Brian C., *The Promise of Artificial Intelligence: Reckoning and Judgment* (Cambridge, MA: MIT Press, 2019).

Snyder, Glenn, *Deterrence and Defense* (Princeton, NJ: Princeton University Press, 1961).

Snyder, Glenn, and Paul Diesing, *Conflict Among Nations* (Princeton, NJ: Princeton University Press, 1977).

Sparrow, Rob, "The Turing Triage Test," *Ethics and Information Technology* 6 (4) (2004), pp. 203–213.

Spatola, Nicolas, and Thierry Chaminade, "Cognitive Load Increases Anthropomorphism of Humanoid Robot: The Automatic Path of Anthropomorphism," *International Journal of Human-Computer Studies* 167 (2022), pp. 1–15.

Steele, Ian K., *Betrayals: Fort William Henry and the "Massacre"* (Oxford: Oxford University Press, 1990).

Steff, R., S. Soare, and J. Burton (eds), *Emerging Technologies and International Security: Machines, the State and War* (London: Routledge, 2020).

Storr, Jim, "Neither Art nor Science—Towards a Discipline of Warfare," *RUSI Journal* 146 (2001), pp. 39–45. doi:10.1080/03071840108446627.

Strawser, Bradley J., "Moral Predators: A Duty to Employ Unmanned Aerial Vehicles," *Journal of Military Ethics* 9 (4) (2010), pp. 342–368.

Sunstein, Cass, and Martha Nussbaum, *Animal Rights: Current Debates and New Directions* (New York: Oxford University Press, 2004).

Swiderska, Aleksandra, and Dennis Küster, "Avatars in Pain: Visible Harm Enhances Mind Perception in Humans and Robots," *Perception* 47 (12) (2018), pp. 1139–1152.

Taddeo, Mariarosaria, "Modelling Trust in Artificial Agents, a First Step Toward the Analysis of e-Trust," *Minds and Machines* 20 (2) (2010), pp. 243–257.

Tallis, Raymond, *Aping Mankind: Neuromania, Darwinists, and the Misrepresentation of Humanity* (New York: Atlantic Books, 2010).

Talmadge, Caitlin, "Would China Go Nuclear? Assessing the Risk of Chinese Nuclear Escalation in a Conventional War with the United States," *International Security* 41 (4) (2017), pp. 50–92.

Talmadge, Caitlin, "Emerging Technology and Intra-War Escalation Risks: Evidence from the Cold War, Implications for Today," *Journal of Strategic Studies* 42 (6) (2019), pp. 864–887.

Tannenwald, N., "How Strong is the Nuclear Taboo Today?" *The Washington Quarterly* 41 (3) (2018), pp. 89–109.

Tarraf, Danielle, *The Department of Defense Posture for Artificial Intelligence: Assessment and Recommendations* (Santa Monica, CA: RAND Corporation, 2019).

Taylor, Timothy, *The Artificial Ape: How Technology Changes the Course of Human Evolution* (Lexington: University Press of Kentucky, 2004).

Tetlock, Philip, *Expert Political Judgment: How Good is it? How Can we Know?* (Princeton, NJ: Princeton University Press, 2005).

Tetlock, Philip E., and Aaron Belkin (eds), *Counterfactual Thought Experiments in World Politics* (Princeton, NJ: Princeton University Press, 1996).

Thompson, Suzanne C., "Illusions of Control: How We Overestimate Our Personal Influence," *Current Directions in Psychological Science, Association for Psychological Science* 8 (6) (1999), pp. 187–190.

Thoreau, Henry David, *Civil Disobedience in the Writings of Henry David Thoreau*, Vol. 4 (Boston, MA: Houghton Mifflin, 1906).

Thucydides, *The Landmark Thucydides: A Comprehensive Guide to the Peloponnesian War*, ed. Robert B. Strassler, trans. Richard Crawley (New York: Free Press, 1996).

Tooby, John, and Leda Cosmides, "Groups in Mind: The Coalitional Roots of War and Morality," in *Human Morality and Sociality: Evolutionary and Comparative Perspectives*, ed. Henrik Hogh-Olesen (New York: Palgrave Macmillan, 2010), pp. 191–235.

Trinkunas, Harold, Herbert Lin, and Benjamin Loehrke, *Three Tweets to Midnight: Effects of the Global Information Ecosystem on the Risk of Nuclear Conflict* (Stanford, CA: Hoover Institution Press, 2020).

Trivers, Robert, *The Folly of Fools: The Logic of Deceit and Self-Deception in Human Life* (New York: Basic Books, 2014).

Tumber, Howard, and Silvio Waisbord (eds), *The Routledge Companion to Media Disinformation and Populism* (London: Routledge, 2021).

Tversky, Amos, and Daniel Kahneman, "Availability: A Heuristic for Judging Frequency and Probability," *Cognitive Psychology* 5 (2) (1973), pp. 207–232.

Tversky, Amos, and Daniel Kahneman, "Judgement under Uncertainty: Heuristics and Biases," *Science* 185 (27) (1974), pp. 1124–1131.

Ullman, Shimon, "Using Neuroscience to Develop Artificial Intelligence," *Science* 363 (6428) (2019), pp. 692–693.

US Army Department, "ADP 6-0: Mission Command: Command and Control of Army Forces, Army Doctrine Publication," *US Department of the Army*, May 17, 2012.

Vacher. J., et al., "Bayesian Modeling of Motion Perception Using Dynamical Stochastic Textures," *Neural Computation* 30 (12) (2018), pp. 3355–3392.

Vallor, Shannon, "Moral Deskilling and Upskilling in a New Machine Age: Reflections on the Ambiguous Future of Character," *Philosophy & Technology* 28 (2015), pp. 107–124.

Vallor, Shannon, *Technology and the Virtues: A Philosophical Guide to a Future Worth Wanting* (Oxford: Oxford University Press, 2016).

Veruggio, Gianmarco, and Keith Abney, "The Applied Ethics for a New Science," in *Robot Ethics: The Ethical and Social Implications of Robotics*, ed. Lin Patrick, Keith Abney, and George Bekey (Cambridge, MA: MIT Press, 2014), pp. 348–349.

Visser, Ewart J. de, et al., "Almost Human: Anthropomorphism Increases Trust Resilience in Cognitive Agents," *Journal of Experiential Psychology Applied* 22 (3) (2016), pp. 331–349.

Von Clausewitz, Carl, *On War*, ed. and trans. Michael Howard and Peter Paret (Princeton, NJ: Princeton University Press, 1976).

Wagner, Alan R., Jason Bornstein, and Ayanna Howard, "Computing Ethics: Overtrust in the Robotics Age," *Communications of the ACM* 61 (9) (2018), pp. 22–24.

Wallach, Wendell, and Colin Allen, *Moral Machines: Teaching Robots Right from Wrong* (Oxford: Oxford University Press, 2009).

Walt, Stephen M., "The Enduring Relevance of the Realist Tradition," in *Political Science: State of the Discipline*, ed. Ira Katznelson and Helen V. Milner (New York: W.W. Norton, 2002), pp. 197–230.

Waltz, Kenneth, *Theory of International Politics* (New York: Random House, 1979).

Warren, Mary A., "On the Moral and Legal Status of Abortion," in *Contemporary Modern Problems*, ed. James White. 9th ed. (New York: Broadman & Holman Publishers, 2008), pp. 113–124.

Watson, David, "The Rhetoric and Reality of Anthropomorphism in Artificial Intelligence," *Minds and Machines* 29 (3) (2019), pp. 417–440. doi:10.1007/s11023-019-09506-6.

Waytz, Adam, John Cacioppo, and Nicholas Epley, "Who Sees Human? The Stability and Importance of Individual Differences in Anthropomorphism," *Perspectives on Psychological Science* 5 (3) (2010), pp. 219–232.

Waytz, Adam, Nicholas Epley, and John Cacioppo, "Social Cognition Unbound: Insights into Anthropomorphism and Dehumanization," *Current Directions in Psychological Science* 19 (1) (2010), pp. 58–62.

Weeks, Jessica L., "Autocratic Audience Costs: Regime Type and Signaling Resolve," *International Organization* 62 (1) (2008), pp. 35–64.

Welch, David, *On the Brink: Americans and Soviets Reexamine the Cuban Missile Crisis* (New York: Hill & Wang, 1989).

Wiener, Norbert, *The Human Use of Human Beings: Cybernetics and Society* (New York: Avon Books, 1967).

The Writings of William James: A Comprehensive Edition, ed. J. J. McDermott (Chicago, IL: University of Chicago Press, 1977), (Original work published in 1909).

William, James, *Varieties of Religious Experience: A Study of Human Nature* (New York: Signet, 2009).

William, W. Calvin, "The Vacher," *Scientific American* 271 (2006), pp. 100–107.

Wilson, Benjamin, "Keynes Goes Nuclear: Thomas Schelling and the Macroeconomic Origins of Strategic Stability," *Modern Intellectual History* 18 (1) (2019), pp. 1–31.

Wirtz, James, "Limited Nuclear War Reconsidered," in *On Limited Nuclear War in the Twenty-First Century*, ed. Jeffrey Larsen and Kerry Kartchner (Stanford, CA: Stanford University Press, 2014), pp. 263–271.

Wittgenstein, Ludwig, *Philosophical Investigations*, trans. G. E. M. Anscombe. 3rd ed. (New York: Prentice-Hall, 1973).

Wohlstetter, Roberta, *Pearl Harbor* (Stanford, CA: Stanford University Press, 1962).

Wolters, Timothy, S., *Information at Sea: Shipboard Command and Control in the US Navy, from Mobile Bay to Okinawa* (Baltimore, MD: Johns Hopkins University Press 2013).

Xie, Tianling, and Iryna Pentina, "Attachment Theory as a Framework to Understand Relationships with Social Chatbots: A Case Study of Replika," in *Proceedings of the 55th Hawaii International Conference on System Sciences* (2022), pp. 2046–2055.

Yong, Ed, *An Immense World: How Animal Senses Reveal the Hidden Realms around Us* (New York: Vantage, 2022).

Yudkowsky, Eliezer, "Artificial Intelligence as a Positive and Negative Factor in Global Risk," in *Global Catastrophic Risks*, ed. Nick Bostrom and Milan M. Ćirković (New York: Oxford University Press, 2008), pp. 308–345.

Zagare, Frank C., "Reconciling Rationality with Deterrence: A Re-Examination of the Logical Foundations of Deterrence Theory," *Journal of Theoretical Politics* 16 (2) (2004), pp. 107–141.

Złotowski, Jakub, et al., "Anthropomorphism: Opportunities and Challenges in Human–Robot Interaction," *Journal of Social Robotics* 7 (2015), pp. 347–360.

Złotowski, Jakub, Hidenobu Sumioka, and Frederike Eyssel, "Model of Dual Anthropomorphism: The Relationship between the Media Equation Effect and Implicit Anthropomorphism," *International Journal of Social Robotics* 10 (2018), pp. 701–714.

Zwald, Zachary, "Imaginary Nuclear Conflicts: Explaining Deterrence Policy Preference Formation," *Security Studies* 22 (4) (2013), pp. 640–671.

Index